Dealing With Deviants

Dealing With Deviants

The Treatment of Antisocial Behavior

Stuart Whiteley
Dennie Briggs
Merfyn Turner

SCHOCKEN BOOKS • NEW YORK

First SCHOCKEN edition 1973

Copyright © Stuart Whiteley, Dennie Briggs, and Merfyn Turner, 1972
Library of Congress Catalog Card No. 73-78298
Manufactured in the United States of America

CONTENTS

Dealing With Deviants

Introduction

DEVIANTS AND THEIR DEMANDS

In 1848 Henry Mayhew, a journalist and commentator on the social scene, wrote a series of articles which were gathered together in his books *London Labour and the London Poor*. Mayhew was fascinated then, as the news-media men have continued to be ever since, by the deviants, drop-outs, petty criminals and ne'er-do-wells of the contemporary London scene. In one chapter he casts his enquiring eye over the inhabitants of the lodging houses, and whilst he can identify the reasons that brought many to this miserable situation— lack of a dwelling, dismissed from a job, or other social failing —he found one group that remained a puzzle to him. They were young men, they seemed not to care about the vicissitudes of their situation, and there seemed no obvious reason for them to be thus on the fringes of society.

'They were', he writes, 'persons naturally of an erratic and self-willed temperament, objecting to the restraints of home and incapable of continuous application to any one occupation. Their condition is not due to drink, nor ignorance nor to the poor situation of their early lives.'

The London lodging houses are much fewer in number today, but sitting on the steps of the Eros statue in Piccadilly Circus, in the Remand Centres and in the coffee lounges of our mental hospitals we can still view Mayhew's 'erratic and self-willed' persons, and we are only a little nearer to an understanding of what makes them so.

ATTITUDES TO DEVIANCE

Deviance is commonly regarded as 'badness' and deserving to be treated by punishment and imprisonment, or as 'madness' and requiring treatment by medicines and hospitalisation

At the extremes of deviant behaviour this labelling and all that goes with it causes the majority of the public few qualms of conscience. The immediate problem is solved in that society is protected from the 'bad' individual by secluding him in prison, whilst the 'mad' individual is saved from the consequences of his actions by being secluded in a mental hospital.

But the solution is only a temporary one, of course, and produces no lasting resolution of the real problems. Indeed the institutionalisation that results from long term confinement in either the prison or the mental hospital gives society yet another problem to deal with ultimately.

In the intermediate group, with whom we shall be concerned in this book and where 'madness' and 'badness' seem inextricably entangled, even the immediate solutions are less clear cut and unquestionably give more cause for concern.

In dealing with such a person the various representatives of society who have to decide what should be done are in considerable doubt about what disposal is the correct one both for the individual and for the rest of society. If he is deflected to the 'bad' end of the spectrum and is contained in a prison, then he is often the subject of psychiatric reports; and if he is sent to the psychiatric hospital he will frequently be there under some legal or restrictive order imposed by the courts— such is the confusion.

In the field of mental health, however, it is now established practice to treat the mentally ill person in the community and to involve members of the public as well as professionally trained workers in the on-going treatment and acceptance of mental disorders.

At the other end of the spectrum there is a definite although less strongly supported and acclaimed movement towards treating the offender more amongst the society from which he has deviated by involving professionals and lay public alike in dealing with the problems of criminality. These tentative moves indicate a changing attitude to deviance whereby such behaviour is being seen more as a matter of concern for society as a whole than as one that is restricted to certain professional areas.

The deviant with whom our book is concerned is in any case less likely to be unequivocably labelled as bad or mad and treated accordingly. He therefore becomes a subject who is less committed to one or other treatment 'stream' and is ideally suited for a new approach. He is a person who, by his repeated deviant acts, constantly comes into contact with the rest of society as if putting himself forward and making some demand on society for recognition and fulfillment of his needs.

The acts often are delinquent, but frequently the offence committed is more in the nature of a social disturbance than a calculated crime. At the same time he seems untouched by the standard reactions with which society has responded in the past, that is to punish him or to treat him medically.

At a superficial level his demands seem simple enough to satisfy. He often asks for material things, such as a new job, fresh clothes, money or accommodation, all of which the welfare or probation agencies can dole out easily. He usually seeks very immediate gratification of these needs, but even that can sometimes be matched. The problem seldom rests there, however. The demands escalate, the frustration aroused by the slightest delay mounts, and the material help provided is often rejected out of hand or soon forgotten.

The tendency to make up for deficits in the social background and to provide good things, whether in material terms or at an esoteric level through giving trade training and educational opportunities, has been one of the main priorities of the probation and penal reform movements but has made little difference to the rising tide of delinquency.

Perhaps it is fair to suggest that the *real needs of the deviant are not being correctly perceived and still less catered for*.

Underlying the direct demands are the hidden demands which the deviant makes, namely to be understood and brought into society as an integrated and useful member rather than be forced to continue to play the deviant role.

THEORIES OF DEVIANCE

Sociologists and others have attempted many and diverse explanations of deviance. In terms of *Functionalist Theory* deviance may be seen as an essential and permanent part of any group or organisation, in which case the surrounding society will need to organise itself to contain and moderate the extent and effects of the deviant sector with little hope of or interest in bringing about reformation or integration. Thus the prisons or mental hospitals are made more secure or less restrictive as the mood prevails, and regulations are enforced, revised or allowed to lapse. We build a psychiatric prison to block one loophole and a maximum security prison to block another, but the emphasis is on containment of the problem.

Alternatively, deviance can be seen in *Social Conflict Theory* as the essential interaction through which social changes are brought about. In other words it is the constant friction between a deviant sector and the rest of society which draws attention to a particular problem area. More than this, it is through the interaction of the various elements concerned both on the side of society and on the deviant side that some resolution of the issue finally emerges. Conflict of this nature therefore should be looked upon as a potentially useful factor in the evolution of an organisation or culture rather than being suppressed as wholly negative.

For instance, the deviant whose deviance takes him entirely away from further contact with society would appear to be rare. In criminal terms he would be a solitary thief who stole sufficient only for his immediate needs, and so successfully that he was not detected. In reality the deviant more usually comes into constant and repeated conflict with society by the very nature of his actions, and the act of deviance tacitly demands some response from society.

Whilst the response of society may be equally constant and repetitive, either suppression or punishment, there is always a possibility that this point of contact could lead to some compromise reaction on the part of both the deviant and society so that some more constructive resolution could emerge.

As an example, the time may be ripe for an individual offender (perhaps he is about to get married) when at last he meets a person, whether a professional social worker or a layman, ready to help with a different attitude from previous contacts, and this may encourage the growth of trust and confidence. The new contact may by chance have a knowledge of an appropriate hostel or hospital that can offer a different kind of assistance and he and the offender begin to work together towards a new way of life. The delinquent act has brought the two parties together, and now it becomes possible for changes in behavioural roles to take place.

Moving from the specific to the general in the consideration of Social Conflict Theory, it is useful to look at the way a society determines what is deviance.

Different cultures have different standards and norms of behaviour, as the work of many social anthropologists has shown. There is no overall and universal acceptance of what should be regarded as a socially deviant act, for the various cultures have their own particular areas of social conflict demanding attention.

We change our definitions of deviance also in a way which keeps alive the conflict and the interaction at the fringes of organised society when the situation becomes static, and lends support to the theory that through situations of conflict society seeks a resolution of its problems.

In the past few years in England, for instance, certain types of abortion which were reasonably controlled by existing laws and kept out of prominence have ceased to be regarded as criminally deviant. The revision of the regulations has brought renewed activity in this sphere and brings the whole question of abortion into a new arena as a social conflict situation for which we now seek a solution on a different (medical and social) level. On the other hand the possession of small amounts of drugs (such as amphethamines) which were formerly freely available is now regarded as highly deviant and delinquent, and directs attention to a sector where young people are making a commentary of one kind or another on the society in which they live.

Approaches to deviance broadly reflect the attitudes of the Functionalist or Social Conflict Theories in their polarity. Either deviants are suppressed and contained, which is seen as an authoritarian control, or they are allowed to work towards change, which is seen as liberal and progressive. The two approaches themselves are in some conflict, and those who determine social policy are uncertain as to which attitude to adopt, with the result that first one opinion and then the other is held as events take their course.

One of us (Stuart Whiteley) recalls with irritation but understanding the consternation and anxiety engendered in a group of Prison Officers from a long term security establishment when, shortly after the implementation of increased security measures following the Mountbatten report, they were sent on a study-day to the Henderson Hospital. Here they saw very similar clients to those under their penal control (indeed, recognised a former prisoner) and were expected to take part in a free and permissive interchange with the latter.

In both the penal field and the psychiatric field there is a tendency to vacillate thus in uncertainty between control and liberalisation, restraint and non-restraint in the approach to those who deviate from the norms of accepted social behaviour. Out of the conflict of opinions one expects that discussion will be stimulated and a more generally accepted ideology will finally evolve.

In the final outcome what happens to the deviant is the resultant of several forces.

11

Not only does he make overt and covert demands but equally so do the various factions of society. There are needs in all of us to punish wrong doers, to elect scapegoats, to assist those in trouble and to be the agents of charity. These needs will have their outlets in the way that magistrates, doctors, probation officers and others in the field work as well as in the wider application of governmental policies responding to what seems to be the demand of the current national situation.

Whilst this book is mainly concerned with a re-appraisal of the *deviant* and *his* demands, at the same time it would be misleading to suggest that any resolution of social conflict situations would result without some change of attitude also on the part of some of the sections of society with whom the deviant is in conflict.

THE CURRENT STUDIES AND THEIR IMPLICATIONS

In this book we look closely at small groups of three kinds of deviants in a prison, a psychiatric unit and in a hostel for ex-prisoners. They are fair representatives of that very large group of deviants who are neither the professional criminals on the one hand nor the criminally insane on the other. The implications of our findings, we suggest, have a wider application in the general field than specifically to the three communities we shall describe.

Psychopaths, addicts, drop-outs, and delinquents, all have something to say through their choice of deviant behaviour, and seek through the resulting conflict with society some answer to their unspoken demands. We have to be more sensitive and receptive to these demands at our different points of contact, whether these are the prison cell, the hospital ward, the probation office or the social work agency.

The *first section* of the book describes the medical approach to social deviance and the evolution of the Therapeutic Community method of treatment. It goes on to describe the application of the Therapeutic Community methods to the young deviants, so often called psychopaths in medical terminology, at the Henderson Hospital in England.

The second section looks at the ways the penal system has tackled deviance and describes at length the development of a Therapeutic Community kind of approach in one prison system in the United States. Although originating in part from some of the earlier 'medical' methods and experiences, this project moved successfully away from and without need of medical interventions. It used consultants of an inter-disciplinary nature and employed rationale and practices from a variety of areas, yet it retained the essential Therapeutic Community nature.

The third section is devoted to deviance seen at ground roots, as it were, in the general community and describes the inadequate and muddled attempts that have been made to accommodate deviants in hostels and institutions. It goes on to describe the development of a more purposive hostel type of approach to the deviant at large, and the spread of this approach into wider fields.

The three approaches described are the same in some respects. They seek to understand and meet the covert demands of the deviant. They have grown out of actual experiences of living with deviants. They are indicative of some of the varied resources upon which society can draw in dealing with social deviants, for each contributor has approached the problem from an entirely different position and with very different facilities to call upon.

The personality of the writers of each of the three sections plays an important part in the way that each has chosen to work. Differences of personality and approach are reflected in the three sections by the way that the material is presented and described. We feel that these differences are noteworthy and illuminating; it would have been a mistake to sub-edit the book into one standard format.

Stuart Whiteley, with a medical training and an orthodox psychiatric background, became interested in group therapy and the methods of the Therapeutic Community in a forward looking but conventional mental hospital. A research project into the incidence of mental illness in vagrants led to a closer interest in drop-outs, deviants and delinquents, and it was in this connection that he came into contact with Merfyn Turner. The idea of working in a residential community for the treatment of deviants was a natural outcome, and he gladly accepted the invitation of Merfyn Turner, then working in this field, to join in the administration of one of the hostels in the Norman House group for the rehabilitation of ex-prisoners.

However, the hostels were run with a different aim in mind than had been Stuart Whiteley's, and the psychiatrist found himself called in only in cases of 'illness' to advise and act executively. He gradually withdrew to find a place in the

already established Henderson Hospital where a population of
deviants was being treated in a way which utilised a socio-
dynamic and team work approach rather than a strictly
medical one, despite an overall administration by the Health
Service.

Merfyn Turner, the son of a Welsh Non-Conformist Minister, was trained as a school teacher but a brief spell in prison
as a Conscientious Objector opened his eyes to the inadequacy
of his fellow prisoners and to the inadequacies of the system
which purported to reform them.

Starting with unorthodox clubs and residential homes for
young delinquents, he became a nagging bystander at the
elbow of the authorities, gradually establishing hostels of a
personalised nature, run in a somewhat paternalistic and
autocratic way but providing a missing factor in the lives and
life-styles of the selected individuals whom he caused to be
deflected his way by the Courts and prison authorities. He
gave a new concept to hostel life and a lead which has been
widely followed in other hostel schemes.

Dennie Briggs first discovered the inadequacies of his scientific training as an academic psychologist in dealing with
delinquents and deviants whilst serving in the authoritarian
setting of a U.S. Naval Hospital. After working with Harry
Wilmer on an experimental Therapeutic Community admissions ward, he was sent by the Navy to Henderson Hospital
where he came under the influence of Maxwell Jones and continued the relationship subsequently upon entering the U.S.
prison service. Maxwell Jones became a consultant retained
by the California Department of Corrections and was influen-
tial in the establishment of wide scale experiments throughout
the prison service there. Briggs was especially impressed with
the non-professionals (the social therapists) at Henderson and
was able to introduce analogous roles for hospital corpsmen
in the Navy and later for prison officers in prisons. As these
role changes occurred, they allowed for hospitalised psychiatric patients and for prison inmates to take on non-professional roles, in which task Briggs fostered and trained them to
become proficient. Naturally activation of the latent resources
of suppressed prison inmates caused considerable threat to
professional social workers, psychologists and psychiatrists.

When he later returned to England and worked with Stuart
Whiteley at Henderson (see the appendix to Part I) he now
found that the psychiatric team approach gave him less scope

and that the professional staff were less responsive to his particular approach, which to some seemed more openly directive than was acceptable in a psychotherapeutic orientation.

In the final chapter of the book we make a comparison of the three approaches with the object of illustrating their potential as well as drawing attention to their limitations. The specificity of each approach is stressed. Rather than competing with or obtruding upon each other, however, the three approaches can be seen as complementary forces in social treatment, particularly where delinquents are concerned.

A new dimension in the treatment of delinquents could be explored by adopting an approach to social deviance which has more awareness of the different needs of the deviant at different points of conflict with society and at different levels of social integration. It is suggested that an integrated and linked system could be formulated which would meet the individual deviant with resources appropriate to his particular demands rather than, as at present, seeking to cope with deviance by one holistic approach.

PART I

HENDERSON
By
Stuart Whiteley

Chapter One

MEDICAL ATTITUDES TO SOCIAL DEVIANCE: MORAL INSANITY TO PSYCHOPATHIC DISORDER

TOWARDS the end of the 18th Century and at the beginning of the 19th Century doctors were turning their attention to certain disorders of social behaviour and describing them as a form of mental illness. Thus Pinel in France, Ettmuller in Germany, Rush in America and Pritchard in England all had something similar to say on the topic. [1]

Pinel recognised as a form of insanity a condition in which there could be a derangement of the moral senses without an accompanying 'lesion of the understanding', whilst Rush gave a more detailed description in which he cited 'these persons diseased who cannot speak the truth upon any subject or tell a story twice in the same way . . . their falsehoods seldom calculated to injure anyone but themselves'.

Nevertheless it was Pritchard in 1837 who crystallised these views with his concept of *Moral Insanity* in which 'the temper and disposition' were affected in persons of 'a singular wayward and eccentric character'. He felt that the condition often dated from 'some reverse of fortune . . . or loss of a beloved relative'. Pritchard's concept separated Moral Insanity from other forms of insanity in which intellect was affected and was widely taken up and held almost to the end of the 19th Century despite the fact that it was somewhat vague and overinclusive.

There were many critics who from the outset tried to view moral development, not as anatomically and physiologically determined but as an abstract issue and dependent on cultural, national and family traits. Rush himself had already posed the problem of where disease ended and vice began in this puzzling matter and this remains the dilemma to the present day.

A plea of Moral Insanity was made by the defence in the trial of the assassin of President Garfield of the U.S.A. in 1881 and sparked off the argument with which we have in later years become so familiar. Does such an 'illness' imply that the subject is not responsible for his actions? The Court in that case rejected the plea and its implication, and this has been the tendency with crimes of some severity, although paradoxically less serious offences (indicating a *less* serious affliction?) are often regarded more liberally by the courts.

The acceptance of a plea of *diminished responsibility* in the English courts since 1957 has gone some way towards putting the problem in perspective although the medical position remains muddled.

The idea of some inborn defect of mind persisted throughout the 19th Century, however, even on the Continent of Europe where the close of the Century saw the awakening of psychoanalytic thought. Koch introduced the term *Psychopathic Inferior* to imply an innate maldevelopment although his conceptualisation tended to spread over into more neurotic behaviour patterns.

In England the inborn defect of moral sense was seen as similar to the inborn defect of intellect of the mentally subnormal and the term Moral Imbecile was finally chosen for inclusion in the Mental Deficiency regulations of 1904. The incongruity of classifying the so-called Moral Imbecile alongside the intellectual Imbecile and hospitalising and treating the two together made nonsense of the situation, but the legislation was not abandoned until 1927, and even after that the descriptive term of *moral defective* was used well up to the time of the Second World War when the term *psychopath* became more generally used.

It seemed as if Pritchard's original declamation had set a medical seal upon the condition, and generations of doctors sought for and came up with varied medical explanations for disordered social behaviour. The preoccupation with physical and inherited causes has nevertheless led to several factors being quite correctly cited as causative agents, and each in turn has added something to our knowledge.[2]

Thus the *brain damage* following encephalitis in childhood, the scarring and irritation of the brain in temporal lobe epilepsy, the minimal brain lacerations that can follow a difficult birth, the slowness of maturation of the electrical wave pattern of the brain, and most recently an abnormal chromosomal pattern are all factors which *may* be associated with socially disturbed behaviour although not inevitably so.

On the purely *genetic* side studies have shown that although there may be evidence of an inherited psychopathic factor in succeeding generations of a family, the genetic influence does not follow the lines of closest blood kinships, and the environment in which the child is reared is felt to be the decisive element.

From the *psycho-analytic*[3] standpoint there has been a tendency to view neurosis and 'psychopathic disorder' as linked, the difference being in the way each reacted to a stress situation. The neurotic expresses his conflict in his intrapsychic turmoil whereas the psychopath, by acting-out, succeeds in evading any deeply felt emotion. The psychopath is thus described as immature in personality and emotional development. He is regarded as fixated at a protophallic level where sex is not yet differentiated, where there will be no developed super-ego and hence no castration fear. Such an individual is impulsive, has no anxiety or guilt, and can be restrained only by external controls because he is lacking in the inner controls of a developed conscience. The early pregenital fixation is emphasised by many psycho-analytic writers, and the deficient super-ego development is linked with the failure to introject the father image.

Shifting a little from this strictly psycho-analytic concept of maldevelopment of social and moral standards, considerable attention has been paid to the disturbed *environmental influences* which may lead to such a maldevelopment.

Bowlby,[4] investigating juvenile thieves, demonstrated that maternal deprivation in the early years *could* result in behaviour of the psychopathic type, but then was much criticised for his statement which was seen as too all embracing and not always substantiated. Bowlby, however, made it clear from the outset that he was only investigating one factor in the aetiology of disturbed behaviour and his findings remain a positive contribution although, like the physical findings, they do not provide the ultimate solution.

Continuing in this field the hostile or rejecting parental attitude has been seen by others to be of primary importance, particularly where the child continues to live with the cold and rejecting parents rather than being separated from them.*

* In the Daily Telegraph Colour Supplement of 12.12.69 and 19.12.69 there is an account of the family life of the girl Mary Bell who was sentenced at the age of 12 for the murder of two other children and described as a Psychopathic Personality. The tragic story is one of repeated family dramas, near-fatal accidents to the child, and episodes

The influence of the father who is traditionally the law-maker in our society is another factor seen as important. Father may be the absent party or, if present, *his* standards may be erratic, misleading or inconsistent giving the child no stable model with which to identify. Finally institutionalisation in childhood with loss of the total family environment is often regarded as particularly liable to be followed by disturbances of social and emotional behaviour, but once more the evidence is two-sided and institutionalisation as a child is not to be seen as an inevitable precursor of later disturbance.

Thus whilst the medical profession since Pritchard has put forward a variety of physical, psychological and environmentally induced causes of disturbed social behaviour these can each only account for a minority of cases.

Nevertheless by 1959 when the English Mental Health Act was reviewed and revised, a situation had been reached where a considerable body of psychiatric thought concluded that in some types of social deviation there was a *medical* entity which should be recognised and designated as *Psychopathic Disorder* and provided for in terms of legislation and treatment facilities as a Mental Disorder alongside Mental Illness (i.e. psychosis and neurosis) and Mental Subnormality.

The (1959) Act therefore broke new ground by taking this step which was hailed as progressive and liberal. The new Act defined Psychopathic Disorder rather vaguely as—'a persistent disorder or disability of mind (whether or not including subnormality of intelligence) which results in abnormally aggressive or seriously irresponsible conduct on the part of the patient and requires or is susceptible to medical treatment'. Legislation provided for compulsory committal for treatment —but only if the patient was under the age of 21, and not beyond the age of 25, which can be an age when the psychopath is at his worst. The Act reflected the continued uncertainty of the profession despite the radical step taken, and the legislation is in fact seldom invoked. New units for the treatment of Psychopathic Disorder have not been forthcoming and instead the validity of Psychopathic Disorder as a medical concept has been increasingly questioned both inside and outside the medical profession.

---

of rejection by a markedly disturbed mother whose dominating personality pushed the more passive and emotionally over-controlled father into a position of little direct influence in the home.

MEDICAL ATTITUDES

Peter Scott,[5] a forensic psychiatrist, reviewed a series of articles on Psychopathic Disorder and abstracted four common clauses from the many definitions:*

(1) The exclusion of subnormality or psychosis.

(2) The long standing duration.

(3) The description of behaviour such as aggressive or irresponsible.

(4) A clause indicating that society was impelled to do something about it.

This composite definition makes no mention of illness although many of the earlier definitions, from Rush in 1812 to Henderson in 1939, had concluded with the statement that the condition was to be regarded as an illness. Scott's opinion was simply that such an individual may be regarded as psychopathic (that is, ill) by a society stimulated to treat him medically, or as a recidivist (that is, criminal) if society was not so stimulated. Nigel Walker, a criminologist, has said similarly that the diagnosis of psychopathy is no more than a social device to deflect towards psychiatric treatment an offender against society with whom it seems inappropriate to deal punitively.[6]

Certainly Psychopathic Disorder does not fit the medical model of illness with a known aetiology, pathology, treatment and prognosis and a more satisfactory way of looking at the condition must be sought if its cause and management are to be better understood.[7]

THE EMERGENCE OF SOCIOLOGICAL THOUGHT ON PSYCHOPATHIC DISORDER

The early philosophical approach which ran counter to Pritchard's medical concept of social deviance was based on the assumption that the development of a moral sense of values was linked with the degree of civilisation of the particular culture or race, and that somehow this development went awry in those cases described as *Moral Insanity*.

Moral Insanity then and Psychopathic Disorder now are seen as something different from simply delinquent behaviour which, although deviant from the general norms, may not be particularly deviant from the norms of a certain district, street gang or family. Deviant behaviour learned in this latter

* The brief but cynical definition of Barbara Wootton, who has little time for the medical concept of psychopathy, reads: 'extremely selfish people and no one knows what makes them so'.

23

way by *differential association* is open to modification and correction by society and by the individual himself when he moves out of that group and its attendant customs and adapts to other standards of behaviour in order to gain acceptance.

The psychopathic deviant is deviant to the ways of his own deviant group, and his behaviour carries a deeper significance than a simple learning of bad habits.

Although a psychiatrist and adhering to the concept of an illness, Henderson had nevertheless departed from the strictly psychological standpoint when he described the psychopath in terms of his observed behaviour in 1939 in his treatise on *Psychopathic States*.[8]

Henderson's three types were:

(1) *The predominantly aggressive psychopath** who acts on impulse often with violence to himself and others with little feeling or rational thought behind his actions.

(2) *The predominantly inadequate psychopath*† who ekes out a dependent existence through an alternating provocative or passive relationship with the authorities.

(3) *The predominantly creative psychopath*‡ who in an eccentric and wayward course through life is capable of strokes of genius and episodes of gross mis-judgement.

Neither Henderson's three types nor his categorisation of Lawrence of Arabia with his curious mixture of daring and despair, melodrama and nonentity, ingenuity and foolhardiness as an example of the latter group have been widely accepted by psychiatrists[9] but yet in general terms they give certain clues to the behavioural meaning of psychopathic disorders.

The types overlap, they are not clinical entities with objective categorisation but if the predominant feature is noted it may indicate something of the underlying drives which need to be understood.

As examples one may summarise:

(1) *The Predominantly Aggressive Psychopath.* He is a creature of impulse, acting on the urges of raw, uninhibited and primitive drives, who may commit acts of pointless violence, or senselessly destroy property. He steals what he sees

* See for example the two assassins in *In Cold Blood* by Truman Capote.

† See for a true-life account *The Unknown Citizen* by Tony Parker.

‡ See both sides of the argument in *Lawrence of Arabia* by Richard Aldington.

rather than what he needs. He lashes out when people get too near. Some of his actions will seem to verge on the psychotic and, clearly, this is the most serious type of psychopathic behaviour and—fortunately—the rarest.

Pete has had several convictions for assault and his violence is getting worse. He has struck out viciously at a man who could not, or would not, give him a light, implying with a mouthful of abuse that he was in some way 'taking the Mickey out of me'. His background is a broken home, orphanage, Approved School, Borstal and prison, with a fair degree of truancy, and rebelliousness, so that the 'authorities' are constantly forced to do battle with him. He has had a little chance to learn what it means to live with—and relate to—people in a normal setting, and seems to have got it all wrong and misunderstands every word, interpreting every act as potentially hostile and so 'gets the boot in first'.

But the primitive violence within is steadily consuming him. He has been badly damaged in brawls, smashed up in cars when drugged and recently he caved in his head when he fell from a bus dead drunk.

(2) *The Predominantly Inadequate Psychopath.* A little higher up the ladder of personality development he is not quite as raw in his behaviour. This is the biggest group and includes all those who can only exist in society provided the representatives of society are in some way directing, controlling, supervising, or caring for them. So he tends to vacillate between a subservient attitude to the Welfare Agencies and childlike rages when his immediate and unrealistic demands are not immediately met.

Usually with a background of isolation and deprivation of family care in childhood, the inadequate psychopath is the persistent petty thief. An erratic worker, he gambles the house-keeping and drinks the Loan Club money—even his deceits and crimes are largely unsuccessful. It seems as if he can only find some degree of contentment or identity when he is, like a dog, on the end of his master's lead, even though he constantly tugs away and yaps at the heels just to emphasise what a fierce animal he is and how necessary it is for him to be on the lead.

(3) *The Predominantly Creative Psychopath.* Less easy to recognise. What was originally meant by this description was the eccentric, off-beat, near-genius who, by strokes of intuitive inspiration rather than formalised reasoning, brought off

great triumphs in business, art, politics or social life, whilst those ordinary mortals about him hesitated through uncertainty or weighed up the pros and cons with caution.

He is a live-wire and sparks off ideas unceasingly, most of which fizzle out in a trice, but some of which light a brilliant— if temporary—flame. Some of the 'whiz-kids' of the business world have built huge empires on the shakiest of foundations, sweeping others along with their enthusiasm, dismissing all criticisms and over-riding the opposition mercilessly. Sooner or later the edifice comes crashing down because judgement and assessment have been totally lacking from the start.

More often than not the creativity of the psychopath is much less spectacular and may only amount to a crazy dodge to make phone calls without payment, or the creations may exist only in fantasy. The pathological liar is such a case. Although there may well be an element of criminal fraud in this type of 'conning', often enough the gain cannot be reckoned in terms of money; it can only be seen in terms of some child-like, emotional gain.

Canon/Colonel/Air Commodore Collins was such a man. With a commanding presence, and outfit to match, he would sweep into a Bond Street gallery, be shown on request a series of old masters, decide on his purchase, with the aid of the art dealer, and leave a cheque with instructions for the picture to be delivered to his country house at a given address. Then he left. The cheque was false but so was the address and there was no expectation of gaining money or property by the deceit— only a brief identity as someone who was a definite member of society.

Even earlier than Henderson, Partridge[10] had preferred the term *sociopath* to emphasise the pathological *social* process and he believed that the latter was a defence mechanism to prevent the individual from breakdown into mental illness when under stress.

This choice of an escape route (into psychopathy) has parallels with the view of Laing[11] and the existential psychiatrists who see in psychosis itself an escape route from unendurable stresses and strains in 'real life' situations. In the case of the psychopath this escape path is nearer a conscious level of thinking.

A youth whose crime was to steal boats described his escape from the emotional pressures of a world which he found at times hostile, unfriendly and inimical and to which he could become frankly paranoid in the following terms:

> When things become too much I have to get away—
> I get in a boat and pull the hatch down over me—and outside is the sea and the wind with nothing and nobody in sight. I feel like a turtle with my home on my back—all I need is around me—food, clothes, a bed—and I can relax.

When the pressure eased he would sail into port and to the inevitable arrest and punishment.

A similar escape path is seen in a sort of wandering urgency which is a common finding in the psychopath. He leaves a trail of suitcases and odd belongings about the place—in lodgings he has left, with a Probation Officer he once knew, at a railway station somewhere as if to establish territorial bases which give some background identity and at the same time provide places to which he might go one day if need be. He muses on the people he could go to stay with—a grandparent in Glasgow—or an old workmate in Southampton—but seldom gets to either.

There is an uneasy awareness of his lack of contact with the existing society and a fear of total disintegration into madness. A feeling of non-recognition, even a fear of not-being. This is often expressed by the psychopath's quick assumption of one identity after another, his changes of name, domicile, mode of dress, appearance, the jargon he uses and the distinctive group he cleaves to—Hell's Angels, Rockers, junkies etc.—all with recognisable dress, an in-group language and a stereotyped pattern of behaviour.

It is a restless search for the psychopath to be *a something* lest he find he is nothing.

Thus Linda wrote to us from prison trying to explain her disturbed behaviour which had got her into custody and requesting re-admission to the Unit saying:

> I thought everything I said, did and thought was not real, that I was not real—almost as though I did not exist—so I could never affect anyone, because I was not real. No one could possibly take me seriously because I was not real.

In similar vein a more controlled new member of the Unit appeared at group meetings one day in a white boiler suit with his name written on the front and said frankly:

> I thought no one could see me like I was so I put this on to make sure you'd notice me.

Uncertainty of his own identity and its potential is seen by Gough,[12] a sociologist, as one of the primary deficiencies in the psychopath. There is a lack of role-playing ability. He has not acquired the ability to see himself objectively from another's point of view and thus be capable of modifying his own behaviour. He cannot predict the consequences of his actions nor understand how society will react to his behaviour. Lacking this ability to put himself in another's position he can form no attachments outside himself.

Halleck,[13] who also discards the concept of psychopathy as an illness, puts forward the idea that the psychopath is not so much incapable of forming relationships but is actively seeking to avoid them. He has no need of others and can 'travel light', free of commitments, ties and feelings of guilt. Indeed, Halleck puts forward the suggestion that society's preoccupation with the psychopath and his behaviour stems from a hankering envy of this appearance of freedom! Halleck goes on to say that it is doubtful if such a 'pure' psychopath exists, however, for if he had no need of people he would take himself off where there were none and remain untroubled. Instead he has doubts of his ability to sustain himself without some dependent link with society, and the constant brushes with the law are symptomatic of this.

The late Jimi Hendrix, a pop singer with a wild and nonconformist image commented to a newspaper reporter:

'Do *you* think I'm free? If I seem free its because I'm always running'.

Although he is the outsider the behaviour of the psychopath brings him into repeated contact with society. Whereas he often says he wants to be a beatnik, junkie, or drop-out and to live apart from society his actions in fact usually contradict this and bring him into constant conflict and contact with society. He assaults society and stays close to it. He rages against authority but seeks it out to strike. He demands freedom and goes repeatedly to gaol. He has no feelings and yet frequently commits suicide. To be truly psychopathic would be to have no need of people and society but to go through the motions of *conformity* so as to remain untouched by people and society, as Halleck has pointed out.

Invite the psychopath to live an authority-less existence (as in a democratic Therapeutic Community) and he is often crestfallen. He can only be whatever it is he wishes if society shows sufficient interest in him to say 'you cannot'. Like a child excluded from the game because he does not know the rules he makes his presence felt and recognised by constantly and repeatedly crashing into the other children at play.

His choice of behaviour pattern appears to be voluntary. He will tell you he wants to be as he is, but one must ask if his choice is authentic and free, or is based on false early conceptions? Does he make a free choice of behaviour knowing alternative ways of behaving or does he only know the way based on his own mislearned experience?

To summarise, the basic disorder in psychopathy is a defective awareness of social conduct and expectations and of the effect of one's own behaviour on other people. For its origins we must look to the factors which may have impeded social learning in the formative years and given rise to *a mislearning of social interactions, communications, conduct and behaviour.* There could be an analogy with *infantile autism* which has been described as 'an inability to receive or transmit the earliest inter-personal communications'. No such inability exists in the psychopath, but for a variety of reasons the earliest communications (between mother and child, family and child, school and the child) go wrong. They may be non-existent, incorrectly or inadequately transmitted on the part of the external world or—on the part of the child—misperceived because of genetic constitution, organic disease, or extraneous factors interfering with the perceptive process at some particularly crucial phase.

In the first three years, for instance, maternal deprivation may be crucial, in the following two years the child may be more vulnerable to disturbed communications from the father.

Cleckley[14] has gone so far as to describe the defective interpretation of social communications seen in the psychopath as a semantic *psychosis* believing in the illness concept but following on a concept of deficient social learning.

In practice, rather than coming upon a specific causal factor, one more often encounters a series of adverse factors, each summating to obscure perception until at a crucial time for that particular individual the ultimate trauma strikes home.

Thus, Patrick, an impulsive thief with a history of sudden violence and a constant chip on his shoulder which made him over-suspicious and hostile, had the following history.

He was illegitimate (possible genetic factor) brought up in the impersonal institutional type of orphanage (deprivation of maternal care) in a socially disturbed area of Glasgow (where the cultural norm was to accept a certain degree of crime and violence). He had one arm crippled by polio (physical inadequacy with his fellows) and would rely on a solitary friend to tie his shoe laces daily. One morning, when Patrick was 5 or 6 years old (a crucial age when he is emerging from the search for a parental figure and moving forward into encounters with fellows and their society), his friend refused to tie the laces.

Patrick as a man could clearly recall the hurt and its consequences, immediate and ensuing. He turned his back on his friend, on fellows, on society and from then on went his own way reliant on no one and grabbing whatever he could whenever he saw it (whether he needed it or not) and seeing threats and rejection in the faces and attitudes of everyone who came near.

Nevertheless, a nagging doubt remains about the validity of the first experience, and throughout life he tests and tests out again the same situation. Someone seems friendly and Patrick responds cautiously, but little by little increases his demands and his needs approaching the ultimate test.

Welfare Officers are bled dry of sympathy and sustenance until they cry, 'not you again'. The casual friend says after another 'phone call 'but my wife and I are going out tonight so we can't have you round' and these are interpreted as the 'rejecting' responses he half fears yet half desires. Having received them again he is assured in his belief that people are not to be trusted, relationships and feelings are fraught with disaster.

Once more he turns his back, confirmed in his early but *mislearned* pattern of what goes on between people at an emotional level.

REFERENCES

1. A review of the early literature on Psychopathic Personality is given in 'A Concept of Psychopathy and Psychopathic Personality: its evolution and historical development'. Maughs, Sydney. *Brit. J. Crim. Psychopathology*, 1941, 2, 329–56.

2. For a comprehensive review of the historical background and aetiological considerations, read the opening chapters of *Ten Studies*

MEDICAL ATTITUDES

into Psychopathic Personality. Craft, M. John Wright & Sons Ltd, Bristol, 1965.

3. Reviewed in 'Developments in the Concept of Psychopathic Personality'. Gurvitz, M. *Brit. J. Delinq.*, 1951, 2, 88.

4. See *Deprivation of Maternal Care* in *Maternal Care and Mental Health* and *Deprivation of Maternal Care* (ed. Bowlby, J.). Schocken Books, New York, 1966.

5. 'Psychopathy'. Scott, P. *Postgrad. Med. J.*, 1963, 39, 12.

6. *Cropwood Conference on Psychopathic Offenders.* Walker, N. *et al.* (ed. West, J. F.) Inst. Crimin. Cambridge, 1968.

7. For a general review of the subject see 'The Psychopath and his treatment'. Whiteley, J. S. *Brit. J. of Hosp. Med.*, 1970, 1, 263; or less clinically orientated in 'Out of Step: The Psychopath and Society'. Whiteley, J. S. Family Doctor Publications, 1970.

8. *Psychopathic States.* Henderson, D. K. Norton, New York, 1939.

9. See *The Psychopath.* McCord, W. M., and McCord, J. Insight Books, London, 1964, where the authors criticise the validity of calling Lawrence a psychopath in view of his 'undermining shyness, his hatred for the horrors of war, and most importantly his pervading guilt and desire for expiation'.

10. 'Current Conceptions of Psychopathic Personality'. Partridge, G. E. *Am. J. of Psychiatry*, 1930, 10, 53–79.

11. See for instance *The Divided Self.* Laing, R. D. Pelican Books, 1965.

12. 'A Sociological Theory of Psychopathy'. Gough, H. G. *Am. J. Sociology*, 1947, 53, 539.

13. 'Psychopathy, Freedom and Criminal Behavior'. Halleck, S. *Bull. Menninger Clinic*, 1966, 30, 127.

14. *The Mask of Sanity.* Cleckley, H. M. 4th Ed. Mosby, St. Louis, 1964. This is a classic book of historical value and literary merit even though Cleckley takes a controversial view of psychopathy as a psychosis.

Chapter Two

SOCIAL LEARNING THROUGH THE THERAPEUTIC COMMUNITY

SITUATIONS in which social learning can take place through the experiences of living closely together with colleagues, making necessary rules for the survival of the group and creating a purposive harmonious and satisfying way of life together, have long been utilised in many countries in the management of juvenile delinquents, the treatment of maladjusted children or simply the fuller education of young people.

The well documented accounts of the Ford Republic, Makarenko and the Gorki settlements, Homer Lane and the Little Commonwealth, David Wills and Q Camps, Neill at Summerhill, and Lyward at Finchden Manor are a few examples.[1]

Such projects always create much interest and arouse more controversy but seldom spread into the wider fields of general usage where society prefers to stick to the traditional and orthodox methods of authoritarian direction and the imposition of behavioural standards from above.

In the field of adult offenders there has been even less experimentation with these more liberal 'living and learning' self-governing situations, yet as long ago as 1837 Alexander Maconochie governor of the Norfolk Island Penal Colony, did set up a crude stage by stage experiment in social rehabilitation, but clearly created so much anxiety and apprehension in his contemporary society that he was recalled and his methods suppressed. What Maconochie had done was to dispense with the uniforms, restraints and authoritarian symbols which in their turn created a set response of hostility and resentment from the prisoners, and allowed the latter to work out firstly how to manage their own affairs by a simple reward system for work done, then how to collaborate as one of a working pair, and finally how to fit into a village community with relative freedom within the confines of the settlement.

Clearly the different aims of these educational, treatment or reformative communities have demanded different methods in practice but the principles of self-determination and the possibilities for self-awareness to develop are the same.

In psychiatry a similar approach—*the Therapeutic Community*—took root during the Second World War and with the passage of time became a widely accepted treatment method. Then, as if on a converging path with the evolution of sociological thought in the medical attitudes to deviance, the Therapeutic Community evolved into a method of treatment for social deviants as its real potential became apparent.

THERAPEUTIC COMMUNITIES IN PSYCHIATRY

The basic idea of the Therapeutic Community is to utilise the interactions which arise between people living closely together as the means of focusing on their behavioural difficulties and emotional problems and to harness the social forces of the group as the medium through which changes can be initiated. How this came about is of some interest.

In the armed forces, psychiatric hospitals of the Second World War a hitherto unique situation was encountered first in the U.K. and then in the U.S.A. as the latter came into the war.

Large numbers of patients of roughly the same age group (young adults) with similar psychiatric illnesses (neuroses), the latter precipitated by a common social disturbance (commitment for war service), were gathered together in one treatment centre.

The population was quite unlike the mixed diagnostic categories and wide age range of the accustomed psychiatric hospital and the situation was ripe for a different approach.

THE PSYCHODYNAMIC MODEL OF A THERAPEUTIC COMMUNITY

At the Northfields Military Hospital in England an experiment with group psychotherapeutic methods had only partial success when conducted on traditional lines.

Then, Foulkes and his colleagues looked at the problem for its unique situation and saw in *the ongoing life of the hospital* and its participant members the medium through which emotional interactions could be expressed, brought under examination and modified. An experiment in large group dynamics and interaction at a community level was consciously *set up* by the psychiatric staff.

Foulkes himself had a psycho-analytic background and retained an analytic method in his approach to the group as he has described in his book *Therapeutic Group Analysis*.[2]

In that book an example of the Northfields method is described and can be here summarised. A general malaise and discontent had fallen on the hospital and was reflected in many ways. A particular centre of disharmony was the hospital band (appropriately enough!). A member shortly to leave the hospital was manipulating the other band members into accepting as his replacement a friend of inferior musical ability at the expense of a more competent musician. The latter, already dispirited and depressed, was inclined to give in and the band seemed powerless to resist the manipulation which could only further their own destruction. Foulkes describes how, by sitting in on the band meetings he, the therapist, came to learn about the overt problems and also to understand the latent undertones of anxiety and uncertainty about many other problems common to the whole hospital at a surface level. He was able to reassure the displaced musician as to his own value and competence, advise the band on a more satisfactory solution to its immediate problem which meant the exclusion of the manipulating member (whom Foulkes calls the psychopath, it may be noted!) and to encourage the band in its function of morale boosting and the facilitation of social events and interaction in the hospital. In turn the general improvement allowed a freer expression among the group members of the scarcely broached fears that many had, such as a rumour that participation in unit affairs may be likely to delay discharge from the Army. Once out into the open these matters could be dealt with more effectively.

Foulkes regards his intervention as 'essentially analytical'. Of the Therapeutic Community at Northfields he has said that 'out of this experiment came the idea that the occupation of any group may be of secondary importance whereas active participation in the group setting may be the essential therapeutic agency. The results of the participation depending on the good or bad effect of the interpersonal relationships which are encountered.'

This essentially group-analytic model with the therapist maintaining a distance, observing and commenting and facilitating problem solution by interpretation of the overt and latent content of the groups' interactions has been carried over into the Therapeutic Community treatment of psychiatric patients, particularly neurotics in hospital settings, and follows a medical conceptualisation of psychiatric treatment.

SOCIAL LEARNING

A SOCIODYNAMIC MODEL OF THE THERAPEUTIC COMMUNITY

Contemporaneous with the consciously introduced North-fields experiment, however, a similar group of patients came under treatment at the Mill Hill Emergency Hospital near London, and out of that experience a slightly different Therapeutic Community model *evolved* with the passage of time.[3]

At Mill Hill the staff were fewer, and in a leading position amongst them was Maxwell Jones who came with a background of the rather organically orientated psychiatric training of the Maudsley Hospital.

Jones faced the identical issues raised at Northfields and tackled his staff problems by a didactic approach in which he lectured to large groups of patients, as if to medical students, on the psychological basis of their physiologically and anatomically expressed psychosomatic symptoms.

He was quick to perceive, however, that the professionals had much to learn from, and with, the patients about the root causes of their symptoms, and soon these large group meetings became a forum for the interchange of opinions and then for the resolution of problems in the daily life of those concerned at a practical level of shared discussion and decisions.

The end of the war brought the end of this particular problem activated by the current social disturbance but also the emergence of a new social problem in the form of returned Prisoners of War who felt and often were emotionally, socially and industrially displaced persons.

Maxwell Jones set up a rehabilitatory community which tackled the resettlement problem by involving local tradesmen, employers, social club leaders and the like in the necessary re-learning and rehabilitatory process.

There was little attempt at formal psychotherapeutic exploration or interpretation in these early days and the same essentially practical and sociotherapeutic approach was carried over into the next problem thrown up by society which was the post-war industrial malcontent and apathy. Jones geared his unit to Industrial Rehabilitation and the exploration of problems in the actual workshop setting. This approach seems facile and superficial now and it was a crucial step to move on from this stage to the appreciation that the actual work situation was of secondary importance to the deeper seated problems that the patient brought to his job; his family disputes, marital disharmonies and personality deviations.

In any work situation such a person would find expression for his discontent, and the unit at Belmont, re-named as the Social Rehabilitation Unit in 1953, widened its horizons and became something of a model and experimental society in which different facets of the individuals daily life could be usefully explored and, if appropriate, modified.

The difference between the type of Therapeutic Community *evolving* at Belmont and that *set-up* at Northfields is reflected in an account of the handling of an incident at Belmont which, like the episode at Northfields seemed to emanate from a general unit discontent and at the same time pose a threat to the on-going life of the Community.[4]

A dissident group of women patients was boycotting unit activities and meeting in a ward kitchen as a splinter group. The integrity of the Community was thus threatened. Jones himself intervened one evening and tried to persuade the dissidents to join a unit social gathering but they refused and he retired. Next day the ward sister intervened because her social therapists were being inconvenienced in their use of the kitchen for essential duties,* and she lost her temper with the kitchen squatters. After each of these staff interventions there was a repercussion in the following day's Community meeting, and on each occasion hostility was expressed by the group members to the male and then to the female authority figure, but the present situation could be interpreted in terms of the personal conflict situations relevant to those concerned in their own lives.

With a better understanding of these unconscious factors the whole group was able to turn its attention to the welfare of the Community and draw up new plans and rules for the use of the kitchen and the incorporation of the women members into the group.

The differences between the Northfields and Belmont models are slight. There is a general and considerable overlap of basic beliefs and techniques, but from Northfields we get the *group analytic model* with the therapist conducting the treatment process from a detached point of view, retaining control and interpreting behaviour in psychodynamic terms. The Belmont model is more socio-dynamic. The therapists are

* This was in 1956 and something of the traditional hospital regime still carried over. Now (1971) the Community residents prepare and serve their own meals and staff members have less hierarchical roles and few separate duties.

multiple representing different facets of the Community life, they integrate at a less detached level and show their own feelings as appropriate, and it is the strength and power of the total Community group which brings about the therapeutic changes. There is more emphasis on *confrontation* of the patient about his behaviour now than on *interpretation*.

Because you are behaving *thus* we feel *this* and our group has suffered in the particular way we show you now—as a result of your behaviour.

The two approaches are not mutually exclusive and a Therapeutic Community will utilise all the processes described at various times, but the basic difference in origin, evolution and orientation is of importance and has some bearing on the type of patient for which either approach is most appropriate.

The overlap could be represented diagrammatically thus:

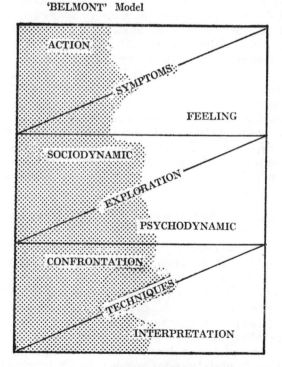

'BELMONT' Model

'NORTHFIELDS' Model

This socio-dynamic emphasis at Belmont was further high-lighted by a comprehensive study of the Belmont unit in the mid 1950's by Rapoport. He outlined four principles at work in the Therapeutic Community.

(1) *Communalism*, by which was meant the sharing of communications, opinions and tasks.

(2) *Democracy*, which extended into a sharing of responsibilities and decisions by joint discussion and consensus taking.

(3) *Permissiveness*, which entailed acceptance of another as he really was—both in his acting-out (anxiety avoiding) behaviour and in his emotionally upset (anxiety experiencing) behaviour.

(4) *Confrontation*, which entails constantly putting before the individual what he is doing here and now in his every day behaviour.

The divergent psychodynamic-sociodynamic differences of approach were reflected even in some of Rapoport's criticisms of the Belmont Therapeutic Community where he saw a conflict between the *psychotherapeutic* aims of the medical side and the realistic *rehabilitatory* goals of the workshop side. There seemed a conflict of purpose between the objective which said 'let us find out *why* you are thus' and that which said 'whatever you are you must *adapt* to these conditions'. There was, too, an unselective application of the treatment which meant that powerful therapeutic tools were often put into the hands of patients unable to learn to use them beneficially for themselves or for others. Finally those who 'did well' in terms of adjustment to this highly artificial society did not necessarily carry over their success into the different situation in the external society.

THE LATER DEVELOPMENT OF THE THERAPEUTIC COMMUNITY

At about this period in time (1959–60) came the revision of the Mental Health Act already referred to in Chapter 1 with its new attitude toward Psychopathic Disorder—but also the wave of new tranquilising and anti-depressant drugs began to make their effects seen in psychiatric treatment.

The Therapeutic Community ideology had been widely taken up after the war by psychiatrists with little else new to offer for the past two decades, and the old, ritualistic and oppressive Mental Hospital regimes which perpetuated and perhaps induced mental disorders had been exposed and

SOCIAL LEARNING

largely discarded. With the advent of the new pharmacological preparations, however, there was something of a return to the former medical omnipotence and therapeutic authoritarianism although the newly gained freedom from restraint for the patient, the respect for his opinion and the opportunity for him to participate in deciding on his future were not altogether lost. The liberal regime of the Mental Hospital became the Therapeutic Community *approach* as described by Clark,[6] in contrast to the Therapeutic Community *proper* which maintained the viewpoint that mental disorders arose from misconceptions and maladjustments in inter-personal reactions and could be treated by exploration of these interactions alone.

The latter school of thought lost support in the treatment of some psychotics and many neurotics who clearly responded better to the new drugs, and whilst some Therapeutic Communities incorporated physical treatments into their own versions of the Therapeutic Community technique, the already less medically orientated Belmont unit moved even further from the general psychiatric field and became a natural treatment centre for the psychopath and his basically social disorder. No medications or physical methods of treatment were used and gradually the individual psychotherapeutic interviews were dropped with deputation of all treatment interchanges to the total Community and its subordinate groups.

THE THERAPEUTIC COMMUNITY AT HENDERSON

Re-named Henderson Hospital* in 1960 or simply Henderson without the Hospital suffix and its attendant implications, the place has become an autonomous unit within the administration of the Department of Health with about 30 staff† who are non-resident and approximately 40–50 'patients' or residents.

* The Henderson is named after D. K. Henderson (author of *Psychopathic States*, Norton, New York, 1939) but out of Maxwell Jones' respect for his former mentor rather than for Henderson's interest in psychopaths.

† Staff List: 4 Psychiatrists, 2 Social Workers, 14 Nurses, 4 Social Therapists (usually students embarking on or part way through a social studies, sociology or social psychology etc., course and seeking field work experience), 1 Psychologist (also the clerical work group leader), 1 Occupational Therapist, 3 Secretaries, 1 Domestic, 1 Porter. There is an attached Disablement Resettlement Officer and also a Probation Officer and Chaplain who attend part-time.

The concept of the Therapeutic Community at Henderson is as now outlined.

In any society tensions arise between people, reactions occur and feelings are stirred. In most situations for the sake of on-going business and peaceful co-existence we can seldom let such inter-personal reactions have free expression and we suppress, sublimate, displace or avoid them; forgetting about it, having a drink, sleeping on it, or taking it out on something else.

In the Therapeutic Community these inter-personal happenings become the medium through which treatment is realised.

The Unit is therefore close-knit, intimate and somewhat encapsulated. Its aims are basically:

(a) to produce a community in which these real inter-personal reactions can freely *occur*, be uninhibitedly *expressed* and be *accepted* by the group

(b) to have an agreed mechanism by which such interactions can then be *explored* to the full

(c) to provide a social system which affords the opportunities for *trying out* different roles and alternative modes of reaction.

The Community is not 'permissive', therefore, in the way of a free and totally unstructured society but is a very specific model which many have criticised as being *too* rigid. But in attempting to meet the needs of the particular type of individual for which it has developed its structure the latter has some important purposes and meaning.

(a) The Community Culture

It takes time to develop the Community Culture, as the historical development of Henderson has shown. Maxwell Jones has said that, in the early days, he was probably fortunate in having an old dilapidated and badly decorated and finished building, for the sense of involvement in a common task was more readily seen and grasped. It may be that some Therapeutic Communities have failed because the staff leaders have pushed an ideological model too quickly for the natural growth and awareness of the participants.

Even within the existing Community there are constant periods of basic re-learning of the method as new members are joining. The Community therefore sways between authoritarian direction and democratic evolution, between periods of rigid rule insistence and almost anarchic free-living as different groups find out for themselves the strength of Community life.[7]

For the longer stay staff these episodes of cultural regression demand considerable restraint and toleration, for there is a natural tendency to move continually forward which may leave behind some of the people for whom this Community is intended.

Clearly it is desirable for the Community to be resident and intimate in its living activities, so that all behaviour becomes subject to scrutiny. The closeness of the Community and the absence of outside commitments and attachments will intensify inter-personal experiences within the Community, but a frequent criticism is that this 'monastic' in-group, with its lack of privacy, unreal seclusion and lack of contacts with outside life, is false and unrealistic.

This is agreed, but the exclusion of outside affairs which frequently serve as defensive blocks to involvement in the treatment situation is purposive. The whole process of Therapeutic Community treatment is as specific as for instance psycho-analytic treatment, and demands equally careful selection of participants.

Of the intensity thus engendered one member has commented 'It's like real life speeded up. You meet in one day things you wouldn't come across in a month outside. They come at you from all sides. Non-stop.'

Great stress is laid on *communication*, and there is constant feed-back of opinions, accounts, goings-on and general information to the total Community group. Much of this takes place in rather ritualised feed-back reports from all areas to the Community meetings, and its very amount and the ritualistic way in which it may be called for can threaten to obscure or divert its purpose.

Thus feed-back reports of a group meeting may be totally blocking the real content of the group, deliberately or unconsciously misconstrued, and themselves prevent real communication. The need to share all communications can undoubtedly become an obsessional neurosis but one has to steer a zig-zag course between the Scylla of little communication and the mistrust that that engenders in all organisations, and the Charybdis of total communication and the implication that no one is trusted to get on with a job in confidence.

Again the particular problems of the social deviant tip the scale towards over-communication if anything. As we have seen there is a considerable undercurrent of uncertainty, suspicion indeed paranoia in the personality* of this individual who feels himself excluded from society. Not to know what has gone on in the room from which he has been excluded (the parental room, the staff-room or another group meeting) may be to increase his tension *beyond* the point where it can use-fully promote a free expression of his anxiety, and result in a fall-back into provocative acting-out behaviour.

The *responsibility* delegated to the Community is consider-able but must be authentic. The Unit itself has to operate within certain boundaries—as part of a hospital group, as a unit of the Department of Health and subject to the overall laws of the land. Therefore the rules made by the Community for its daily life must be within that framework. We cannot legalise pot-smoking for instance nor decide on the annual budget allocation. Equally, the decisions that such a con-glomerate group can take are purely limited to basic social behaviour and interactions. In some Therapeutic Communities decisions are taken by the group on the prescription of medication but this demands specific medical knowledge beyond the scope of the majority of the group and seems a false situation. Decisions taken as to who shall be admitted or discharged are a different matter, for—in our particular case —strictly medical considerations do not enter the problem, and if an individual is perceived by the group to be in need of medical attention there is no hesitation from the group in turning to its medical members and requesting that they get on with whatever they deem reasonable, e.g. a transfer to an orthodox hospital.

Decisions particularly about the discharge of patients who have transgressed rules are sometimes felt as anti-therapeutic and 'wrong' by the staff whose natural inclination remains to care for and make allowances for the 'patients'. But it would be disastrous to the total ethos to over-ride or unduly in-fluence the decision of the group once made. Nevertheless such decisions, whilst often seeming punitive or scape-goating, are not taken lightly. They arouse considerable feelings of anxiety, guilt, depression and foreboding in the group and this drawing of the line by his peer-group will often be a turning point in

* In a study of Personality Traits in Henderson residents, by the use of the Cattell 16PF Inventory, significantly high scores were shown in the factors measuring suspicion, apprehension, tension, imagination, and significant tendency towards lack of self-control, emotional stability and shyness (O'Brien, M. Unpublished research, 1968).

the career of someone who has constantly pushed and provoked the authority just a little further and usually had
authority give way in the end.

The general *atmosphere* of a Community meeting can be
rowdy, infantile in its exchanges, primitive in the feelings
expressed and unsophisticated in its conduct. There is the
ritualistic call for feed-backs from various areas concerning
yesterday's events, the brusque interrogation of those who
have offended against the code, and haphazard discussion of
certain forthcoming events—matters that require review or
amendment of existing regulations.

The situation is regressive. These are adults with unformed
or misformed patterns of social behaviour, playing out a game
of social interaction and learning from it.

'A crash course in living' was the apt description of one girl.
'You learn in six months at Henderson what you should have
learned, say between 6 and 10 years old.'

Indeed the Therapeutic Community situation, and particularly the Community meeting, is reminiscent of the Piaget[8]
concrete stage of development (6–10 years old) when social
awareness and the need to fit into a social system, in play, at
school and with other children and their attendant spheres of
influence is developing. The earlier *egocentric* stage is being left
behind but the stage of *adult integration* not yet reached.

At such a stage the *Rules of the Game* seem more important
than the game. The testing out of existing rules, the manipulation, breaking, amendment and avoidance of or total com-
pliance with rules are important to the child in his learning of
how to assume a responsibility from within rather than be
subject to the imposition of rules from without.

In the Therapeutic Community the rules are simple rules of
behaviour—don't take drugs, don't bring drink into the Unit,
don't be violent, don't be in the ward of the opposite sex after
midnight and so on.

There are rules which remind one of the purpose of being
here—attend groups on time, do your share of the housework
etc.—and odd rules which a particular situation may require
and which somehow become incorporated into and used by the
system.

For instance, at one time there was considerable horse-play
with fire-equipment, and a rule was introduced to say that such
interference (which could have dangerous consequences) meant
instant discharge. Perusal of the records for a follow-up

research some years later demonstrated that a considerable number of people had been discharged 'on fire-rule'. In fact the Unit was not full of arsonists but this was another rule around which there could be considerable acting-out. To *touch* the fire-hose was a symbolic way of crying enough and leaving, or it could be a test-out of the Community's strength or attitude to oneself.

Some of the arguments around rules broken seem ludicrous but the emotions and manner in which they are expressed must be seen in a more basic light.

A group arguing whether Yeast Tablets are 'a drug' (and therefore illegally taken by Joe who must come up for consideration of discharge) may be composed largely of ex-junkies and law breakers, but the basic argument they are working out is not about drugs but about the meaning of social contracts between people and the expectations that such entail.

Similarly the Community must be seeking for the meaning behind a particular breach of the rules. A resident may contrive a situation which, however much we like him, places him in breach of a rule which carries a discharge decision. It cannot be smoothed over. He is telling us that he must leave but he cannot take that step himself. To persuade such people to stay on often leads to increasingly severe disturbance. Also, the decision once made, the rule once invoked should not be reversed in the heat of the moment. At this stage of leaving the 'child' must know that No means No. He becomes confused if the parent body is erratic in its implementation of rules. He needs to learn and know the limits. Only at a later (adult) stage can he *interpret* the rules.

The rules are nevertheless complex—there are instant discharges—'unless there are good reasons why this should not be so'—but in any case you can 'sleep-in for the night'—and if you don't break the slightest rule again you are likely to be 'allowed two weeks extension' on your discharge to organise your leaving!

In other words these basic rules are considerably used by the Community to bring behaviour into focus, explore it, try out and test out reactions almost in an academic way, but it is a necessary game, for the alternatives may be the more dangerous acting-out behaviour in which serious rules—assault, murder, damage—are broken to test out society itself.

The *sense of Community membership* is quickly acquired by newcomers (if there is a strong on-going culture). Not much is

demanded of them to be a member, and usually the first transactions are seen in respect of themselves and the total Community. They can dip in and out of Community affairs without
too much emotional strain, and the Community is the first and
rather shapeless object of transference. But it is an important
transference object, as we shall see later, and it is to Henderson
that people relate rather than to Doctor X or this or that staff
member.

The sense of emotional involvement with the Community is
vital for this type of treatment to be effective. The idea that
important matters 'must go to the Community', that the
Community is the ultimate court in disputes and the depend-
able holding situation in troubles, and that a Community
meeting can be called at any time of the day or night if the
situation warrants it gives back-bone to the Therapeutic Community concept.

It is a continuous, stressful, 24-hour process of self-
perception.

'You can't switch it off', explained one member to a newcomer. 'If I go home at weekends I'm still living Henderson
and I want to get back to see what's going on. I dream
Henderson.'

Comments are sometimes made that the pace is too intense
and that there is no relaxation, but the social phenomena
arising in this context are not very different from social
phenomena arising in other organisations where groups of
people came together to work at a common project—in industry, colleges, or even government. The Henderson system
gives members a unique opportunity for examination of these
phenomena.

(b) The Mechanisms of exploration

The day starts with a Community meeting which largely
seems to bind the Community together, remind the members
of their purpose and re-affirm their ties much as a morning
school assembly or daily church service.

Any examination of interaction in the large Community
meeting favours the sociological conceptions already outlined,
but then the day takes its 'medical' form. Small groups
assemble for a psychotherapy session. This tends to be centred
around a doctor but differs from orthodox group-analysis in
that there are multiple therapists—staff from various areas of

the Community and those members of the resident group who may have been in the Unit some time and are now preparing to leave but able to act very effectively in passing on treatment to newer members joining. The small groups are thus open-ended, they tend to follow a style of here and now observation and the interpretation of behaviour, but because of their constitution and the overwhelming sense of all that is going on in the total Community much material is inevitably related to those events which are strictly speaking outside the group-room.

In the small group the various members have a closer and deeper contact with psychotherapy. It is more sophisticated than the Community meeting and demands more of them in terms of maturity. Transference to one or other of the staff members looms greater but is still shared in a group setting, which is a further safe-guard for these people to whom feelings seem particularly fraught with anxiety and danger.

Transference to the whole Community has already been alluded to. Transference reactions to 'the Staff' as a whole arise from a group feeling. There is an analogy again with psycho-analytic practice for there are many times in Therapeutic Community exchanges when it is as if the Community was composed of two persons only—the analyst (the Staff) and the analysand (the residents)—so clearly are the group feelings united on the one hand and demarcated on the other. This interaction of 'the Staff' and 'the residents' also demands attention and understanding for useful interpretation and exploitation.

Under threat from a united residents' onslaught or beguiled by a manipulative psychopath, a new or unsophisticated staff member can fail to see the latent psychodynamic mechanisms and go over to the residents' point of view, split off from his staff fellows, be open to personal confidences between himself and the residents, and be a disintegrative factor in the staff's therapeutic role. This is not to say that staff should never disagree, but in their disagreements they must be aware of the disastrous implications this can have on watching, testing and waiting children when the 'parents' quarrel.

The group and its interactions personifies the disorder for the social deviant, for here he takes and/or is allotted a role to play. The scapegoat, the misfit, the authority or the rebel, for instance.

In the small groups he takes up a share in group feeling or

sees others doing so and tries to follow. The groups are more controlled than the Community meeting, perhaps more inhibited by social conventions and very much a learning process for the individual, about how he may now look into himself.

When new members join the Unit they initially go to a group where the Medical Director, a small staff team and a representative of the resident Community conduct the group, loosely, but nevertheless directed towards exploring and illustrating by what is going on how such events can be turned to a useful learning experience for the newcomer.

In this new members' group much of the early apprehension about the seeming lack of medical care and authoritarian controls and, or, support are worked through. The newcomer gradually sheds his expectancy of external control and direction and assumes the readiness for personal exploration.

This is the first time that the 'Medical Director' has been referred to by title. It seems paradoxical that a democratic community should have such a hierarchical head but he serves an important psychotherapeutic purpose, and this is enhanced by the first encounter in this particular group.

All staff and residents are referred to anyway solely by Christian name, no staff uniforms are worn, clothes adopted tend to be fairly inconspicuous in their determination of social class, and Staff make no particular demand for preferential treatment.

Thus the hierarchy is hidden in everyday transactions but someone has to serve as the all bad father, the one who rigidly sets the rules, the ever-loving mother, the heroic elder brother and the understanding kid sister. Staff fall into these roles partly by dint of their personality but largely because of the posts they occupy in the Community. It is important to be aware of these transference possibilities and use them to the full.

A new admission, an adopted ungainly, 'dropped-out' boy in constant conflict with his father who had expected more of him and had now thrown him out requested a 'travel warrant' to his distant home the first week-end. Such free passes on the railway are not lightly agreed and smack much more of the traditional welfare services of the orthodox hospital. It was put to the Community but Charlie insisted that he now saw everything clearly and was going home to clear things up with his parents. The Community rather half-heartedly agreed he should have the warrant, but at a meeting from which I

(Medical Director) was absent. He told me of the decision and
somewhat irritably I scolded him for his lack of self-sufficiency
in seeking a warrant instead of hitching, pretending so soon
that all was clear to him, and finally putting me into the
position in which I would have to step back from my Community role and play the role of a proper doctor in signing a
travel warrant for him.

> 'The Community said I could have it—why are you against
> it?' he asks.
> 'Have you been in this situation before where you must have
> things right now and it causes trouble—with your parents for
> instance?'
> A moment's reflection. 'My mum would give me things but not
> my father. He's like you—says I must work for it. He's earned
> it and I have to. Never let me have a thing, he wouldn't.'

It is put to Charlie that to enforce his claim will really take
him and me out of Therapeutic Community treatment and
reinstate the old model of hospital doctor and hospital patient
that he knows so well. The group takes up the issue until
Charlie finally says:

> 'After you've explained that—I'll respect you less if you give
> in now—but I still must have it!'

The next few days in all groups he attends he brings out his
dilemma—whether to commit himself to the Community
treatment or stick to his inner needs for a personal parental
attention. The warrant is signed and waiting for him to pick
up but the day preceeding the journey he sprains his ankle,
which would make it unwise to travel as all agree.

Other groups have other purposes (there are groups where
the family is brought in or married couples attend, those soon
to leave get together and those who have left continue to
meet) but they still tend to the medical model of exploration.
Thus in the afternoons the Community break into work groups.
The work accomplished is no more than that necessary for the
on-going life of the Community—cooking, building and furniture repairs and maintenance, some clerical and research work,
preparing a magazine, decorating and generally improving the
living situation with 'fine art' works and *all* the staff (doctors,
social workers, nurses etc.) are involved in these actual working situations.

Work groups tend to be freer from medical control, and each

has its own system, but on the whole there is an agreement that what is important is not the work so much but some period of examination during the afternoon of *how* the work was done, who reacted in what way to the situation, how people got together, took or gave instructions, co-operated or rebelled.

Some groups rigidly work at their task and then rigidly attend to the problems (maintenance), others are looking at the problems as they go along (magazine). There is a free choice of work groups which means that different levels of maturity tend to plane out. Like collects like, and the tasks chosen are usually appropriate to the maturity levels. This means that staff too must appreciate the various modes in which these groups can operate, differently but still effectively for their members.

Some people are lost in the morning verbal groups but can effectively work (really and psychotherapeutically) in the afternoon groups at a slower and less pointed pace, rather like children in play therapy.

Sometimes the harassed individual needs to retreat for a while into a basic work group where he can mess about with paint instead of 'talking about his problems'.

The medical mode of exploration is carried over further into ward meetings and into meetings which can and frequently are called at any time by people in trouble or around a crisis situation. The tradition is that if a problem arises—Jack is depressed and tearful, Bill and Ben are drunk and threatening to break up the television room—the appropriate group (ward, workshop, the whole Community) forms a group then and there and tries to solve the immediate issue practically and *at the same time* explore psychotherapeutically how such a situation arose and what are its implications for those concerned and for others.

A criticism of this group-psychotherapeutic approach to the more practical aspect of living in the Therapeutic Community is levelled by those who feel that the experience of living in and through the problems that arise is enough of itself and that 'all that psychotherapy crap' should have no part, and that the satisfaction of getting on with and finishing a good job will bring rewards equal to any psychological insights.

However one of the basic objectives of the Therapeutic Community is the exploration of behaviour, and since this at least is something of value that the medical side has to offer, it seems a wasted opportunity not to spend a considerable time in trying to find out *why* things happen as well as facilitating them to happen.

(c) *Role-playing opportunities*

One of the more obvious opportunities that the Therapeutic Community affords is for the individual to shed his patient role and try out a therapist role, and the open-ended group as opposed to a closed group with its members all at a similar stage of maturity development gives full opportunity for this.

Sometimes this therapist role is adopted too readily as a defence against personal involvement or as an attempt to gain favour with whoever is seen as the 'real' therapist, but in the ward meetings, workshops and crisis meetings in particular where staff are few or totally absent the insightful and sincere individual who may act in a therapeutic way can be highly effective, and such meetings may be beneficial to all concerned as an experience in actual self-determination.

The need for the social deviant himself to be involved personally in the exploration or modification of deviance in others has been widely stressed, and the Therapeutic Community gives ample scope for such.

For a new admission the first new role to adopt is not to be a patient and dependent on hospital care and attention, or not to be a delinquent and dependent on penal care and attention —or both.

This can be a difficult change to make. A very institutionalised girl complained tearfully on the second day that 'there were no cups—so how would she drink'.

True there was a shortage of cups—they get broken, or left around, but others in the group saw no problem. Some drank from empty milk bottles,* others had bought personal cups in Woolworths, one or two had made mugs in the pottery room and she was immediately offered a loan of all or any and suggestions about how she might do similarly for herself, which she was able to implement by the next day.

---

* The milk-bottle drinking has its own connotations of course. One very immature dependent and violent young man who always drank from the bottle and one day flung his bottle across the meeting room smashing it left having gained a certain improvement. He returned to a hostel (for alcoholics) where the warden told me he continued to drink from a milk bottle 'like at Henderson' until he said he had now had enough of institutional life and left to find a flat (and crockery presumably) and is getting on well at an independent level of existence.

SOCIAL LEARNING

At a more basic level the complicated structure of the Therapeutic Community allows considerable opportunities for role-playing. With about 40 residents the Community has a committee of 20 or more posts and each area, ward or workshop will have representatives and small sub-committees for entertainment, administration, etc. as well as various ad hoc committees which may be appointed to look after certain problems, e.g. to re-arrange the catering service and negotiate such with the hospital management.

The jobs carry real responsibility, anxieties, rewards and difficulties. The Chairman is called out to deal with severe problems as would be a doctor on call. The catering officer has to organise supplies and cooking for a difficult group to whom the basic feeding act has psychodynamic undertones too. The Ward Representatives see to the emotional well-being of their colleagues as well as keep records of attendances and absences.

The jobs change around at monthly elections, and usually there is much competition for prestige posts such as the Chairman or the Selection Committee which interviews new applicants.

The foreman of a work group, this month in a position of authority, may be the tea-boy next month. He has a chance to try himself out up and down the hierarchical scale, to see himself (or someone exactly like himself) from another point of view, to feel what authority is like as well as to know dependence, to be in control as well as to be controlled.

The simple shifts bring out simple attitudes. A habitual Borstal Boy shoved into the works' foreman position (for he was a good manual worker) finally said, 'I can't do this—I need to be *told* what to do—I'm not comfortable having to decide.' This was reflected in his life outside the workgroup and in the outside world.

With the jobs seen as primarily experiences in alternative roles this system of allocation and re-allocation does not make for administrative efficiency, but that is not the prime motive.

SUMMARY

The Therapeutic Community represented by the Henderson model therefore is one which has evolved in response to social demands and disorders. Dealing with social problems by the examination and adjustment of social forces it can take realistic decisions and has authentic responsibility for its own well-being within the confines it sets itself.

HENDERSON

The structure of the working day and the mode of operation emanates nevertheless from the more medically inspired group-psychotherapeutic techniques developed in the treatment of psychiatric disorders.

How in detail the day is structured and the modifications of behaviour achieved is probably of secondary importance to the opportunity that such a Community offers for positive identification with a large group which can represent a microcosm of society—provided that in some way this is linked with a process which seeks to understand how and why certain situations come about. In other words the Community must become Therapeutic.

The structure and mechanism of Henderson *today* is given. Tomorrow it may be different, but so long as time is spent in examining how and why it has needed to become different that is what matters. When a Therapeutic Community becomes settled, comfortable and static, free of anxieties, rivalries, guilt, anger, depression, love and hate it has lost its purpose.

REFERENCES

1. See in Chapter 1 of *Reluctant Rebels*. Jones, Howard. Tavistock Publications, London, 1960; or, more fully, read *Homer Lane and the Little Commonwealth*. Bazeley, E. T. Schocken Books, New York, 1969. *Throw away thy Rod*. Willis, D. Gollancz, London, 1960; *Summerhill*. Neill, A. S. Penguin Books, London, 1960; *Mr. Lyward's Answer*. Burn, M. Hamish Hamilton, London, 1960.

2. *Therapeutic Group Analysis*. Foulkes, S. H. Allen & Unwin, London, 1964.

3. The early experiences are described in *Social Psychiatry: A study of Therapeutic Communities*. Jones, M. Tavistock Publications, London, 1952.

4. Read more fully in 'Some Therapeutic Functions of Administrative Disturbance'. Rapoport, R. N., and Skellern, E. *Administrative Sc. Quarterly*, Vol. 2, No. 1, June 1957.

5. *Community as Doctor*. Rapoport, R. Social Science Paperbacks (Tavistock Publications), London, 1952.

6. 'Therapeutic Community: Concepts, Practice and Future'. Clark, D. H. *Brit. J. Psychiat.*, 111, 479, Oct. 1965.

7. See in ' "Democratization" and Authority in a Therapeutic Community'. Rapoport, R., and Rapoport, R. *Behavioral Sc.*, 11, 2, April 1957.

8. *The Moral Judgement of the Child*. Piaget, J. Harcourt Brace & Co. Inc., 1932.

Chapter Three

EXPERIENCES IN THE THERAPEUTIC COMMUNITY: THE RESULTS OF TREATMENT

THE previous chapter has described something of the Therapeutic Community structure and illustrated how the dynamics of the Therapeutic Community can be viewed at any time in three planes, namely:

(1) at the *Community* level with its fluctuations of overall mood and state of well-being in which it assumes very much the role of the composite authority figure, the transference agent, or the archetypal parents;

(2) at the level of the *small* group which is the exploratory level seeking to understand in the here and now activity the feelings of the individual in respect to his fellows and particularly as determined by the influence of the overall Community;

(3) at the level of the *individual*, which is the ultimate aim of the whole procedure. The reaction of the individual is a product of the attitude taken up by the parent Community and his own state of awareness in his perceptions of the here and now situation, and this will be described in the present chapter.

At first the interaction tends to be between the newcomer and the total Community, only later, after the exploratory and almost academic experiences in the small groups, does he venture to emerge more as an individual and discuss his deeper feelings to other individuals both here in the Unit and around the key figures in his real life situation.

Thus at a new members' group Sue is talking about the difficulty of getting accepted into the Unit and has spent the first weekend out with virtual strangers she met in a pub and became 'steaming drunk' as she puts it. She 'cannot remember' anything about her early life with her parents except that for much of it she was living away with grand-parents. She complains that the parents undertook to have her born and therefore should have considered her wants more. It is put to her that *we* the Unit undertook to have her but it is difficult to meet or consider her wants when she goes away from us to others, indeed that in this unsatisfactory weekend activity there has been something of a repetition of early childhood feelings vis-à-vis the parents.

At the same group Dina, an adopted girl with very similar family problems but who has been in the Unit several months and attends now more in the role of a co-therapist, is able to talk about her personal feelings to the doctor in the group, relating him very much to the powerful and controlling figures she saw in her parents but at the same time finding a level of communication between her and him where she can put forward ideas for her future life, ask advice and accept comment.

In the reactions of the individual we see a re-creation of the early social and emotional learning experiences with a 'second chance' now to get the situation into perspective.

For the individual coming into a Therapeutic Community it can be a liberalising but at the same time frightening experience to be part of a society where the habitual authoritarian controls exerted by others from the outside are shed and the possibility for independent action is experienced.

Thus Terry, an explosive, impulsive and near psychotic youth with a history of Approved School and Borstal confinement and more recently a lengthy stay in a Mental Hospital where he had frequently to be transferred to a locked ward because of violent acts, became increasingly agitated in this first week at Henderson by the absence of evident controls. With no locked ward to be moved into and no ready tranquillising drugs freely dispensed, he had considerable fears of his own ability to retain control over himself. He ran away and spent the next three days travelling about the country in a country bus on a Rover's ticket before being able to return to the Unit and commit himself to a lengthy, sometimes anxiety-ridden, but finally successful treatment course.

A very similar individual spent his first week looking into every room, behind every door, and into every cupboard like a frightened animal in a new cage. Then he was able to say, 'If I stay here I'll go mad—it's the uncertainty—I can't stand not knowing what's going to happen next', and wisely he elected to leave.

This emergence from under an umbrella of restrictive yet protective authoritarian control can often be seen at the Selection Group interview where a prospective applicant for admission is interviewed by a representative group from the Community members. At first he answers questions as to why he is here, and what are his needs in terms of 'my psychiatrist says'—'the Probation Officer told me'. As the interview proceeds and his opinion is sincerely sought, his views allowed and often heartily agreed with by someone present, he begins to see that real control and responsibility is held by members of the group not dissimilar to himself and is not just invested in the few staff members present. He begins to offer more of himself, and when it is finally put to him that he has as much choice in making the forth-coming treatment contract as does 'the hospital', it may be the first time this fostered-out, ex-Children's Home, former Approved School and now 'remanded on bail for medical report' subject has been allowed an opinion about his future independent of the authorities.

Nevertheless there is a heavy fall-out of new admissions in the early days of treatment and some 20% leave in the first two weeks. This is for a variety of reasons—too much anxiety engendered by the apparent absence of external control, a flight into health occasioned by the thought of prolonged and arduous treatment, or sometimes increased despair at the same prospect or unwillingness or inability to shed the deviant pattern which is so well-known for an unknown and uncertain pattern of behaviour.

In the series followed up later in this chapter only 13% stayed longer than six months, 38% longer than three months.

Failure in terms of further convictions or further psychiatric admissions was more likely to be seen in those who left before the three month mark, although not to a significant degree. These earlier leavers were not strictly comparable to those who stayed longer (and therefore could not serve as a strict control group) for they tended to be more criminally inclined than psychiatrically affected.

Of 24 in the series who left in under 14 days, 15 had relapsed (into conviction or psychiatric admission) within the two year follow-up period, one had committed suicide actually in hospital and two others died in traumatic circumstances before three years were passed. Eight (33%) were free of relapse of any sort at the follow-up time despite this very short stay.

The early weeks are usually the most disturbed so far as the Community is concerned, for the new member is testing out. He tries to make the situation *viable* in the terms of Whitaker and Lieberman.[1] He persistently continues in his known (and deviant) method of behaviour, trying to gain collusion from those around him and confirmation that he has really no need to change. Thus his repetitive drinking, rule breaking, violence or whatever continues and brings him into repeated conflict with the Community. The pressures of the group, accepting, yet confronting, interpreting, pointing out, suggesting modifications, understanding and facilitating problem solving will be a different reaction from the authoritarian suppression he has hitherto provoked, and he may come to see that for him also there can be the possibility of a shift in behaviour roles in this different type of society.

If he continues to act-out, then the Community-imposed sanctions mount in parallel with his misdemeanors until it becomes clear that he must change his pattern if he wants to stay or—if he wants to continue in his old ways (and he is welcome to do so)—he must leave.

Because of his continuing misdemeanors, he may repeatedly be faced with a discharge vote. The votes are counted for and against, with abstentions going in his favour. The cry of 'Watch the abstentions, mate' may be the warning light, for this floating vote can and will finally swing over to a discharge decision.

When the initial testing out period is over, however, the individual who has elected to stay will then seize the Community with a hungry mouth. He becomes highly involved in all Community affairs, takes on as many jobs as he can, is active in all the meetings, and keen to air his knowledge of the Community and its customs to visitors. He picks up the in-group jargon and folk-lore and sees in Henderson the early promise of all that has been denied him in life.

It is a stage of *positive transference* (to Henderson as a whole) where everything about the Unit is good, but whenever stresses and strains arise and he may be confronted with his own behaviour, or if feelings come poking hurtfully to the surface, he resorts to the old acting-out behaviour.

A smash-up, a piss-up or a lost weekend in London punctuates his otherwise assiduous attention to Community duties such as gathering together ward-mates for a group meeting in his role as a ward representative, or making and reading out to the Community meeting a summary of the events at a previous day's meeting in his role as a group secretary.

This stage can last for the first 2–3 months, at which time there may be a shift in behaviour to a state where the persistent emotional upsurges become too strong and too persistent to be easily thrust aside. He begins to experience feelings and the old acting-out and emotion-avoiding behaviour peters out. He has gained sufficient strength from the group to allow such unpleasant feelings to emerge, but not yet sufficient reassurance to deal with them effectively. He blames the Unit for 'giving him more problems than when he came in', he can see no hope for himself and regrets his lost links with past behaviour. The Unit is no good, in a mess, and has let him down. His colleagues are bloody fools and the staff useless. Now is the stage of *negative transference* to the Unit, and this too can be a time for flight. However at this time the depressed, resentful and seemingly abject individual may be the backbone of the Unit. He now fetches other patients into groups, not because it is his job as the ward representative but because he feels it is right for them to be there. He restrains the acters-out, he is learning the meaning of control for himself and exercising it appropriately on others.

The working through of the depression until final leaving is a stage of dis-involvement in the Unit. Often the patient will have 'gone through' the Committee from cafeteria assistant to Chairman and now be on the side lines with no Committee post and watching a new generation flex their muscles in the power battles. He is consolidating what he has learnt, but again there may be occasional forays to the old haunts and the old life as if to see if such places and people still exist, to test out if he really has changed and to assure himself that a niche still exists if the new life fails. An old pattern of behaviour has been discarded but a new pattern may not have been fully acquired or established yet.

Leaving frequently tends to be a messy, half rejecting, half rejected affair, and the first months outside the Unit difficult.

Roy, seen some 18 months after leaving, says 'I went through a ropey stage when I left. I had a phase of dressing up and acting queer. I couldn't stick a job and kept getting pissed and then I took the usual over-dose—you know in the street so I'd be picked up. I spent a week in an ordinary mental hospital and you know I knew what they were all up to—staff and patients—the games they were playing—and I thought what the hell am I doing here?'

He walked out and had been in steady employment and with a more stable social life ever since.

In the Rapoport[2] study the success rate judged at 6 months was 31%, although at discharge an expected success rate of 61% had been estimated. However by one year after discharge there had been a reassertion of the lessons learned, with success now assessed at 41%.

STAFF REACTIONS

New staff joining the Therapeutic Community go through very similar experiences to the new resident.

They are more mature and more sophisticated in their reactions but they have periods of initial zeal, disillusion with the ideology, and then a realisation that there is a great deal of value here but that it is hard work indeed to dig it out and the rewards are limited and not spectacular.

Considerable strain is put upon staff, for they are forced into a position of self examination by the residents with whom they are in constant therapeutic interaction and by their colleagues in daily staff meetings and after-group discussions and seminars. They must be aware of their own roles and feelings and considerable time should be spent in training, for the strength of a Therapeutic Community is at the ground-roots level throughout the whole working day. It must not be hived off into special sub-groups conducted by the experts.

The personal problems as well as the personal attitudes of staff soon come out in the Community interactions and require time to be put aside for group exploration of these difficulties in staff meetings separate from the meetings with the residents. These can be difficult and tense situations, for a staff member will find himself in the position of someone being treated rather than in the privileged role of the therapist, and reacts as his particular personality determines, for better or worse.

RESULTS OF TREATMENT

So far the specific nature of Therapeutic Community treatment has been stressed and the consequent need for care in selection of people for whom the experience would be appropriate and beneficial.

Grant[3] and his colleagues found that subjects who would not normally be considered as suitable for psychotherapy by reason of persistent acting-out, lack of verbal ability and low intelligence could become disturbed and their state worsened by an intensive psychotherapeutic regime.

Similarly Craft,[4] in a controlled experiment with young delinquents of low or subnormal intelligence, compared the outcome of a group treated along Therapeutic Community lines with one treated in a benignly authoritarian but traditionally directive way. The latter group did best in terms of fewer convictions in the follow-up period and Craft concluded that 'perhaps short-term attempts to change personality (*in that particular sample*)* merely leave patients in a confused and bewildered state in which infantile aggressiveness and demands for immediate gratificaton come more readily'.

On the other hand Miles,[5] with a similar sample of subnormal offenders, demonstrated that a therapeutic community group showed a superior outcome to an authoritarian-treated group in terms of increased ability to form and use inter-personal relationships.

Craft was measuring reconviction or rehospitalisation as criteria of failure.

A further experiment by Grant[3] at Camp Elliott compared the outcome of treatment in high maturity subjects with those of low maturity. Two types of therapist were employed—those skilled in therapeutic community methods and those of an authoritarian disposition.

The high maturity subjects did well with the therapeutic community therapists and badly with the authoritarian therapists—and vice versa—low maturity subjects did badly with therapeutic community therapists and well with authoritarian therapists. Selection of appropriate regime was as important as selection of candidates.

A FOLLOW-UP OF HENDERSON LEAVERS

The results of psychotherapy are always difficult to measure. Follow-up interviews suffer from bias if the interviewers are from the institution under test, and there is the additional hazard of the interviewee's desire to please the questioner. This was particularly noted in our original attempt to make follow-up assessments. Discharged members still had a strong identification with the Unit and presented themselves in an artificially good light (as relatives pointed out), as they perhaps felt at that moment of reminiscence rather than after a well-considered reflection of past events. In psychopaths there is perhaps a particular tendency to live for the moment, but a final barrier to the interview follow-up was the other particular quality of the psychopath—his vagrancy. Only

* Author's italics.

52·4% could effectively be traced and be found in when the interviewer called.

A more objective if less illuminating method was therefore chosen, and the Criminal Records Office and the Ministry of Health Psychiatric Index was utilised to provide definitive follow-up information. A conviction of sufficient severity to be entered on criminal records or an admission to a Mental Hospital which was automatically registered on the Ministry of Health index were the two criteria taken to be indications of a failure in social adjustment (if *either* was present).

The group followed-up were 122 consecutive male discharges during a 12 month period of 1964–5. They were all people referred to the Henderson with the diagnosis of psychopath, character disorder, personality disorder or similar term and were admitted after being screened by the Community Selection Group which in a group interview lasting about two hours seeks to assess the subject's motivation for change, his awareness of his own social defects and the need to do something about them, and his capacity for gaining insight and emotional growth. It also assesses his particular ability to function in a group therapy setting and whether or not the Therapeutic Community at that moment feels capable of coping with the newcomer. Thus after a period of extreme violence in the Unit a man with a long history of impulsive violence would most likely be rejected.

Psychotic, subnormal or brain damaged subjects are excluded by a pre-interview perusal of referral letters, but such are seldom referred to Henderson now because of the well-known function and purpose of the Unit.

The characteristics of the group followed-up are shown in Table 1. They are a mixed bag of young social deviants whose deviance ranges through impulsive violence, delinquency, sexual perversion, inability to work, addiction, alcoholism, deceits or simply an inability to get on with fellows, families or employers.

The predominant syndrome with which the subject presented in this series, where such could be determined, is also shown in Table 1. The letters of referral were examined, three syndromes were categorized and the predominant syndrome for each case was then selected.

Thus, by *affective syndrome* it is meant that depression, apathy, tension, hypochondriasis, insomnia or ideas of suicide were stressed.

EXPERIENCES AND RESULTS

The *thought disorder syndrome* emphasised bizarre ideas, suspicion, paranoia, obsessions, odd beliefs and social withdrawal.

The *action syndrome* laid emphasis on the criminal activity, addiction, sexual disturbance or other such acting-out behaviour in the history.

The overall results showed that 40·1% had remained out of further trouble in that they had neither been convicted *nor* admitted to a Mental Hospital in the follow-up period which was for a minimum period of two years and over three years in some cases. In all but fourteen some data concerning subsequent history was available. As three of these had been contacted at one year and two were found to have emigrated, only nine (7·3%) were totally untraceable after leaving the Unit.

TABLE I

Background features: (122 consecutive discharges)

Age on admissions				Matrices IQ			
18–22	.. .. ..	56	46·0%	less than 85	.. .. ..	1	1·2%
23–27	.. .. ..	33	27·0%	86–95	.. .. ..	5	6·0%
28–32	.. .. ..	16	13·1%	96–105	.. .. ..	12	14·5%
33–37	.. .. ..	12	9·9%	106–125	.. .. ..	56	67·5%
38–42	.. .. ..	3	2·4%	126–135	.. .. ..	9	10·8%
43 and over	.. ..	2	1·6%	more than 135	.. ..	0	
		122	100·0%			83	100·0%
				failed to take test	..	39	
						122	

Background features (continued)	No.	Total	%
Childhood experiences			
Broken home under 16 years (any reasons)	48	122	39·3
Institutional period (non-penal) under 15 years ..	30	115	26·0
Irregular school attendance due to sickness	11	118	9·3
Irregular school attendance due to truancy	26	118	22·0
Irregular school attendance due to other reasons ..	10	118	8·5
Irregular school attendance due to all reasons ..	47	118	39·8%
Grammar/public school level reached	33	114	28·8
Some G.C.E. passes gained	21	115	18·2
Convictions as juvenile	38	122	31·1
Approved school committal	15	122	12·2

Background features (continued)	No.	Total	%
Marital status			
Married	36	122	
Divorced/legally separated	2		
Total having married at any time	38	122	31·1
Occupational status			
Highest steady job attained: (Hall Jones scale of occupational prestige)			
Class 1: Professional/higher administrative	0		
Class 2: Managerial/executive	1		0·8
Class 3: Inspectoral/supervisory (higher)	4		3·3
Class 4: Inspectoral/supervisory (lower grade) ..	11		9·0
Class 5a: Routine non-manual	21		17·2
Class 5b: Skilled manual	16		13·2
Class 6: Semi-skilled manual	36		29·5
Class 7: Routine manual	31		25·4
No job	2		1·6
	122		100·0%
Less than 1 year in any one job	48		43·2
1–2 years in any one job	21		18·9
Over 2 years in any one job	42		37·9
	111		100·0%
Not known	11		
	122		
Previous psychiatric admissions (122 cases)			
Previous admissions to Henderson	17		13·9
Previous admissions to all psychiatric units including Henderson	66		54·5
1 admission	36		
2 admissions	12		
3–4 admissions	7		
5 and more admissions	11		
Syndrome cluster in referral letter:			
Affective syndrome predominates	27		23·5
Action syndrome predominates	45		39·1
Thought disorder syndrome predominates	3		2·1
Mixed affective/action syndrome predominates	30		26·1
Other mixtures	10		8·7
	115		100·0%
Not possible to determine	7		
	122		

Background features (continued)	No.	Total	%
Previous criminal history (adult over 17) (122 cases)			
Previous convictions	87		71·3
On probation for previous offence at time of present referral	45		26·8
Having had imprisonment as adult	52		42·6
Admitted following present court proceedings (and referred due to such)	33		27·0
Admitted on an Order of Residence (Sect. 4 C.J.A. 1948)	21		17·2
Admitted and on probation (includes above)	57		46·7
Of the 87 with previous convictions:			
1 conviction	18		20·6
2 convictions	19		21·8
3–5 convictions	30		34·4
6 or more convictions	20		22·9
Includes crimes of violence/damage ..	18		20·6
Includes taking and driving away	24		27·6
Includes sexual offences	12		13·8
Having had imprisonment as adult	52		59·7

PREDICTING SUCCESS

With the idea in mind that the Therapeutic Community is a very specific treatment procedure and not applicable to a comprehensive range of deviants the study turned more to an exploration of prognostic factors.

The total group was divided into *success* (no convictions or psychiatric admissions in a 2-year period of follow-up and *failure* (conviction or psychiatric admission in the follow-up period) sub-groups, and the items in the social background, delinquent and psychiatric histories were compared in the two groups.

The factors significantly associated with a *better outcome* were that a better grade of school had been reached, more success in school had been achieved in terms of examination passes gained, and this evidence of stability and ability to achieve results was reflected in the occupational and inter-personal spheres.

Thus those with a better outcome had shown more occupational achievement in terms of reaching a skilled manual job (class 5b) or an inspectorial/supervisory job (non-manual) (class 3). They had also shown greater stability in work in terms of holding one job for at least two years.

More of this group had married than had those in the poorer outcome group, and in the latter were two divorces but none in the former.

Factors which were significantly associated with a *poorer outcome* were more usually present in the previous criminal history, but the fact that the subject had spent a period in an Institution during childhood (non-penal and before the age of 15) was so associated.

TABLE II

Prognostic factors	Better outcome group			Poorer outcome group			χ^2 (1d.f)	p.
	No.	Total	%	No.	Total	%		
— Institutional period (non-penal) before 15	6	50	12·0	24	65	36·9	7·86	0·01
+ Grammar/public school attained	22	47	46·7	11	67	16·4	10·9	0·001
+ Some G.C.E. passes gained	14	49	28·5	7	66	10·6	4·9	0·05
+ Held one job over two years	26	46	56·5	16	66	24·2	10·7	0·005
+ Having attained class 3 or class 5b (or higher) occupation	13	50	26·0	7	71	9·8	4·43	0·05
+ Having married (at any time) vs remained single	22	50	44·0	16	72	22·3	5·3	0·025
— Previous conviction (adult over 17)	28	50	56·0	59	72	81·8	8·4	0·005
— Over two convictions (adults over 17) ..	13	50	26·0	37	72	51·4	6·8	0·01
— Approved School and adult penal committal	1	50	2·0	13	72	18·0	5·99	0·025
— On probation at time of referral	7	50	14·0	38	72	52·7	17·43	0·001
— On probation at time of admission	11	50	22·0	46	72	63·9	19·15	0·001
— Admitted on Order of Residence (Sect. 4.CJA 1948)	4	50	8·0	17	72	23·6	4·01	0·05
— Admitted following current Court proceedings	7	50	14·0	26	72	36·1	6·2	0·025
+ Affective syndrome predominant	18	49	36·8	9	66	13·7	8·1	0·005

EXPERIENCES AND RESULTS

In addition (but not at a level of statistical significance) the better outcome group were more likely to be older (over the 18–27 group) to be above average in intelligence (I.Q. 106+), and the occupation of the father was more likely to be in the successful middle occupational classes (classes 5b and 3).

In both groups the incidence of broken homes of any kind before the age of 16 was high, as was irregular school attendance. Truancy showed a tendency to be more frequent in the poorer outcome group.

Factors which were significantly associated with the poorer outcome were a history of previous convictions, recidivism as measured by more than two convictions, and the fact that the subject had been to Approved School and adult penal establishment also. Other factors were that already he was on probation at the time of referral to Henderson (from a previous conviction) or was on probation when admitted, was admitted on a Probation Order of Residence or was admitted and hence referred in connection with current court proceedings.

The types of crime were similarly distributed in the two groups, but although a juvenile criminal record was more likely to be found in the poorer outcome group the level was not significant.

Slightly more of the better outcome group had had previous psychiatric admissions but not to a significant degree. A similar trend was shown in previous out-patient attendance, both adult and Child Guidance.

However, there was a significant difference in presentation in that a better outcome was associated with a predominance of affective syndrome in the presenting symptomatology. Although action syndrome was common in both groups it is more likely to be the presenting feature in the poorer outcome group.

REFLECTIONS ON THE DYNAMICS OF THE THERAPEUTIC COMMUNITY

Voluntary participation in treatment is more likely to be associated with a successful outcome, as the figures for those subjects admitted in connection with current court proceedings or on various forms of probation clearly show.

Positive involvement in Unit affairs with support for the ideology and identification with the aims of the Unit has previously been considered to be related to success, and an assessment of positive or negative involvement (rule breaking, avoidance of treatment groups, lack of participation) was made from the case summary. Although no level of significance was reached, there was a tendency for the better outcome group to show a more positive involvement and the poorer outcome group to be negative or indifferent.

When the use of the Unit facilities (Disablement Resettlement Officer, Psychiatric Social Worker, a 'future planning' group) to plan leaving properly in terms of job seeking, accommodation finding, further arrangements for after-care contact, were considered the better outcome group showed a higher proportion who had left in a planned way.

The poorer outcome group had more often left abruptly or disappeared without a word. Those discharged by the Community for rule-breaking, although more likely to be found in the poorer outcome group, were not significantly so associated. Such rule-breaking may sometimes be interpreted as a 'neurotic' way of terminating treatment.

DELINQUENTS AND THE THERAPEUTIC COMMUNITY

If we consider separately the 87 delinquents with a previous history of (adult) convictions, the number who were reconvicted within 2 years were 49 (56·3%) (1964–5).

This can be *loosely* compared with the 64% reconvicted in the 2 years following Borstal in a study made by Hood[6] (1960), or the 62% reconvicted in 2 years a group of *homeless* Borstal boys aged 17–20 selected by Miller[7] (1960–1) for a residential and group psychotherapeutic community setting.

Of the 87 in the series who had a previous history of convictions, 39 (44·8%) relapsed and were re-convicted in the first year after discharge, and by the end of the two-year period 49 (56·3%) had been convicted. So far as the records made it possible to check, 53 (60·9%) had been convicted by the end of the third year after discharge from Henderson.

The group of 37 which was free of further convictions for the two-year period was compared with those who had been convicted in this period. There were some differences between the groups in that those who relapsed and were subsequently reconvicted were more likely to have experienced a broken home, to have been in an Institution or been to an Approved School in childhood, but these differences did not reach a significant level.

EXPERIENCES AND RESULTS

The main factors which were found to be associated with subsequent failure were the factors related to previous criminal behaviour. Thus, the group subsequently re-convicted had a significantly higher proportion who had had over two convictions prior to the Henderson admission, who were admitted to Henderson in connection with current court proceedings, and who were admitted on a Probation Order of Residence; these subjects were recidivists, probably little motivated, and considered to need some control from the external authority of the Courts.

The group who remained free of further convictions after discharge had more often had a previous history of psychiatric admissions, they presented with a more affective symptomatology, and their ability to plan their leaving was significantly associated with the better outcome.

THE INFLUENCE OF A PSYCHIATRIC HISTORY IN THE PROGNOSIS OF CRIMINALITY

The psychiatric component of the previous history and its influence on criminality could be examined further by comparing the group which had had previous convictions only with the group which had had previous convictions and previous psychiatric admissions.

As it happened, the previous psychiatric history of one case was uncertain, and he was excluded, which left equal numbers in the two groups.

No. of previous convictions	43 with previous convictions and psychiatric admissions	43 with previous convictions only
1	8	10
2	7	12
3–5	15	14
6 or more	13	7

Those with a history of convictions and psychiatric admissions also were older, more had married, and their psychiatric component was reflected in the greater proportion of affective syndrome in the symptomatology, although action syndrome was still predominant. They could become more involved in the Unit and a planned leaving was significantly associated.

In the first year after leaving Henderson there was a greater

67

reduction in the number of convictions in this group than in the other, and in the second year significantly fewer were re-convicted from the group which had the previous psychiatric admission history. Thus, in the delinquent group the presence of a previous history of psychiatric admission appeared to be a good prognostic sign as far as the likelihood of reconviction was concerned.

From the first to the second year the psychiatric admission rate of the previously psychiatric group decreased in parallel with the decreasing conviction rate, whereas the psychiatric admission rate for the group which had not previously had psychiatric admission was maintained at virtually the same level from first to second year.

Admission to psychiatric hospitals was a new aspect of behaviour for this latter group who now appeared to have acquired a psychiatric label in addition to their criminality.

	43 with previous convictions only	43 with previous convictions and psychiatric admissions
Psychiatric admissions in year one	9 (20·9%)	15 (34·8%)
Psychiatric admissions in year two	8 (18·6%)	8 (18·6%)

A GROUP WHO FAILED ADMISSION

During the initial search for an adequate control group a further group of 50 consecutive cases who had been selected for admission but then failed to attend for admission were considered but rejected for the different features they were to display.

As a group they had a similar incidence of previous psychiatric admission to the 122 who were admitted. The incidence of adult convictions was lower, but the delinquents were a little more recidivist, and there was a particular increase in crimes of violence, damage and taking and driving away offences. They were a younger group and in childhood had had more experience of broken homes but less experience of non-penal institutional life, although more Approved School commitment.

They presented with the same action syndromes predominant but with a marked increase in the prominence of the *thought disorder* syndrome. This was significant [χ^2(1d.f)=11·2.

p < ·001] when compared with the presence or not of thought disorder syndrome in the total series.

THE NATURAL HISTORY OF PSYCHOPATHIC DISORDER

There are many psychiatrists who regard psychopaths as untreatable or at best only to be managed and controlled until some hoped-for maturation takes place.

It is commonly held that the psychopath 'burns-out' in middle life, but the extensive follow-up by Lee Robins[8] of deviant children, many of whom were later to display psychopathic behaviour patterns, suggests, that while overt anti-social behaviour may diminish with the years the psychopath can be just as destructive within the narrower confines of his family for many years. The psychopathic drive may be replaced in middle life by a more neurotic seeming depression, and this can be the time when psychotherapeutic treatment becomes more pertinent.

On the other hand, death by violence and by suicide is high in the later years.[8] In the present series there were five violent deaths within three years of discharge. Suicide was the verdict in three cases and the other two were fatal accidents associated with an overdose of drugs.

Craft[9] has made a comprehensive review of the outcome of treatment in various centres. The type of treatment was largely custodial management and the settings penal but he concluded that 'even among extreme samples of psychopathy a substantial number improve with the passage of time or treatment or both'. He drew attention to the fact that in two separate groups of subnormal offenders treated by himself on a benignly authoritarian and directive regime and followed-up later, 58% of the group followed-up after five years, and 40% of the group followed-up after three years were in open employment and out of hospitals or prisons. He stresses the need for long-term facilities for support in the outside community and ready re-admission to the parent hospital if stresses become too great.

Of 900 treated in the penal setting of Herstedvester,[10] Denmark, where the treatment follows some therapeutic community principles modified to fit into a prison setting, 87% were finally able to leave the institution (after being committed on an indefinite sentence) and to function in the outside community. Gibbens[11] et al. in (1959) following-up criminal psychopaths found that 24% of their sample had received one or no convictions during an eight-year follow-up.

On the less custodial and more dynamic side of treatment, comparative figures are hard to come by. McCord and McCord[12] report that milieu therapy has changed the behaviour of some (juvenile) psychopaths in terms of decreased aggression and punitive views of authority, increased internalised guilt, increased behavioural control and increased realistic self-perception. However permanent these measured changes will be they leave to future research.

AN INTERPRETATION OF THE RESULTS

Our own research suggests that whilst the previous criminal history remains an important indication of prognosis, particularly of poor prognosis, the factors which give evidence of some personality maturity and emotional potential are useful indicators of a good prognosis.

The philosophy of Henderson and similar Therapeutic Communities has always been to work on the 'not sick' part of the subject, with the aim of establishing that part of his personality more securely, and that being achieved the 'sick' —socially deviant—part will have less *raison d'être*.

Thus the person most likely to benefit from this type of Therapeutic Community treatment will already have shown some ability for achievement in school, occupational and interpersonal areas, and this despite possible early disturbance in the family.

The one less likely to benefit will have often experienced more deprivation of the early social learning opportunities in the home and family in terms of institutional life as a child, but will have been a non-achiever at all stages thereafter and in a somewhat passive-hostile relationship to society, so that his life is a series of commitals to Approved Schools, Borstals or Prison, Probation, Courts and now to hospital. At Selection Group he so often answers to the question 'why are you here?', 'Well ask them —they sent me —they said it would be best — I don't know do I?'

The Therapeutic Community is a regressive situation in which the early social learning experiences of the five to ten-year-old can be repeated. The affective, emotion-experiencing subject is able to become involved in this situation and use it productively to restructure his interpersonal relationships and behaviour in a more personally satisfying and socially acceptable way. The subject who has less personality resources cannot let himself become involved in this situation, which he fears may be a further emotionally traumatic experience, and he stays on the outside and repeats the provocative testing-out patterns of behaviour until even this permissive and therapeutically orientated society responds by rejection or increasingly punitive controls. He is then confirmed in his feeling that society is not to be trusted, and it may be that the experience is harmful in terms of later increased psychiatric disturbance.

In the Henderson community these less intelligent or less mature personalities probably become more disturbed as a result of competition with their better endowed fellows, and it may be that they would benefit more in a Community of their peers geared to a less intense or less stressful pace and with less ambitious goals.

Selection must therefore be based on positive features rather than negative ones such as a 'last chance' or 'because further imprisonment will clearly do no good'. The positive prognostic factors here indicated can be seen in terms of progressive levels of emotional maturity similar to the I-levels described by Grant in seven stages of emotional and personality integration, from total egocentricity to a mature capacity for interpersonal relationships (Sullivan *et al.*).[13]

In the present study, the group of failed admissions comes nearest to that category of character disorder, with the lowest emotional integration and for whom treatment procedures remain in doubt, and for whom some external and containing control seems to be indicated.

The persistently acting-out personality as represented by the poorer outcome group has reached a somewhat higher level for emotional experience, but his consistent acting-out is a sustained emotion-avoiding act and, as has been shown, the intensive type of Therapeutic Community may prove a disturbing and non-beneficial treatment approach. It may be that the treatment needs of this type must first be met in terms of management in supportive hostels and the like. More authoritarian and directive regimes, with less responsibility given to the subject, may have to be established before any maturation or social learning can proceed.

In the late Sir David Henderson's terminology, this latter may be seen as the *'inadequate psychopath'*, the former (who in this study were the failed admission group) as the *'aggressive*

HENDERSON

psychopath', which leaves the third category of *'creative psychopath'*; if this can be stretched to accommodate those whose creations are largely phantasy, unrealistically and hopelessly ill-conceived as well as often regarded as deviant by the society in which they live, then the affective, feeling, potentially able but emotionally disorganised subject of the better outcome group can be included. Clearly, he is at a still higher level of emotional maturity and the Therapeutic Community offers a good chance of further integration and progress towards maturity, but different regimes with different aims need to be developed for the other two categories, as the succeeding chapters will show.

REFERENCES

1. Read the theory of *Group Dynamics in Psychotherapy through the Group Process*. Whitaker, D. S., and Lieberman, M. A.
2. *Community as Doctor*. Rapoport, R. (Social Science paperback) Tavistock Pub., London, 1967.
3. See *Current trends of Individual and Interpersonal approaches to Rehabilitation of the Offender*.
Conference on Mobilising Resources towards Rehabilitation of the Offender, New York, 1963.
4. Described in *Ten Studies into Psychopathic Personality*. Craft, M. Wright, Bristol, 1965.
5. 'The Effects of a Therapeutic Community in the interpersonal relationships of a group of psychopaths.' Miles, A. E. *Brit. J. Criminol.*, 1969, 9, 22.
6. *Borstal Re-assessed*. Hood, R. Heinemann, London, 1965.
7. *Growth to Freedom*. Miller, D. Tavistock Pub., London, 1964.
8. *Deviant Children Grown Up*. Robins, L. Williams and Wilkins, Baltimore, 1966.
9. 'The Natural History of Psychopathic Disorder'. Craft, M. *Brit. J. of Psychiat.*, 1969, 115, 39.
10. Read an account in 'Treating the untreatable'. Sturup, G. K. *Proc. R. Soc. Med.*, 1948, 41, 765.
11. Gibbens, T. C. N. *Proc. Roy. Soc. Med.*, 1969, 62, 57; Pond, D. A., and Stafford-Clark, D., *J. Ment. Sci.*, 1959, 105, 108.
12. *Psychopathy and Delinquency*. McCord, W. M. and McCord, J. Grune and Stratton, New York, 1956.
13. Sullivan, C., Grant, M. Q., and Grant, J. D. *Psychiatry*. 1957, 20, 373.
14. *Psychopathic States*. Henderson, D. K. Norton, New York, 1939.

Appendix to Chapter Three

THE COMMUNITY MEETS:
A VERBATIM TRANSCRIPT

VISITORS to our Therapeutic Community often ask after sitting in on a Community meeting 'was that a typical group?'

It is a difficult question to answer. It is not all dynamic inter action and inspired interpretation in the Therapeutic Community. Some days the proceedings drag, are a waste of time or a bore. Some days everyone needs to take a breather and the groups are funny and lighthearted, other days they may be paralysed by an outburst of violence or stifled by ill-judged staff interventions.

The following group was tape recorded for no particular reason except that we were casting about for other means of examining group material at the time. It has good and bad facets—in that respect it is typical. It is presented in full to show how slowly the themes evolve—the commentary introduced through the discussion and marked ◆, allows a quicker résumé of the proceedings.

Staff names are italicised and their positions stated.

The more important steps are set in italics, and the pattern of analysis follows very much the Whitaker and Lieberman[1] 'Focal Conflict Theory' which can be summarised as follows:

THE FOCAL CONFLICT THEORY OF GROUP DYNAMICS

The group as a whole expresses some conjoint and shared unconscious problem. This is its *Disturbing Motive*—its worry —which is often expressed in guarded terms initially. Solutions are put forward by the group and some of these are *Restrictive*; they meet the superficial needs but do not get to the core of the unconscious problem. They produce a stalemate and are discarded if the group is to progress. Other solutions are *Enabling Solutions* which allow the expression and emergence of the hidden problem but in their turn mean that the real and basic anxiety, the *Reactive Fear*, is exposed. The conflict between the *Disturbing Motive* (in this case, we cannot get our work done) and the *Reactive Fear* (if we get our work done we shall be committed to work for life, have to answer for the consequences etc.) is the *Focal Conflict Situation* of the group.

HENDERSON

The problem moves forward in a succession of steps and stages as little by little *Enabling Solutions* allow more and more of the *Reactive Fears* to be dealt with effectively rather than blocked by *Restrictive Solutions*.

THE GROUP

The setting is the large Community Meeting room at 3.00 p.m. on a Friday afternoon. Staff and residents come together at this time under the chairmanship of the P.L.O. (Project Liaison Officer), a resident elected for the month to supervise the workshop projects. At this particular time in a wave of self-liberalisation we had thrown out a more rigid system of attendance in stereotyped work groups and were looking for a work situation where people could feel more free to involve themselves meaningfully in a common and shared task which they could enjoy. In fact things were going badly. The old system of a rigid and restrictive regime seemed to be missed.

There were about 30–35 residents in the group and about 12–15 staff of various professions from doctors to social therapists, including nurses, social workers and workshop instructors.

A Community Meeting is always chaired by a resident and tends to follow an agenda of sorts which may be rigid or flexible as the situation demands and the chairman can function.

This particular meeting has a fairly restricted scope and a definite task which is to review the workshop situation, unlike the more open morning Community Meetings where administration and psychotherapeutic intervention often occur and seem to vie with each other for priority.

Nevertheless as in all the Henderson procedures the socio-dynamic forces which lie behind the incidents discussed are given due attention.

Jane (the Project Liaison Officer) *What about today's work group?* By the end we had 19 people in.

Ron (Workshop Instructor) We got 19 people, *but we had to wait until very nearly five and twenty past before almost anyone came.*

David   We were saying last week that we need more definition, more information, so that we could look at what was really happening. I think perhaps *if we could improve our records* . . . Perhaps Simon and Jane could use a register system. We could *at least examine in more detail* what was happening.

APPENDIX: THE COMMUNITY MEETS

Marie   That's what we intended to do in Research . . . I was under the impression Simon was keeping a register but then this week I found he hadn't done it.

David   *I don't think records are the answer to this,* but they may help us to be more specific by seeing who are regular attenders and who are not. Keeping records is not an end in its self.

Margaret (a Psychologist) Do people have any ideas as to *why there's such a poor attendance?*

Jane   Well, I think today it's very much to do with the way things *have been over the last two days . . . people want attention, but don't know how to ask for it.* Is Shaun here now?

Shaun   Yes

James (Doctor) And Simon?

Sam   What's happened to Basil?

Marie   He's typing away in Research—he's writing an apologetic letter about the library. He's writing to the Community *apologising for not carrying out his job.*

Simon   (*coming back into the meeting*) *Martin said he is too tired to attend and Cedric is not interested.*

◆ (1). The *Disturbing Motives* are expressed by both staff and residents. The work programme is not being carried out and we don't know why, nor do we know what to do about it.

Restrictive Solutions are put forward which can solve the overt problem but leave the latent problem untouched. They are poor solutions and are discarded. ◆

Pam   Is Colin in?

Betty (an Occupational Therapist) *Has there been any change in the pattern this week,* you know in any one area . . . are a lot of people going into the 1.15 meeting and then not going on into the project groups . . .

Stuart (a Doctor) *It seems to me with each group we have to work a week ahead . . . you know, paint one room, or make one chair. So we can actually see what we do with a small group of people, but unless we can get people to commit themselves, it's very difficult.*

◆ (2). These are *Enabling Solutions* different approaches which may be profitable but are not taken up—yet. The residents ignore them. ◆

Jane   I'm fed up with asking the question—'Why weren't you in work', or 'Why aren't you in the group'. . . Towards the end of the week I feel like hell!

Stuart	Don't you think you're turning too much to each individual group? The Community only works in the overall 'work room'. A lot of people don't at the moment come to the Community meetings.
Marie	I'll tell you one thing, Jane, when Simon and yourself are discussing things and trying to give out work it's such a confusion that people get bored and walk out. *If there could be something already prepared—you know—jobs allotted we could get on with it. I'd like the work pinned out nice and neatly . . .*
Jane	But, in fact, I usually do go and see Simon before the 1.15 and talk over the work with him.
Shaun	There is a possibility it could be more clearly defined . . . I think we agreed on one point that *Ron and Tom should come here with a list of things that need doing.*
Dennie (a psychologist)	Is it possible right now, *Ron*, that you and *Tom* could give us any indications of what is needed next week?
Ron	*Yes. I could run off a list* of chairs and tables, etcetera, that really needs to be done next week.
	But it's a group that needs some kind of continuity, and it's very difficult when people come in from a quarter past one to two o'clock and then leave things like this. I think what it needs is a nucleus of a minimum of about four people to commit themselves, either for whom we ought to say that they have a project of their own to do and commit themselves to that project, or to say if they do not have a project of their own, accepting one of the projects that was there. Such as a chair—and come in every day until the chair is completed and then go off somewhere else.

◆ (3). More *Restrictive Solutions* which get us nowhere towards solving the basic problem and in any case the staff member seems to block this approach.◆

Jane	We've tried this . . . somehow it happens for a day or so and then fades out.
Tom	What about the new people . . . couldn't we support them?
Dennie	Jane, *could we try a more positive approach* and instead of scolding people when they don't follow through their commitments, *could we have some people make some commitments*, talk about what are the things that would prevent them from fulfilling their commitments, and then see how we could help them.

APPENDIX: THE COMMUNITY MEETS

◆ (4) The previous *Enabling Solution* is now taken up again—but blocked again by a staff member. Why are they doing this? What *Reactive Fear* can these solutions be arousing in staff?

Ron	Yes, it seems to me that this is fine. . . . This is what I would like to see, but it does require x number of people to take on commitments, and have a meeting afterwards when this can be discussed. But in our present system *it's quite impossible even to plan this.* What I would like is the work that we've undertaken at the moment with these six people. They were going to carry through a project and we haven't seen them since. Now, and this is a problem, I think, if we take on painting a room, then we need to be able to get together and plan and get on with it and talk about the problems of doing it.
Dennie	*Could we try, as an experiment* for next week, to plan right now a small project, and have people commit themselves? And let's find out how their commitments might break down and how we could prevent it. Let's try a small project for a week and see what happens.
Betty	Is each person sticking with this for one week?
Dennie	Yes.
Sam	The painting of A7 sitting room?
Bill	Well, I'm working on A7 lounge now.
Sam	Well, there's only one job left to do there, isn't there?
Bill	Yes, *I've no intention of doing anything whatsoever about it today* . . . .
Dennie	Could we take this as an experiment for a week and see what we could learn from it? The painting of A7 sitting room for instance, Sam?
Sam	*I don't want to commit myself to that job,* I want to commit myself to maintenance.

◆ (5) The group begins to take a step forward—but quickly retracts when pressed, into its former defences.◆

Dennie	*Well, is that a project that might take four days next week?* What about it—who would be willing to commit themselves for three or four days next week as an experiment to see if we could work something out. Anybody?
Terry (a nurse)	I'd be quite happy to have a go.
Bill	It's going to take a whole week. We'd need at least four for a week.

77

HENDERSON

Dennie	O.K. *Terry* has volunteered. Are there three others?
Jean (a Psychiatric Social Worker)	Well, I'm involved in it already. . . .
Dennie	Do you want to commit yourself for next week?
Jean	Well, I said that I would already, haven't I David?
David	Sorry, I forgot.
Dennie	How about two more people? Pam? One other?
Betty	Is there anyone who hasn't managed to get into a group?
Bill	*I guess it's five now. Terry, Pam, Jean, me and who else?*
Dennie	Let's try something, Pam, Could you think of two things that might come up next week that would interfere with you painting four days next week. Can you think—could you name two things that might—you know like you might get upset on Tuesday and stay in bed, or something. What would be two real things that might stop you?
Female voices	Colin! Cyril!
	[LAUGHTER]
Dennie	How would they stop her from. . . .
Female voice	I didn't say anything about it.
	[LAUGHTER]
Dennie	Pam can you think of any two things . . .
Pam	I can't guarantee that nothing is going to upset me.
Dennie	Let's take it as a possibility.
Pam	No!
Dennie	They won't?
Pam	No!
Dennie	You're saying then, that next Friday in this meeting you will carry through your commitments and nothing will stop you?
Pam	*Why do you have to ask me these questions?*
Dennie	I thought we wanted to try. We'll ask each of the five.
Pam	*I can't think of anything.*
Dennie	How about *Terry*. Would you? How many days next week will you be able to work?
Terry	Well, I'm not on selection on Wednesday. So the only thing that would stop me is the beginning of Tuesday when there's the staff meeting.
David	Well Pam, are you sure Colin and *Terry* won't upset you?
Pam	. . . there will be a time when I'll want to stay in bed, you know.

78

APPENDIX: THE COMMUNITY MEETS

Dennie	Let's just say hypothetically. . . .
Pam	I can't say—*I don't know about next week, because this is this week, because I don't know what will happen.*
Jean	How about this feeling you were talking about in the meeting yesterday, that *you'd really like to do things for just one day*, Pam.
Pam	No, *I said not for ever and ever! I don't like the idea of sticking with it for about a month, but I don't mind something for a short time.*
Ron	Well, we're asking you to undertake something for one week.
Pam	Well, that's obvious. I mean—for goodness sake!
Ron	Right, well will you be able to do it?
Pam	Yes!

◆ (6) Staff keep the pressure up hopefully and this begins to break through. Finally Pam expresses the real *Reactive Fear*—that commitment to something means being tied 'for ever and ever'.◆

Dennie	Jane, can you record this somewhere, so that next Friday we can have some facts?
	[PAUSE]
	I am trying to be very serious, and some of you aren't. Could you record this somewhere and then next week we can review this and we can call on Pam to give us an account of what happened?
Jane	Yes, I can do that.
Dennie	(talking to Allan) What about—I'm sorry I don't know your name—*can you tell us what is one thing that might come up next week that would stop you from painting?* Can you think of anything?
Jane	Football.
Sam	Yes.
David	Yes.
Dennie	That's only on Tuesday.
Sam	Yes.
Dennie	So on Tuesday you won't expect him in on the painting. What about Thursday? Can they expect you to come in Monday, Wednesday and Thursday?
Allan	Yes.
Dennie	What might come up on Monday, Wednesday or Thursday that might interfere? Can you think of anything?
	[PAUSE]

HENDERSON

Allan	*If I got bored* on Monday or . . .
Dennie	O.K. What can we do as a community to help you on Monday if you got bored and don't show up for work? What can we do?
Allan	Sometimes I won't get bored by going to work on Monday. It will be Wednesday.
Dennie	O.K. What can we do on Wednesday to help you so on Friday you can carry it through?
Allan	You know, I think I could use a discussion at the end of it.
Dennie	But let's say Wednesday, if you don't show up at the 1.15 what do you want us to do? Leave you alone? Come and find you and talk to you? Because we want you to have a successful week. How can we help you if it doesn't work out that way? For instance, *would you want* Sam *to come and look for you* at the 1.15 on Wednesday if you aren't there. Or anybody? [PAUSE]
Allan	I don't think—not at the 1.15—no, perhaps afterwards, when I felt better.
Dennie	2 o'clock. 2.30. 3? What do you want us to do to help you? Or nothing? [LOTS OF NOISE HERE] Can anybody help me? Does anyone know what I'm trying to say?
Philip	Well, *what happens* Allan, *if you go off swimming?*
Allan	When I go swimming? If I feel like it?
Philip	Yes.
Allan	I'd go then.
Philip	You'd go swimming?
Fred (a doctor)	What do we do then?
Allan	I'll be back in time for 2 o'clock.
Norman	We want these groups to go from 1.15 not from 2 o'clock because we want them finished at 2 o'clock.
Terry	We stop at 2.30 and then talk about what happened on Monday, so that we could somehow see that Allan gets in on Wednesday.
Allan	Sorry, I can't quite hear you.
Terry	Well, if we meet at 3.30 after we've worked and perhaps talk about what had happened—what was going to happen on Wednesday.
Allan	Yes.

APPENDIX: THE COMMUNITY MEETS

Betty	*Do you think you'll be able to give some clues so that we know when you've been pretty bored with the group?* You are going to be able to say when it's been difficult?
Allan	I feel confident enough for that to be personally interested.
Marie	This is, of course, if he feels that way but of course, he doesn't even know yet.
Dennie	You see, *what I'm trying to say is almost everybody knows what it feels like inside to fail, because we've all failed, but most people here do not know what it's like to succeed.* And all that *I'm trying to say is, could we set up an experiment* where three or four people could commit themselves? We'll try in the Community to succeed, and then next Friday you can tell us how you felt? What was it like? *What was it like to succeed for a change instead of failing* all the time?
	[PAUSE]
Someone	For me this is a waste of time.
Pam	If somebody makes certain commitments, if these people are sure that they're going to be committed now. If somebody else makes sure that these people definitely do it.
Terry	Can you see something perhaps happening to you on Tuesday, Pam, because if Sam and Bill go to football. . . .
Bill	I won't be going over to play football, because Tuesday we'll start painting.
Sam	I'm not in the painting group . . . sorry, go on Simon.
Terry	On Tuesday we start painting.
Bill	If Allan goes off to football, the group will be too small to start.
Philip	If you don't go to football, Simon goes up the wall because there's nobody practising football.
Jane	*Would it be more realistic to commit yourself to four days?*
Dennie	Right, or three days, whatever is real so . . . one day . . .
Pam	If people are playing football, can't that day some other people who aren't playing football do the painting?
Bill	I'm worried that we can't get the job done in a week anyway. Well, personally, *if I see that we're not going to get this job done in a week it's going to box me up for a start.*

[CHORUS OF VOICES]

Shaun (talking to Bill) You're breaking a commitment you've already made, which is to play football on Tuesday.

Fred   What time will you be finishing?

Sam   We have a discussion, you know about 3.30 to 4 o'clock.

Dennie   But don't you think that if we set this up for five people on Monday, Wednesday and Thursday, don't you think you could finish the job if we could rely on five people for three days?

Bunny   We've got five. We've got yourself, *Jean*, Pam, *Terry* and Allan.

Dennie   We could allow you to take Tuesday to fulfil your other commitment.

Pam   *What about making it a job that must be finished and saying that somebody is responsible for having organised it,* that people are there every day . . . ?

Dennie (interrupting) Are you volunteering?

Pam   Yes.

Dennie   Great. How can the group help Pam follow through. I mean this is great. . . .

Voice   By being there.

Pam   If you felt like just going swimming, would you just —float off?

[LAUGHTER]

Fred   . . . last seen disappearing in a south-easterly direction. . . .

Jane   Do you think that you'd be able to go to Pam before you, you know you float off?

Allan   Yes.

Jane   Yet, this is one thing that might prevent you coming in if you felt like going swimming. You know, sometimes in the past you've taken off in the afternoon. *If you felt like going swimming, do you think you would be able to see Pam before you went?*

[PAUSE]

or do you get that pissed off?

Allan   *Yes.*

◆ (7) With Allan a similar conflict situation is worked through, *Restrictive Solutions* and then *Enabling Solutions* are given.

His fear of non-involvement in the group and having to 'float off' is expressed and it can be countered by the group's awareness of the problem and its readiness to support him.◆

APPENDIX: THE COMMUNITY MEETS

Dennie	Well, why don't you just give him some leeway? Why don't you just say Monday, Wednesday, Thursday? 1.15 to 4 p.m.?
Allan	I've been to three of the 1.15's. It's not as if it's just the 1.15.
Shaun	*It's possible that the first day is never very difficult, but the subsequent days are.*
Dennie	That's what we're going to find out Shaun.
David	Well then a discussion period as well as examining what has happened. Could we predict it in a sense more specifically what difficulties we're going to have the following day? Or the next day. . . .

[PAUSE]

Dennie (talking to Bill)	Could we tighten this down a little bit more? What might prevent you from showing up on Monday or Wednesday or Thursday. Can you think? Can you imagine anything? What could we do to help you if you get pissed off Wednesday, and don't show up?
Bill	I'm not sure.

[GENERAL CHATTER]

Stuart	What about your visitors from Australia, or something like that, maybe?
Bill	I object to my visitors from Australia being brought up again—they get me a bad name.
Jean	Well, what about if you are going away this weekend? . . . Will that affect you?
Bill	I'll be back for the 1.15 meeting on Monday.
Shaun	*What would happen if the group does something the way you don't like it being done?*
Bill	I'm not sure. Discuss it, I suppose.
Betty	Well, what about what you just said, *your anxieties about the job not going on schedule.*
Dennie	Well, say on Wednesday afternoon *Terry* didn't show up, he had to go to the nurses' meeting and Pam's in bed and only one wall's done . . . then what? What would you do then?
Bill	*Yes, that pisses me off.*
Dennie	O.K. what would you do then?
Bill	Well, the thing I would like to do now if *I'd thought the job was not going to get done. I'll piss off.*
James	Is there any other alternative that you would do?
Bill	I don't think I would.
James	You're in the bathroom. *Terry* at the nurses' meeting.

	Allan's scrubbing. Pam's in bed. What alternatives could you see, other than pissing off?
Bill	. . . Pam or Allan . . .
Marie	*Well, why can't you continue it on your own?*
Bill	Oh, no, as I said if I thought the job wouldn't get done —*I'd get very discouraged.*
Marie	Do you need people there to make you, to help you work?
Bill	. . . Yeah.
Dennie	Well, *you've already got some help because everybody in your group has tentatively agreed they want to succeed, haven't they?*
Allan	Yes.
Dennie	So you've got something to build on, haven't you?
Bill	Yes, but I've . . .
Dennie	. . . which you didn't have this week.
Bill	. . . the pledge . . .
Philip	Why, did you think the rest of the group might get pissed off?
Bill	Well, I think it's . . .
Philip	*Could it be*, Bill, *that they get pissed off because it's your idea and not the group's ideas?*
Bill	Um. *Well, maybe I try to lead a bit and they might be a bit pissed off with me, but I don't know what the colour scheme will be* and I'm quite prepared to consult people. . . . I'll do the work, but this sort of thing. . . .
Dennie	Pam is going to help you to organise things because she's taken the task of seeing that it's done.
Bill	Well, this is great. I mean that's . . .
Dennie	So you'll be.
Male Voice	A7 It's their lounge, and it's up to them to discover what colour it's going to be.
Bill	*I'll do the work, but I don't pretend to be much on artistic* . . .

◆ (8) Bill finally expresses his *Reactive Fear* which is the fear of things not being done properly which leads him into over-control of the situation or total avoidance of the situation.◆

Female Voice	. . . what colours are available?
Stuart	This is an important factor—is the material available?
Bill	Let's stick to one problem. On Monday they're going to wash down the walls. On Tuesday they'll undercoat. On Wednesday should we slap on the paint or wait

	until they discover what colours they decide on. Or shall we decide what colour we want?
David	Well, A7 could have a weekly ward meeting on Tuesday.
Sam	Well, we're having one today to discuss the new ward and, yes, perhaps we could discuss it then and let people know about the colour on Monday.
Jane	Could we just ask *Ron* what colour is available?
Ron	*There's only one colour available!*

[LAUGHTER]

This is the point I was trying to make earlier on. I didn't mean it as a job. We should sit down and make our plans and then we could have any colour. But if you suddenly want to start painting tomorrow, you'll have to use the colour that's available.

Fred	What's available?
Ron	The only colour available is magnolia.

[GENERAL NOISE AND CHATTER HERE]

Bill	I thought of this problem before. If by Tuesday it was suddenly decided what colour we'd like . . . .
Ron	*Well, now you need to give him about a fortnight!* . . .
Fred	What colour do you want—do you know?
Paul	Have you got any white? Magnolia's an off-white. . . . If you want pastel colours you'll have to stick in some colouriser tubes.
Bill	Well, this was suggested by someone else.
Sam	If we have the ward meeting this afternoon and decide on the colours, could we have the colours by Monday?
Pam	We need a fortnight.
Shaun	Is it really important for us to decide on the colours now. . . .
Fred	What colour is magnolia, anyway?
Female Voice	It's green.

[GENERAL CHATTER]

David	What about Shaun's point? O.K. . . . *we want the group to succeed*. What about the situation when the group doesn't want to succeed as a group thing.
Ron	The way to deal with it is to get these half a dozen people together and then meet at the end of each day and talk about it. *But I don't think that all this backchat here is going to solve all this at all.*
James	Well, not if we've only got magnolia.

[LAUGHTER AND NOISE]

HENDERSON

Shaun	We've only got magnolia. . . . *we go ahead with the experiment.*

[GENERAL CHATTER]

James	Haven't you got to do something we like doing? *There's no sense otherwise in doing it surely?*
Anna (a social therapist)	*Can't we learn from this situation and now plan* that we want to do the sitting room in these colours? . . . after a fortnight.
Philip	*While we are waiting for the colours, can't we strip down the walls and wash off, and then move on to something else, say A7 bathroom?*
Bill	If we had two colours. One white and the door in something else.
Ron	This is not much of a problem. The odd bit of paint for a door is no bother.
Paul	*Could we mix colours?*
Ron	No. Colourisers don't mix with the type of paint we've got.
Jane	What door paint have you?
Ron	We've only red and white.
Simon	*I think we should really find out what colour scheme we want and all the things we want, rather than try and use the paint we have.*
Stuart	We've got enough paint for the wood work. It's just the two walls and the ceiling.
Ron	Not the ceiling.
Stuart	*How much paint do you think we need?*
Ron	Approximately three gallons.
Betty	How much will that cost?
Ron	I could get it through the trade for about £9.
Stuart	£9?
Marie	Get it through the trade — £9!
Ron	*£3 per gallon, for what kind of paint.*

◆ (9) The *Enabling Solutions* have brought the group to a point where they are keen to get on although some of the staff and some of the patients still express *Reactive Fears* which block the progress. ◆

Stuart	I thought we could get it ourselves.
Simon	Isn't emulsion paint a bit cheaper?
Bill	Well, let's get one thing straight. Can I suggest that it is decided by A7 that we have a magnolia as

	background, and blue or red, or something that we've got?
Pam	He's only got magnolia. He's just said that.
Bill	Well, he also said he's got blue, red and white. Only we should have magnolia all over.
Simon	What does the rest of the group think?
Allan	I'm not staying in something like a fridge or anything like that.
Marie	*Why don't you paint it white and make it into something by putting things on the walls.*
Paul	*Can't you mix* the red with the white and make it pink?
Ron	With ordinary paint surely you can do that—*you can't do that with non-drip.* . . . Almost any colour would be O.K. for gloss paint for the doors.
Terry	Well, *what colours, Ron, can we get in the future?*
Ron	Well, *this is a problem in itself*, you see. We'd . . . we could use all one colour. Or two colours and we can do doors as well.
Jane	Well, *have you any other colour* to do one wall so that you have magnolia and something else.
Ron	*. . . I doubt it.*
Margaret	Are you sure now that we couldn't get it by the end of next week? *We could spend a few days* cleaning it down, etc.
Ron	I'm quite sure *it will take 10 days to two weeks*

[LAUGHTER]

Male Voice	Can you come and see us on Monday and talk this over?
Jane	Why not see what paint we have over there? We could have stripes and a pattern on one wall.
Bill	Can A7 agree that we have magnolia and any other colour?
Betty	The whole idea of the weekly project. How does this. . . .?
Ron	*We're determined to destroy it. We'd manage to destroy all the efforts* to have a weekly project . . . but we can't do anything in the way of decorating because you decide that you are going to do this and do it in this colour tomorrow. You can't do this.
Tom	We decide what colours we want and then. . . .
Simon	We just decide on the colour scheme we want . . .

James	What is this group going to do in this coming week, do you think?
Male Voice	Why not do a bathroom?
David	*What does the group feel about doing a bathroom?*

◆ (10) Now some staff members (the two instructors) more clearly seem to block the progress—for reasons not here interpreted but perhaps inherent in the whole workshop situation at the time. They see the newer workshop projects getting out of their dominance and control—patients having no need of them as therapists as it were—their own anxieties are aroused about their value in the Community. The group, however, presses on and they take no further part in the discussion. ◆

Shaun	Are you going to ask me about the colours of the bathroom. We're avoiding the whole issue. *It's nothing to do with colours, the important thing is getting something done in this place for a change.*
Philip	Colours do matter. It's important that people do what they want to do.
Simon	I suggest that we paint something we don't have to look at.
David	*We agree on something and then immediately we are confronted with a hostile reaction to stop the group.*
Pam	I didn't know all this was going to happen when I was asked to organise the thing. I can see your painting that room and then everyone going off and moaning.
David	*It may come from outside the group, but it's also inside the group.*
Shaun	*When the group starts functioning the group itself has to cope with that sort of thing.*
James	You can't do it without paint, Shaun.
Sam	*We'll do the experiment for a week with the colour we've got and then if we want it another colour we could paint it again.*
	[GENERAL NOISE AND CHATTER]
Betty	What's the alternative now, I mean . . . you hold together as a group on your original commitment and do it magnolia for a week or . . .
Simon	If you want to paint something magnolia, *paint something which I won't have to look at.* I have to sit there —go and paint A8.
	[LAUGHTER]
David	*I don't see why this group can't wait for a fortnight* and in the meantime do a bathroom. It's just as essential.

APPENDIX: THE COMMUNITY MEETS

James	It's not a terrible lot of fun doing a bathroom, David. I don't want to do the bathroom. I want to do something else.

[GENERAL CHATTER]

Pam	*We're committed now.* It's not much fun starting painting for a few days, then stopping and then going back for a few days.
David	This is assuming that it's not going to succeed. This is . . .
Pam	I was assuming that as he started off by saying 'is anyone willing to do this thing for four days'—he meant get through it and that's the end . . . that's fine. The idea of starting something, getting through that and starting something else, is too much. *This is my own thing, but I don't want to get that involved.*
Male Voice	Why?
Pam	*I don't want to paint for the rest of my life.*

◆ (11) Now that we seem to be going ahead there are quick relapses into the *Reactive Fears*. Pam's fear of involvement, anxiety about the group's ability to succeed and weak *Restrictive Solutions* come forward.◆

David	*It's not a question of painting.* It's a question of having a successful project—achieving something as a group.
Pam	It's not a question of achieving anything, I just don't want to do it.
Shaun	*Yes, this is about experiencing success isn't it?* you want something. . . .

◆ (12) David and Shaun try to focus on the main problems still and keep things going.◆

Cyril	Only we ain't got the paint. Just see how these four people get on and just what sort of jobs they do, and what ideas they come up with for instance during these two weeks.
Bill	*I don't agree.*
Philip	. . . you've got some paint. You start painting with that bloody magnolia paint—*every brush stroke we'll be saying 'Oh Christ'* . . .
Bill	The problem is we're doing this project . . . As far as I'm personally concerned. May I put a suggestion up? Can A7 decide on what sort of colours they would like? Exactly what colours people want to use. Get it ordered . . . for a fortnight from now. *We'll start from*

	scratch in a fortnight's time. . . . . Allan will you do the same?
Allan	Eh? But I want to join in and do the project.
Bill	Sorry.
Allan	But *I want to join in.*
Bill	*Would you leave it for a fortnight* and start over again?

[GENERAL NOISE HERE]

◆ (13) Bill's fears return and he canvasses Allan who is uncertain —he *is* bored but he wants to join in, but even the reluctant and blocking Simon is overcoming his fears and puts forward an *Enabling Solution.*◆

Dennie	But all the same, I think this is defeating the whole idea. *The idea was that*—I think it was *Stuart* or somebody said, *could we think about a task for a week,* that is feasible, that's successful. We're trying to find people to volunteer so we can learn from them. We need something in the form of structure to make this afternoon successful for people. We're trying to set up something so for one week we have some ideas, *but to postpone it is defeating the whole thing.*
Simon	*Well, fair enough. Let's think of another project which we have the materials to do.*
Paul	*Let's paint Rooms 5 & 6,* they're about the same size, then you can paint them magnolia.
Bill	I might find . . . in a fortnight's time, you know after A7—we'll decide what colours then. *In a fortnight's time I might be prepared to go ahead for another week.*
Dennie	That could be a second project.
Bill	But *at the moment we'll do rooms 5 & 6.*
Pam	And no more?
Fred	Can you all agree then on starting rooms 5 & 6 on Monday? *We'll paint them all magnolia.*
Bill	*We're cleaning the place first.*
James	Sure.
Dennie	And then *keep in mind this idea of all keeping the group together and doing two or three weeks, planning for A7* so that they can order paint. A7. . . . meanwhile must decide about the paint.
David	Yeah. Well, perhaps now we could hear what's going to happen.
Female Voice	*Join in the happy family.* . . .
Betty	Perhaps you could think about what has happened

90

	today and then think perhaps what do you expect to happen tomorrow that might upset the concept of where you can go on to.
Dennie	How much it will take to follow our commitment, but at least you will know more than you do.
Stuart	Well done.
Jean	*That's called bringing the group to successful conclusion.*

◆ (14) They reach a compromise to get on with one job as a group with some confidence in themselves and a feeling of freedom of choice about the future.◆

Male Voice	You were saying, *Jean*, that. . . .
Jean	I was saying there will be selection on Wednesday afternoon, but *Brenda* will do that so I'll be in.
Terry	We won't be able to start until 2.30 on Wednesday because of the staff meeting.
Jean	The only thing is that . . . what should we do if there would be just *Terry* and myself here and we would have to do it on our own?
Bill	Rooms 5 & 6 where you can see what you're doing.
Paul	Well, if you want to get it done quickly you could close the partition and it will look as if you're getting it done.
Jane	Anyway . . .

[END OF TAPE]

If anything there was too much staff activity in the group, nevertheless the staff had real anxieties about the work situation and were expressing these.

Dennie Briggs, who at this time was working at Henderson in a temporary capacity with a loosely structured role focusing attention on the workshop programme, was acting here in a directive way (as perhaps befits his personality and accustomed methods) but at this point in time the Community was seeking some direction and his method of working seemed appropriate.

On the whole the staff picked up the theme and worked as a team to develop the 'Enabling Solutions'. They were considerably aided by David and Shaun, two wise and insightful residents, and in Allan, Bill, Pam and Simon we see real shifts of behaviour as the facets of the problem peculiar to each of them is explored and 'de-fused'.

The reaction of the two workshop instructors showed a split in

HENDERSON

the staff team. They felt themselves losing power and control to the residents and other staff moving in on their field. All therapists (and parents) feel some anxiety when the patients (or children) no longer seem to need them. Other staff members here also expressed some anxiety at things going ahead too fast but the instructors became the scapegoats in this particular group, which was unfortunate and made later for bad staff relationships (in fact both had left within six months).

Workwise no great task had been accomplished but a lot of emotional feelings around a real life situation had been explored almost in a model way.

These explorations would not rest here or be lost if no one commented on them at once, for the same people involved are meeting again and again in the continuous and on-going psychotherapy. In the total Community Meetings, in the crisis meetings, in a ward and in the more consciously psychotherapeutically structured small groups of the morning the events of this group would be alluded to and related, for instance to Pam's inability to commit herself and settle into an adult mature and lasting relationship with Colin (with whom she lived along with their 2 children), and to Bill's vascillation between demanding dependence on his over-protective family and a state of total collapse and disaster whenever he moved away from them and assumed responsibilities for himself.

Simon's feeling of uselessness and hopelessness which confined him within the protective but frustrating world of mental hospitals and Marie's need to obsessionally and ritualistically keep things under control are also brought into prominence.

On the workshop side it seemed that more structure and direction was called for by the group and gradually more and more structure and rigidity crept in—but not to the constrictive level of previously, and we began to function without specific workshop instructors. The groups needed leaders, and in the end staff members with particular interests at a hobby or do-it-yourself level managed to take over as work group leaders.

REFERENCES

REFERENCES

1. *Psychotherapy through the Group Process.* Whitaker, D. S., and Lieberman, M. A. Tavistock Pubs., London, 1965.

PART II

CHINO, CALIFORNIA
By
DENNIE BRIGGS

Chapter Four

A 'PENAL APPROACH':
COMMUNITIES IN PRISON

The masonry, the materials, the proportions and
the architecture are in harmony with a moral unity
which makes these dwellings indestructible so long
as the social form of which they are the symbols
endures. The prison surrounds me with a perfect
guarantee. . . . Nothing will demolish it, not blasts
of wind, nor storms, not bankruptcies. The prison
remains sure of itself, and you in the midst of it sure
of yourself. And yet it is this spirit of seriousness in
which these structures were erected which is the
source of their self-esteem, of their mutual reserve
and understanding; it is of this spirit of worldliness
that they will perish.

JEAN GENET *The Thief's Journal*, 1949

LIKE madness, criminal acts were once considered the work of
demons. Alongside other revolutionary movements, fundamental changes in the theories of the causes of crime occurred
in the latter half of the eighteenth century. In the United
States, the Quakers introduced the practice of confinement as
an alternative to corporal punishment. At the Walnut Street
Jail in Philadelphia, the groundwork was laid for prisons as
we now know them. Here, at the close of the eighteenth
century, the idea was introduced that criminal behaviour
could be changed by doing something more than removing social
offenders from the community and confining them in gaols.
In a solitary cell, the Quakers reasoned, the prisoner would
realize that he had done wrong and would become penitent.

But as more people were confined and new places for
confinement were built, the harmful effects of the prison itself
became apparent. Early attempts were made to separate the
older criminals from the younger, the latter being seen as
more susceptible to change, both for better and for worse.

It was not until well into the twentieth century that soli-
tude, silence and penitence were abandoned in favour of work,
disciplined conduct, schooling, trade training and religious
instruction.

Yet the continuing necessity of coercion showed, and still shows, the lack of self-motivation to 'reform' on the part of most offenders. Prisons continued to attempt both to deter the criminal and to rehabilitate him; and to grow in size and in numbers. The large numbers of men who participated in rehabilitation and who were reconvicted shortly after being paroled persuaded many prison staff of the impossibility of changing criminals. This resignation to the futility of attempts at reform is an attitude which still constitutes a major obstacle to progress.

By the first half of the twentieth century prisons had become one of society's greatest and most expensive burdens, with the smallest returns, either as protection to society or as deterrents to crime. Many were soon to become national scandals.[1]

But soon, too, the Borstal system was to become the great hope for preventing young offenders from entering criminal careers. In the United States, similar youth 'reformatories' were then established, the new institution at Bordentown, New Jersey, becoming the model for others.

Meanwhile, more encouraging developments occurred in small 'schools' and camps for disturbed and delinquent children and young people. These efforts showed that seriously disturbed behaviour could indeed be modified, if made early enough, with skilled practitioners and in a special 'non-repressive' total living situation.

BEGINNINGS OF THE 'NEW PENOLOGY': THE CALIFORNIAN EXPERIENCE

Soon after the outbreak of the Second World War, Californian prisons erupted, revealing conditions that had been dormant for years, conditions characteristic of prisons everywhere. Prison reform in California was marked by a series of sudden and dramatic changes. The solutions offered a model of reform that was to affect prisons all over the world.

Prisons at San Quentin and Folsom, traditional bastions of high security surrounded by walls and patrolled by armed guards in gun turrets, were largely autonomous under politically appointed wardens, often police officers, who ruled with absolute, unchallenged authority. A series of devastating riots at San Quentin called national attention to prison conditions in California, generally rated among the worst.[2]

Earl Warren, a youthful, energetic district attorney, was

intimately familiar with conditions in the prisons and the lack of opportunities for ex-prisoners in the community. Campaigning for the governorship, he promised alieviation of these dreadful conditions. Promptly upon taking office he convened a special emergency session of the legislature which enacted a new penal code and established a central prison authority, the Department of Corrections, which was to become the prototype in its field. This action brought the prisons and ultimately the paroling authority together, under a director, responsible to the governor.

The new penal code provided for indeterminate sentences. Under this provision, the time of release from prison was fixed by an Adult Authority, which at first reported directly to the governor. It had absolute power to set sentences, supervise parole activities, and could alter sentences within the provisions of the new legislation. Now, under a total state prison system, the length of sentence could partly be determined by the prisoner's behaviour —at least in theory.

Under the new code the Director of Corrections was appointed politically. Warren, however, established a civil service examination open to competitors throughout the nation. From the successful candidates, Warren chose a distinguished career penologist as the first director, Richard A. McGee. He became the only chief administrator in California to serve under three different political administrations, and for the next twenty years successfully provided continuity and long range planning. Warren, after becoming Chief Justice of the U.S. Supreme Court, commented that McGee's appointment had been the wisest he had ever made.

McGee chose as his deputy an innovative and courageous academic psychologist from Stanford University, Norman Fenton. Correctional reform in California was quickly characterized by long term planning rather than the suppression of immediate disturbances in the local prisons. Administrative structures with strong centralized control and uniformity among the few existing prisons marked the early stages of reform, whilst eventual de-centralization, greater local autonomy and individuality were longer range accomplishments. Staff selection, training and development were early achievements, together with the recognition that prisoners had psychological and social defects which could be modified by means other than suppression, physical restraint and moral reformation.

Fenton introduced clinicians into the prison system, as well as diagnostic facilities. Reception-Guidance Centres, an early innovation soon to be duplicated in many other states and countries, were established along with extensive building programmes, which brought into being specialized environments for prisoners with varying needs. Classification systems and centralised authority for the transfer of felons among the various prisons made separation of the younger, impressionable felons more effective. As new institutions were built, younger inmates were housed together in separate institutions.

Within the prisons themselves, extensive programmes were developed to carry out the clinical recommendations of the reception centres. An impressive attack on illiteracy was undertaken with all prisoners. Schools with qualified teachers were established in every prison, replacing the former use of inmates. Diplomas were awarded from local school districts to minimise the stigma of a prisoner having obtained a formal education while in prison. A wide variety of vocational training programmes was instituted to equip prisoners with employable skills. A series of industries was set up to provide practical work experiences for prisoners, to decrease idleness and to contribute to prison maintenance.

The difficulty of acquiring sufficient numbers of counsellors to work with the expanding prison population, and in recruiting professionals in the various helping professions, led to other innovations, chiefly by Norman Fenton. With the system of silence removed and the general acceptance that talking was a good thing, to whom could one talk? An early practical solution was that non-professional or lay counsellors, properly chosen, trained and supervised by the limited number of professionals, could conduct useful group counselling sessions. Soon, over two-thirds of the prisoners were seated weekly in circles of 10 to 12 men or women, with a prison officer, accountant, secretary, medical technician or any prison employee who had volunteered and been chosen as a group counsellor.

Important decisions about the prison careers of the inmates were taken out of the hands of individual people, and put into committees. Thus a classification committee made decisions about the choice of programme for the inmate and any subsequent changes. A disciplinary committee considered and acted upon any serious rule-breaking. A panel of members of the Adult Authority reviewed and interviewed each prisoner when his minimum sentence had been served, to set the further time to be served and to establish parole conditions.

Custodial personnel were given respect, increased authority and new uniforms. Formerly known as prison guards and by a number of inmate euphemisms, they became officially known as 'correctional officers'. They could now cautiously, but safely and officially, engage in dialogues with the prisoners, and begin to explore new roles and relationships, whereas in the past even talking to a prisoner had been regarded as suspect.

As new institutions were opened, further attempts were made to get away from the stigma of prisons and move in the direction of rehabilitation. They took on new names. The California Correctional Facility for young trainable prisoners was the first newly constructed one, then the California Men's Colony for older, more recidivistic individuals, and the California Conservation Center, to coordinate a vast system of forestry camps to fight fires and conserve natural resources. The California Medical Facility (similar to Grendon Underwood) with a psychiatrist as superintendent, was built, where prisoners who needed extensive medical and psychiatric attention were confined. More recently, the California Rehabilitation Center was established exclusively for the rehabilitation of those men, women and young people who were addicted to narcotics. The new administrators of the 'institutions' were called superintendents rather than wardens, and were either selected by civil service examination or were career appointees by the Director of Corrections. All these major executives were career penologists, who had worked up through the system, unlike the political appointees of just a few years ago, who had changed with each administration.

The introduction of clinically-oriented people did, however, introduce a new element of conflict in the daily operation of prisons. It caused a division of responsibility, and there was competition for custodial or administrative control of the inmates. A split occurred between the clinical and custodial responsibilities. It was like a family, where the father is the disciplinarian and consequently the 'bad object', while the mother is the more accepting and 'good object'. The clinicians tended to explain and often tolerate or overlook rule infractions, in the interests of establishing an atmosphere where prisoners could talk freely and perhaps come to understand their own behaviour. The custodial staff had an orientation whereby strict discipline was called for, believing this would 'correct' delinquent behaviour. As children do, the inmates readily seized upon the division of loyalties for their own advantage and manipulated one force against the other. It was only recently within the correctional agency that more formal attempts were made to heal the schism by creating new roles, sanctioned by new civil service classifications which blended administrative, clinical and custodial control functions into single positions. At some institutions employees were now called 'correctional programme supervisors' at the lower or working levels, managed by 'correctional programme administrators'.

SERENDIPITY: THE CALIFORNIA INSTITUTION FOR MEN AT CHINO

Much earlier, at the time of the prison riots at San Quentin, a separate innovation was being dramatically undertaken at the site of a new high security prison in Southern California. A 'San Quentin for the south' was being built at Chino, near Los Angeles, to accommodate the rapidly expanding population and crime rate. Before it was finished, Kenyon Scudder was appointed superintendent. He immediately and boldly defied politicians and bureaucrats and ushered in the most dramatic example of the 'new penology' that followed. As was portrayed in a film entitled 'The Unchained', he established the largest open security prison in the world, his 'prison without walls'. Single-handed, Scudder developed his individual attitude and administration characterised by the title of his book, *Prisoners are People*, and ran his prison largely on humanitarian lines. This venture, the only exception to the dark era in California penology, was to cause a great deal of controversy among penologists, as well as focus attention on California's new lead in prison reform.[3]

Scudder selected fifty bright young men, nearly all recent college graduates, with little or no knowledge of prisons, and trained them personally for new roles among inmates of the new institution. He returned the lorry load of traditional grey paint to the prison administration and engaged a well-known architect and decorator to design colour schemes for the interior and exterior of the new prison under construction. Walls and cells were now in pastel colours blending with the mountain ranges and the desert surrounding the prison. He stopped construction on the great wall which was to surround the prison. The gun towers, already built prior to his arrival, were never manned except by inmates, when they were used as aircraft spotting posts during the Second World War. He chose to make the prison a minimum security institution which eventually housed 1600 men at one time.

The new superintendent immediately became personally involved with the inmates, offering numerous opportunities for increased responsibility and participation in decisions regarding their welfare and the administration of the new institution. He invited them to his home, built within the grounds, for meals and social gatherings with his family. He provided a pair of gaudy pyjamas for each new arrival, to go with the pastel coloured room he would be assigned to. He and his new staff slept over-night in the same housing unit as the inmates when the first group were brought from San Quentin, to demonstrate the trust they had and to form the beginnings of a new and different relationship between staff and inmates which was to characterise the prison. And he further allowed the men to abandon the drab prison-issue denims and wear their own clothing on visiting days with their families, when they were allowed to picnic under grape arbours.

The appointment of E. J. Oberhauser to succeed Scudder ensured the continuity of his ideals. One of Scudder's original fifty bright young men, who had remained with him at Chino, Oberhauser was known by inmates and staff as 'Obie'. He was also well known for his enthusiastic support and practice of the founders' ideals of humanism and innovation, for his ability to transform these beliefs into the reality of a rapidly expanding prison service. As he was to say to me later, with his gangling legs up on his desk, when he interviewed me as a prospective new employee, 'We haven't had any new ideas around here for the past two years.'

RESEARCH AND EVALUATION

Meanwhile the Department of Corrections, under McGee's continued leadership and administrative expertise, and with the active backing of two subsequent political administrations, had rapidly developed a multi-million dollar yearly programme. Earlier the main efforts had been confined to getting its own house in order, coping with the cataclysmic population in the prisons, then planning a more effective prison system. The Director's staff now began to experiment with alternatives.

The California Legislature authorised and financed a series of experimental projects to investigate the effectiveness of psychological and sociological interventions for certain prisoners. A 'Special Intensive Parole Unit' project (SIPU) was begun, to test the effectiveness of increased parole supervision. The size of parole case load was varied systematically in several geographic regions of the state, and parole agents were given clinical assistance.[4] The project was extended to two of the institutions, both to test the effectiveness of individualised case work approaches to later parole performance, and to see if the prisons themselves had any effect in changing criminal behaviour. Did an ostensibly more permissive and open atmosphere like the one established at Chino have a measurable effect on changing criminal behaviour compared with a more openly repressive one like San Quentin? The Mannheim-Wilkins studies of open versus closed Borstals suggested that open institutions might make a positive difference. Such differences, if they existed, would be important for planning future prison architecture as well as for new programmes. San Quentin and Chino were then selected as contrasts for a long term project.

The Intensive Treatment Programme, IT as it was called, emphasised individual case work approaches for a random sample of adult felons. Eight well-trained and highly motivated social case workers, a supervisor with considerable experience and a clinical psychologist were hired for each of the projects. They were given twenty six men each with whom to work, in contrast with the traditional case load of approximately three hundred assigned to the counsellors in the remainder of the institutions.

At Chino, the twenty six men assigned to each counsellor were housed in one dormitory or 'wing' of a larger hall, where the counsellor had his office for closer proximity to the men. The men remained in the programme from six to eighteen months and were seen minimally once each week for an individual interview to discuss their problems. Some counsellors supplemented the interview with additional ones and with small group psychotherapy with the men, and sometimes included their families. Information between counsellor and inmate, except for gross security matters, was privileged, a new concept in prisons. Weekly psychiatric consultation and

A 'PENAL APPROACH'

regular clinically-oriented staff meetings were instituted. The men and their 'controls' were given psychological tests prior to, during and after the treatment phase of the programme. Both groups were to be followed for two years upon parole.[5]

With the development of the correctional agency into an even larger and more expensive enterprise, and experiments with new approaches to incarceration which, if successful, would entail even more extensive expenditures, the legislative analyst Fred Lewe asked for the creation of a research division to evaluate the total correctional programme and to design alternatives to incarceration. The 1957–8 Legislature authorized and financed a division of research to evaluate the effectiveness of the agency and to conduct and evaluate experimental programmes for future planning.

McGee brought into the Department an experienced psychologist, J. Douglas Grant, who was attracting national attention from his research into a new classification system for offenders, called 'interpersonal maturity levels' or 'I-levels', and a new approach for treatment, 'living-groups'. His work was with confined offenders in the U.S. Navy and Marine Corps. Financed and operated by a combination of research and action programmes, the projects had already demonstrated the effectiveness of new classification and treatment schemes in an operational setting with military offenders. They remained to be tested with another population of offenders.[6,7]

Grant, the only chief executive on the Director's staff who had not grown up in the system, recruited and hired a research staff also largely from outside the field of corrections, who brought with them fresh ideas to old problems. His initial task was fourfold: to evaluate present programmes and bring them together, to try experimental approaches, to furnish the Director's planning staff with systematic knowledge, and to participate in planning long range strategies for changing delinquent behaviour.

His early goal was to formulate a prediction or risk device. The distinguished criminological researcher, Leslie Wilkins, was brought to California from the Home Office, and soon a 'base expectancy' was established whereby each prisoner, during the reception process, could be assessed as to calculated degree of risk of return to criminal behaviour upon release from prison. It would now be possible to begin to think of which groups of inmates to concentrate on for which kinds of intervention,

103

thus maximising the overall effectiveness of the prison system.

Grant's second undertaking provided extensive use of his new classification system, where each inmate could be rated on a scale as to the nature of his overall relationships with other people and with important aspects of his environment. The shape these relationships took seemed to be the crux of his criminality. Interviews with felons led to a paper and pencil test which placed newly arrived felons into high and low interpersonal levels. Grant had shown in his earlier studies the power of systematic classification of both offenders and staff in rehabilitation programmes. He found that rehabilitation could be greatly enhanced when offenders of similar maturity levels were placed together in an intensive interaction programme. The findings supported and enlarged Wilkins' 'lad on lad effect', and pointed towards using the destructive inmate culture for positive gains. The classification of felons by maturity levels to be used in programming, he suggested, could be maximised if the staff conducting the programmes were selected as having similar maturity characteristics as the offenders.

With a risk prediction device and a classification system, new approaches could be designed and systematically evaluated. Grant's next major concentration, while waiting for the follow-up studies of the intensive parole supervision and individual casework approach in prison, was to begin to study the effects of changing the structure and expectations of the correctional environment. His own earlier work with small 'living-groups' was seen as shifting emphasis away from a professionally dominated one-to-one approach, to one which maximised the positive effects of inmates upon each other. The staff could now explore new ways of assisting a 'group process' to emerge, and all activities could be realigned into a total rehabilitative effort. Many of the preliminary results from the earlier treatment projects suggested that other forces in the prison, especially the effects of the inmates upon each other, might be negating the influences of the individual casework approach, or it might be inappropriate.

THERAPEUTIC COMMUNITY APPROACH

The impetus towards wide-scale interest in the therapeutic community approach in prisons was generated by Dr. Maxwell Jones who came to Stanford University Medical Center as

A 'PENAL APPROACH'

visiting Commonwealth Professor of Social Psychiatry for one year. During this time he was retained as a consultant to the Department of Corrections, and in this capacity he visited many prisons and gave seminars expounding his ideas and experiences. In one of his lectures in the Isaac Ray series, delivered to the American Psychiatric Association, he surveyed prevalent thinking on the causes and treatment of delinquency, and then sketched the essentials and probable course of development of a model for a therapeutic community in prison.[10]

> There is also a growing interest in applying the therapeutic community . . . to prison inmate populations. What would the application of this community treatment approach amount to in practice? This question could be best answered, I think, by initiating a small pilot project involving, say, 80 to 100 inmates, with a core staff having a particular interest in this approach, who have volunteered for such a project. This staff would comprise both custodial and treatment personnel. Their special training would ideally be 'on the job', in a group setting where they could be involved collectively in a daily community meeting of all inmates and staff followed by a staff meeting at which the staff-inmate interaction in the community meeting could be discussed in the presence of an experienced supervisor. In addition, each correctional counsellor should have a daily group meeting with the inmates for whom he is personally responsible. Such groups should, if practicable, be limited to about ten inmates. If one of the custodial personnel can also attend as a co-leader, this has considerable advantages for training and coordinating the custodial and treatment roles. The correctional counsellor may wish to continue individual treatment with some of his caseload, and this is in no way incompatible with the group and community meetings. These therapeutic activities should all come under an overall supervisor, preferably by a psychiatrist familiar with penal problems (pp. 135-6).

Dr. Jones suggested a 'transition period' to train staff and establish a 'therapeutic climate' in a prison setting. He began to specify some of the requirements for the staff and for the administrator for the projects.

> Preparation of this kind may take at least six months if the staff is to achieve some awareness of such transference

105

phenomena as countertransference and ego defenses, in
addition to the simpler aspects of group dynamics. The staff
would come into contact with the inmates outside the specifically treatment situation but all inmate behaviour should be
regarded as the stuff of treatment, particularly in those cases
where the acting-out of problems is common. A feedback of
information from the field of everyday behaviour to the group
meetings would be an essential part of the learning process for
the staff, whose skill in relating intragroup and outside
interactions can be developed in this way.

The staff would require further meetings for the examination of their own interpersonal difficulties and for the discussion of their roles, role-relationships and the over-all culture
of the treatment unit. Here again a skilled supervisor is
necessary, someone who is familiar with psychoanalytic and
penal practice and with the social science field.

The supervisor-teacher may and probably should be
involved in the whole treatment programme. Ideally he should
participate in and supervise the community meetings, and in
the succeeding discussions. There is some advantage, however, in having an outside analyst to take the staff meeting,
as this can lead to a degree of objectivity which is not possible
if the analyst is also a full-time staff member. In any case, it is
probably unwise to attempt too much in the way of 'treating'
staff members, and the discussion should be largely limited to
questions which concern the inmates and the staff's feelings
and difficulties about them . . . But perhpas the most important single factor in the establishment of a therapeutic climate
is the personality of the leader. . . . Of first priority would
seem to be the need for selection and training of the prison
personnel for work in living group situations (pp. 136–40.)

Selection of the appropriate inmates for a treatment programme was an early consideration, and thought to be of
extreme importance.

The inmates selected for such a therapeutic community
project in the first instance should probably come from the
short-sentence first-offender group. Ideally, they should be
picked out in the course of the preliminary assessment in the
reception-guidance centre. They should have a relatively high
social maturity rating and favourable treatment prognosis,
as assessed by a psychiatric screening interview. This would
seem to be particularly desirable if the group is to be involved

in the further training of a volunteer staff, as we have suggested above. Staff training should be much more effective if
the initial interpersonal difficulties and training needs were
first dealt with in a relatively 'treatable' group, after which
the staff should be better equipped to deal with the more
disturbed type of inmate (p. 137).

Many opinions were expressed as to the size of the treatment unit in a prison. On this, Dr. Jones commented briefly,

> The size of an inmate group is a controversial question.
> Clearly, much depends on the clinical state of the members,
> and cultural and ethnic factors are also important in determin-
> ing the optimal size. So, too, are the composition and training of
> the staff group and their own feelings in the matter. It is to be
> hoped that the research programmes in correctional depart-
> ments will include studies of the optimal size of inmate living
> groups.* (*footnote: we are here considering minimal security
> personnel living units as a ward community and not the cell
> structure associated with more stringent security programmes.
> Research into the effects of the latter on both inmates and
> custodial personnel might be of even greater importance.)
> In the meantime, planning of living conditions in both
> hospitals and prisons tends to be largely intuitive or deter-
> mined by prejudice, although supposedly based on experience
> and economic necessity. Nevertheless, there seems to be a
> growing agreement that administrative units in both hospitals
> and prisons should not exceed 400 to 500 inmates. There is
> less agreement about the size and composition of living groups
> where essentially therapeutic (interactional) considerations
> are paramount (pp. 137–8).

Finally, Dr. Jones speculated on how such a therapeutic
community in a prison might evolve and some of the shapes it
might take.

> The aim at first would be to avoid preconceptions or at least
> to be prepared to examine critically the attitudes held by the
> staff, to see what validity they have. This examination of
> staff attitudes and beliefs would be a necessary prelude to any
> attempt to observe objectively what was happening in the
> interactional field involving both inmates and staff. Later by
> sharing these observations with the inmates and inviting them
> to do likewise, it should be possible to open up communications
> and enhance the status of the inmates. This process is aided

by the sharing of tasks in a work situation, by frequent informal contacts between staff and inmates, and by a living demonstration of an open and inquiring outlook which is not based exclusively on a desire to bring about change to a 'better' way of life. A community which seeks to share its problems by verbalizing them implies a belief in the value of open expression, that 'talking is a good thing'. This would appear to be a preconception of the sort we have said we are anxious to avoid, but it is an essential prerequisite of any therapeutic community. Many prisoners feel that talking is a bad and highly dangerous procedure, and a long period of informal contact and shared work may be a necessary step before anything approaching a personal topic can be raised. It is here that the inmate peer group can often do much by its own informal observation and discussion of relationships and events, for the sanction of the peer group is likely, in the early stages at least, to carry a considerable weight. The staff must be given sufficient freedom of action within the social structure of the prison to be able to identify with the inmates and their problems rather than with any preconceptions of the prison authorities. Thus, the idea that the content of the group discussions may be used by staff to influence the Adult Authority and possibly extend the term of imprisonment not only will lead to a serious block in communications but also will create anxieties among the staff which would limit their effectiveness in group meetings. However, if this idea appears to be in some people's minds and to be hindering free communication, and if this is pointed out perceptively by a staff member, it can form a useful starting point for shared discussion on the nature of the relationship between inmates and staff.

It is the creation of a set of circumstances that will encourage social interaction, accurate observation, and free discussion which can be seen as the chief task of an experimental unit of the sort we envisage. The purpose of such a unit would clearly be to aid the individual's return to society and the prevention of further incarceration. In the first instance, at least, moral assumptions would be avoided—a thing about the establishment of a 'better' way of life, or even a greater sense of social responsibility, implies that the staff's value system is *ipso facto* the only proper one. In a society where moral values and cultural concepts are so varied, not to say confused, as in our own, it is difficult and surely unwarranted to uphold any one simple model.

A 'PENAL APPROACH'

I would anticipate that such a community would, in time, develop its own characteristic culture based on the discussion of frequently recurring problems and the conscious attempt to reconcile the various divergent viewpoints involved. The community, both inmates and staff, would gradually establish and clarify the roles of its members and their role-relationships, and new inmates would more quickly be drawn into the collective perception of their role. One can conceive of a culture having specific merits for the task of rehabilitation, and this would certainly be a great improvement upon the familiar custodial prison environment.

Along with this, I would anticipate the development of psychotherapeutic skills. Group discussion could not easily be limited to an evaluation of literal events; the staff and to a lesser extent the inmates would tend to become aware of aspects of interaction outside full consciousness as well as conscious motivation would be pertinent, for example, in problems of stealing and would tend to alter the significance of such behaviour for many of the group members. Such incidents would also call for confrontations and living-learning situations as described in the last chapter.

It seems to me that in considering crime we are dealing with a situation where anomalies of growth and various neurotic difficulties overlap with profound problems of differing and often competing cultures. A multidisciplinary approach would seem to be indicated if the complexity of the phenomena are to be dispassionately examined. What happens in this living situation might be compared to what happens when the staff meets daily to discuss *their* problems. The culture becomes more defined, emotional problems can often be resolved, and the personnel are trained to observe. Also staff come to have a feeling of identification with both the staff and inmate groups which increases their feeling of security and hence their tolerance of anxiety. One is tempted to say that maturation, treatment and training can all be identified in this process.

The sort of fluid structure I envisage would favour the gradual development of a culture well suited to the more explicit tasks of observation, training, education and rehabilitation. It would also, I think, favour the emergence of methods of treatment particularly suited to the personality problems of prisoners. It may be that increased knowledge and experience will show that the type of 'therapeutic community' or 'living

groups' advocated in this thesis is relevant to the problems
of those individuals with the lower personality integration
levels (that is approximately two thirds of the prison population) in particular. I believe that such people can, in some
cases, 'mature' or achieve a higher level of personality integration within a therapeutic community. For inmates with
higher levels of personality integration, increasing use of
analytical psychotherapy, both group and individual, may be
necessary if optimal treatment conditions are to be achieved
(pp. 140–3).

Superintendent Oberhauser was quick to see the potential
of this approach but also realised the difficulties that would
arise in applying such radical ideas in the traditional prison
setting. He made facilities available for a variety of experiments. He offered the site of a forestry camp in the mountains
for a small total treatment effort. A therapeutic community
was established there for 104 inmates, especially selected.
Next, a series of experiments was begun at Chino with inmates
who volunteered, to see the feasibility of restructuring por-
tions of the prison so that inmates and staff could experiment
with new roles and ways of operating their own units. Could
staff and inmates in a prison setting collaborate in a treatment programme? Would large group meetings of a total
living unit be possible? The number of fifteen had thus far
been considered the optimum size for safety. To what extent
could you experiment with new roles for the non-professional
staff, mainly the correctional officers, who were closest to the
inmates physically but most distant in relationships? Would
security be endangered by the restructuring of roles? And what
type of person would respond?

The mounting problem of the youthful, aggressive offender
seemed appropriate for study under the conditions specified
by Dr. Jones. This type of aggression and activity was a precursor of the emergence of more widespread protest and violence among dissident youth. This group was also presenting
numerous problems in prison. Previous studies in California
prisons indicated that many of these young men, once confined as adult offenders, became progressively more violent,
both while in prison and upon parole in the community. In a
relatively short time, typically their delinquencies moved
from offences like 'joy riding' to burglary, robbery with
weapons, assault, and even to murder. During the four years

of the project to be described a dozen young men were included who had been convicted of homicide, murder or manslaughter. Young men selected for the project frequently had extensive, but short, juvenile histories. Many had been confined in youth institutions. Two thirds had been in the armed forces, many having been given this 'alternative' by a sentencing judge at the age of 17. Most of these men had not been able to tolerate the armed forces and had received bad conduct discharges. The type of men selected for the project comprised 40% of first admissions to the California Department of Corrections. They caused serious management problems while in prison and usually had to be confined in institutions with higher security, in single cells.

It was necessary to establish an atmosphere in which a group of rebellious, active, bright young men could evolve a system and a way of life which would allow them opportunities to examine the effects of their behaviour on one another, on the total community, and on small segments of it; to accept, discard, control or change what they experienced. In this process, they might discover for themselves the futility of their delinquency and learn alternatives. This new behaviour, we believed, could serve them effectively outside prison. What conditions were needed for such an atmosphere?

Even though the project was located in the grounds of a minimum security prison, with only a single, unmanned fence for peripheral security, there were additional facilities for temporary control. A medium security unit with single cells, reasonably isolated from the rest of the institution, was available and used on occasion to remove a resident from the project for short periods of time. Maximum security was available nearby, but never used. Escape from the institution was a serious matter, both in terms of the anticipated reaction by the public and for the additional felony offence, carrying two years minimum, which it placed on the inmate involved. The availability of these additional controls, in addition to the original sentence and the prospect of parole, was an important factor initially in assisting the residents to form a more immediate reason for changing. As the project progressed and developed its own means, they decreased in importance.

A typical candidate was Bob who was committed to prison for robbery first degree at the age of 21, and sentenced from five years to life. He had been arrested once previously at the age of 20 for drunkenness, and given a ten dollar fine. There was no juvenile history. Late one afternoon he drove his 'souped-up' car into a service station-garage for inspection.

> As the attendant entered the garage, the defendant accosted him with a sawed-off shotgun and ordered him to lie on the floor. . . . Defendant took the cash box keys from the victim's belt and after the victim indicated which was the proper key, defendant struck him on the back of the head and stated: 'You had better be out or I'll blow your brains out. . . .' Defendant took $65.00 and fled. He surrendered himself to the Sheriff's office the next morning and confessed committing the robbery. . . . He stated he had stolen the shotgun from a relative and that it wasn't loaded. It was also revealed that he hit the victim over the head because he panicked over the possibility that the victim might notify the police.

While in the Reception-Guidance Centre, Bob made the following statement: 'When I went to court, the District Attorney made me out to be a bad guy and said to the Judge to make an example of me. So he did. I don't believe I should have got such a rough sentence.'

He continued not to look at the crime itself but attempted to justify it, 'The money I got, I bought food for my family, but I know that this is no excuse.'

The judge, more enlightened and concerned with rehabilitation than many, said, 'This crime, while serious, is not a true example of this defendant's conduct. We feel a minimum term will bring about an early rehabilitation.'

Bob left school in the tenth grade and had average intelligence. He had lived in Southern California all his life. His parents were separated when he was but a few years old. His mother remarried and there were two stepchildren from that marriage. None of the family had been arrested. The caseworker noted that Bob 'had some sexual difficulties during adolescence', but no details were given. Most adolescents have some. His later experimenting with homosexuality caused one of the most serious incidents in the four years of the project. At 19 he married a girl his own age. Soon thereafter he went into the Navy, serving three years and receiving an honourable discharge. His wife had two children but he was never certain if they were his or not. Difficulties began after his discharge from the Navy. Financial worries about supporting his wife and two children mounted, and he was unable to settle down to the slower pace and monotony of civilian life.

Nevertheless, he worked for his stepfather as a carpenter's help for two years but felt that the stepfather placed too many personal demands on him, and so he left the job. Just before his arrest, he began drinking excessively and going around with younger men who were delinquent.

Another candidate selected, George, was committed for robbery second degree at the age of 22, and sentenced from one year to life. The probation officer reported that a man appeared in the Sherriff's office in a small town late one evening with a man in his fifties whom he had found beside a country road. The man had told him he had been beaten and robbed by two men. 'The alleged victim appeared to be dazed and smelled of an alcoholic beverage and was unable to walk.' It was later found that he had broken a leg and had a bloody nose. Later, the victim said he had been in an argument with the two suspects and had left the bar with the two men in his car, one of them driving it for him. The car was driven into a ditch by one of the two men. A passing motorist stopped and transported all three of them back to the small town where one of the men took his own car to get the victim's car out of the ditch. The victim claimed they drove past his car and proceeded onto a side road where the two young men stopped, and ordered him out of the car. One of the men then grabbed him by the leg and the other by the arm, dragged him from the car, twisting his leg. The victim claimed he was then struck on the head and rendered unconscious. When he regained consciousness he crawled to the highway and was picked up by a passing motorist.

The owner of the bar, when questioned later, said he remembered the victim and the 'Roberts boys' leaving together after one of the boys went broke gambling. It was further revealed that Mrs. Roberts, who lived in the area, had a son and a nephew living with her. It was rumoured in the community that both were deserters from the U.S. Army. The two young men were taken into custody and readily admitted to both the robbery and desertion from the military.

George stated at the time of his admission to the Reception-Guidance Centre,

> My cousin and I were drinking pretty heavy at the time of the crime. I don't think this crime should have been committed, but it was. Due to the fact that we left with the victim and he ran off in a ditch, we went back to get my car to pull

CHINO

his out. During the time, my cousin, the victim and myself
got some more beer. I started to get back in the car. Then I
hit the victim, then my cousin hit the victim and said, 'Get
his wallet'. I believe that if we had both stopped to think this
would never have happened. I have never been in any trouble
before and my cousin hasn't either. I, myself, know I wouldn't
commit any robbery for $12.00. But I did, actually we didn't
even need the money. I would say it was an on the moment
decision. Because we were drinking with the victim, and he
wanted us to go with him so I guess that's how it happened.

George, also a native Californian, had no juvenile history,
had left school at the age of seventeen, just before graduating,
and had tested out at ninth grade with average intelligence.
At the time of his arrest he was living with his aunt. The parents were separated and the mother's whereabouts were unknown. He had married a girl of eighteen, divorced her three
years later, and had never held a steady job. He was technically
in the army at the time of his arrest. The social worker
stated,

> The father was a heavy drinker and gambler, and the
> mother was usually pre-occupied with extra-marital relation-
> ships. George was usually present to witness them. His own
> marital relationship foundered due to his wife's identical
> pattern of behaviour to the mother. His interpersonal rela-
> tionships developed severe feelings of inadequacy, insecurity
> and hostility which tend to make him over-react to stressing
> situations, for example; leaving the Army, AWOL, using
> alcohol to escape his feelings of inadequacy, and his impulsive
> behaviour in the present offense. Dependency needs are in
> direct conflict with his independent wishes. He constantly
> strives to prove to himself the ability to function in the
> adequate male role but becomes threatened at the idea of
> accepting the responsibilities that accompany that role, and
> loses his immediate dependency gratifications.

While in the Reception-Guidance Centre, George said he
wanted to learn auto mechanics but the counsellor thought this
was not a mature outlook, thought that he needed an occupation with more stability—he recommended that George
learn plastering.

A third offender, Gene, was selected for the project at the
age of 21, following his first conviction as an adult offender.

At three one morning, Gene was arrested in Los Angeles, along with two others, attempting to rob a sixty year old man. The three struck the old man on the head, causing multiple lacerations, contusions, and a possible concussion. The incident aggravated an existing heart condition for the victim, who later died. The three were eventually given jail sentences of less than one year and then put on three years' probation. Six months later, at 2 a.m., Gene together with three different youths, broke into a supermarket and stole several cases of beer. They were pursued and caught by the police, but Gene escaped and was not arrested until three months later. He was then sentenced with attempted robbery as a probation violation and with burglary second degree, carrying six months to twenty years and six months to fifteen years, the sentences given concurrently. He had used a club as a weapon in the robbery. On arrival at the Reception-Guidance Centre, Gene said,

> I was involved in an attempted robbery charge and received probation and was doing all right until a few months ago when several of us guys were involved in a grocery store burglary. I could probably think of a hundred reasons why I shouldn't have done it but that's all it would be is excuses. I knew better, and maybe while I'm in here I can do a little growing up.

His arrest history was brief, consisting of minor thefts at the age of eighteen. At seventeen he was caught fighting in school, stealing hubcaps from cars and violating a curfew. He had average intelligence and completed the twelfth grade, although he tested at 9.4 years. Gene was the oldest of four children, the others being all girls. He had not been married, had never been in the military service and had never held a full-time job.

These three young men were typical of those chosen for the project to be described in more detail in the chapters that follow.

REFERENCES

1. Excellent summaries of the recent history of prisons can be found in the several papers composing the special issue of *Key Issues*, entitled, 'The Future of Imprisonment in a Free Society', vol. 2, 1965.

2. See Duffy, Q. T., *The San Quentin Story* (Pocket Books Inc., 1951) for a descriptive account of the conditions and reform at that prison.

CHINO

3. Eaton, J. W., *Stone Walls Not a Prison Make* (Springfield, Charles C. Thomas, 1962) gives a documentation of the history of the California Department of Corrections.

4. See *Special Intensive Parole Unit*, phases I, H, III, and IV research reports 1956 through 1966. California Department of Corrections.

5. See *Pilot Intensive Counseling Organization* projects reports (series of 4), California Department of Corrections 1958 through 1961; also *Intensive Treatment Project reports*, phase I. 1958, 66 (2 volumes).

6. Grant, J. D., and Grant, M. Q., 'A Group Dynamics Approach to the Treatment of Nonconformists in the Navy'. *Annals of the Amer. Academy of Political and Social Science*, 1959, 322, 126–35.

7. Sullivan, C. E., Grant, M. Q., and Grant, J. D., 'The Development of Interpersonal Maturity: Applications to Delinquency'. *Psychiatry*, 1957, 20, 373–85.

8. Jones, M. S., *Social Psychiatry*, London, Tavistock, 1952; *Social Psychiatry in the Community, in Hospitals and in Prison*, Springfield, Charles C. Thomas, 1962; and *Beyond the Therapeutic Community*, Yale U. Press, 1968.

9. Wilmer, H. A., *Social Psychiatry in Action: A Therapeutic Community*, Springfield, Charles C. Thomas, 1958.

10. The Isaac Ray Lectures delivered by Maxwell Jones were subsequently printed in ref (8) 1962.

Chapter Five

A TRANSITIONAL THERAPEUTIC
COMMUNITY IN A PRISON

As society evolves, its institutions must change to
meet new needs and to conform with advancing
knowledge. The traditional prison has not been a
notably successful institution except in carrying out
its most elemental purpose—that of incapacitating
the convicted offender for brief periods of time. In
this day when asylums have become mental hospitals, and no disease or social condition is considered either too hopeless or too horrible to defy
the onslaught of scientific examination, the prison
—nay, the entire administration of criminal justice
—must submit to review, research, imaginative
innovation and experimentation.

Richard A. McGee

Transitional phase: establishing a new culture

A time of transition, one year, was allowed to train staff
and work out procedures for the daily groups.* The counsellors and I had been working with groups of inmates who had
shared in planning the project. They volunteered rather enthusiastically to begin it, but were not included in the research
findings reported in chapter six. As 'culture carriers', these
men performed the very important task of starting and developing the project. As the first candidates, who were ran-
domly selected, were brought into the project and got under
way, the 'culture carriers' gradually left it.

During the transition year, we experimented with different

---

* My own formal training had been primarily in social and clinical
psychology. Just before being employed on the research staff of the
California Department of Corrections, I spent eight years in the U.S.
Navy participating in two research/demonstration projects in psychiatric units in naval hospitals with acutely disturbed military personnel
in the U.S. and in the Korean theatre. I also had spent a month with
Dr. Jones at Henderson and had visited other hospitals in the U.K.
where pioneering methods in social psychiatry had been developed.
(See ref. 1.)

numbers for the final project. Experience was gained of units from twenty to one hundred and four men. When the number was below twenty men there did not seem to be enough happening to hold their interest or for the community to function well; and when it rose over fifty there seemed to be too much happening to use the group processes and social interactions for change.

We needed to know how convicted felons in prison would take to a culture which required 'feedback' to operate. Would they see this as 'snitching'? Would they be able to violate the well established 'inmate code of ethics' and feed incidences of delinquent behaviour publicly into the meetings? If men were encouraged to talk openly about their current anxieties at being in prison, would their feelings erupt and get out of control? Could you contain anger and hostility in large groups? What would happen to staff control if inmates talked too freely?

Early large group meetings were viewed with considerable anxiety by the custodial officials. The first meeting with over twenty men was a cautious experience. Extra custodial officials were stationed nearby in case anger erupted and became unmanageable. But as the meetings continued and no ill-effects resulted, everyone relaxed.

Having just come from a mental hospital, and not having been in a prison previously, and seeing the prisoners as similar to youthful patients I had known, I frequently referred to them as 'patients' without realising it. Later they confronted me in a meeting, calling me 'doctor'. I found that some liked the idea of being seen as a patient — sickness was more acceptable than badness —others resented the implication. Wasn't it, after all, enough to be bad without also being seen as mad?

FIRST PHASE: FIRST AND SECOND YEARS

The counsellors at first, understandably, had strong vested interests in keeping the residents in a dependent relationship. Some became interested in learning how to increase participation on the part of the men. I think few, if any, realised the extent of the internal shifts that were to occur within them and how this would affect their lives.

We held meetings with the counsellors to help them work in groups. We engaged the assistance of outside consultants. Maxwell Jones was retained as the primary consultant to assist the development of the project. In addition, he held meetings with the staff of the institution to show them how the new project was part of a widespread trend in rehabilitation. The Superintendent held separate meetings for the institutional personnel to explain to them what we were attempting to do, to put the project into the wider context of the institution, and to give it his personal sanction. The correctional officers were most apprehensive about these large daily group meetings. They feared the inmates would take over. In the past, their fears had been justified, however irrational they might have seemed. When pilot studies had begun at Chino, the previous year, which eventually involved over one hundred inmates plus staff meeting together daily, group meetings in excess of fifteen or so had not been permitted in prisons for security reasons.

One counsellor, who remained with the project the longest, recounts vividly an episode early in the project's history, illustrating mutual learning and how the men 'trained' the staff. The counsellor had remained in the housing unit this particular evening after working hours, to have an interview with one of the men, when he inadvertently became involved in an early 'crisis group'.

> B., R., and G. came in to have a meeting. They related what had taken place earlier in the afternoon in a meeting with them, Briggs, and Mr. C. (associate superintendent) re: possibility that G. and E. were going to escape. It was suggested to me that they should have a meeting with E. included. They went and got him and others joined in the meeting as it went along. Both men seemed nervous but seemed to get much involved and get much consolation from the jug of coffee which seemed in constant passage around the group. G. had gone to E. and told him bluntly what had taken place. The escape idea was discussed for a time and the discussion backed off to the other men in the project, the staff and then to his wife. This talk was a continuation of the small group earlier in the day. Frankly, I was very sceptical at pushing a meeting with G. but he laid it out on the line and told E. he should talk it over with the other men. E. agreed and so did the rest of the group. E's first reaction was surprise, especially that R. would come, as they had had an argument recently and E. was convinced that R. and he were on the 'outs'. They discussed their feelings quite freely with R. emphasizing that

people in the project do care about E. E. then started talking freely and shared his feelings; the project, the staff, his wife, playing the big shot, gambling, escape, cards and dominoes (illegal gambling). It was evident that they understood him and he knew it. The group did not lecture or preach. When E. stated that he felt he would be yanked out of bed in the night and shipped to San Quentin as an escape risk, the group accepted his feelings without trying to prove that he wouldn't be transferred. He would have to see for himself. The group asked E. if he felt he could bring this up in the large group in the morning. The thought was threatening to him but when the men offered their assistance if he needed it, E. stated he would do the best he could. The group ended at 10:15 for count. This was a rewarding experience for me. P.S. the group felt that E. needed a job in the project and suggested he try to get on the screening committee!

In its own administration, the project, in its early stages, reflected the newly created schism in correctional institutions between custodial and clinical staff, the latter sometimes referred to as 'care and treatment'. As the project began, the correctional officers who had been assigned previously to the housing unit were retained with the project. They reported to custodial superiors and saw their roles primarily as keeping the housing unit orderly and enforcing institutional rules and regulations.

Entries in the staff log by the officers at this time reflect their concerns:

H. was involved in an incident in the mess hall at the morning meal. Lieut. on duty was called and a disciplinary report was written.

Numerous persons left the unit early for evening chow without authorization, taking advantage of the new officer on duty.

L. (a resident) advised this officer that benzedrine, nutmeg, etc., were brought into the housing unit on Friday afternoon.

B. failed to do his maintenance assignment. S. brought bread into the unit from the mess hall and states so to the other men in front of the officer. B. again failed to clean the TV area after he was requested to do so. Stayed on his rack (bed). Given a reprimand.

R. was 5 minutes late for the 6:35 count. I counselled him

and he was very apologetic about this and said, 'It won't happen again.' I noted this in his record.

There are dumbells (for weightlifting and against prison rules to have them) between the beds of S. and K. These formerly belonged to H. (implication here is that H. sold them to either S. or K.).

We were offered the institutional laundry as a workshop, where it was hoped that the men could see finished products of their own work and at the same time learn an employable skill. We were wrong. Most of the men selected for the project had poor attitudes towards work and learned no employable skills; the majority could not tolerate supervision. They were often sacked from jobs because they could not get to work on time, reported to work inconsistently, or would become easily bored with routine of any sort. The Superintendent's staff believed that the laundry might be a suitable place for the men to work out these difficulties and that improved quality of the laundry services would have a good effect on the image of the new project. For twenty years the laundry had been bad and everyone had to use it.

The men worked in the laundry until the work was completed each day, returning to the housing unit at 3 p.m. for the community meeting. The laundry supervisors attended the meetings sporadically. When they participated in the community meetings, they were highly critical and punitive in their attitudes towards the men, carping about them and expecting support for their attitude from the project.

Daily community meetings, one of the most vital aspects of the project, brought to focus social behaviour in the community and became the place where membership status was attained and defined. These meetings were also the place where confrontations would occur, between the men and staff, between the men and, eventually, between staff members.

The meetings opened with a resident reading a log, which the men themselves kept, recording significant events which had happened during the previous twenty four hours. The meetings then proceeded spontaneously. The community could take up matters read from the log, or ignore them and introduce new matters not in the log. There was no designated leader of the meeting, but the men did turn to me frequently asking for guidance and interpretations. I participated as I saw fit and often took a few minutes at the end of the meeting to summarise it, to raise questions about what had happened or not happened, or to share some of my own feelings, observations and beliefs with the community.

The meetings opened on time, they were compulsory for all the men and for the staff who were on duty. They took priority over everything else, and when a man was absent, the meeting did not begin until he was there, seated on a chair. At times when the structure was well defined, or there was no crisis, I participated little or not at all, except for the summary, which might just be a sentence or two. I sometimes took notes in the meeting, which I used for the critiques that always followed the meetings, and which provided a record for the men and for my own learning.

The counsellors held small psychotherapy groups whenever the men could be freed, often one or two evenings each week. Each man was assigned to a counsellor, who looked after his 'case'.

The correctional officers assigned to the housing unit rarely attended any of the meetings. In this they were supported by their superiors who did not want them to be confronted openly by the inmates. They were reluctant to become involved in the discussions as they believed that open confrontation would jeopardise their authority and, further, that this was not their job. Such encounters clearly belonged to the counsellors. I began a weekly meeting just for the officers, to understand them better, to help them to talk about their conflicts and begin to find a role for themselves within the project.

A correctional officer made the following notation in the staff log at this time:

> I believe that Sgt. H. has been appointed as overseer for the unit in an attempt to bring it back into custody's fold. Several of the men mentioned that they had been harrassed and pressured by him. A. (correctional officer in the housing unit) is quite concerned by the philosophy of the project. He is disturbed over the age old question of serving two masters and needs support. Can we talk about this in the Thursday afternoon officers' meeting?

The early community meetings focussed on matters relating to becoming a prisoner, the frustrations of institutional life, the inadequacy of the food, the restrictions on movement, the men's anxieties about when they would be paroled, their fears of what was happening to their families and ties outside prison while they were confined, and the discrimination they anticipated as 'ex-cons'. We were concerned with planning details of the project.

As things began to stabilise and new men arrived, the ones who had started the project became more circumspect, were identified with broader aspects of the project, and began to align themselves more with the staff.

The community meetings now moved towards two focal points, the frustrations in the operation of the laundry and those encountered in the housing unit. Both centred round the residents' relations with the staff, and staff not yet related to the project, but intimately associated with it, with the daily lives of the residents.

In time the men developed production skill and could operate the laundry with fewer men in less time than the previous group of older inmates. The laundry staff, accustomed to many years of 'sweat shop' standards with an overabundant manpower source, continued to maintain a skeleton group of older, 'con-wise' inmates whom they ascertained had skills and dependability acquired through apprenticeship and loyalty, qualities which, they maintained, the project inmates lacked. They were naturally apprehensive about the stability of operating the laundry with this young, impulsive, aggressive group and wanted their own core group on whom they could rely when the project failed, as many of the institutional staff believed it would.

A correctional officer noted in the staff log:

> This evening we discussed the laundry situation and I feel that H. has some good observations, and reasonably good ways of handling the situation. Most of us felt it would be a good idea to have an inmate inspector. I do not feel that an inspector or foreman is necessary, but Mr. A. (laundry superintendent) should set up standards and his staff should hold these standards by means of an inspection.

The new men, being bright, alert and highly delinquent were also eager to become totally involved, but were kept from moving into certain key jobs held by the inmates who were not in the project. They began to make time and motion studies of each operation in the laundry and, with the assistance of an industrial psychologist whom we hired for them as a consultant, laid out an impressive blue print for more efficient production in the laundry. They soon found that the amount of skill required was considerably less than that claimed by the staff of the laundry. The older so-called skilled laundry operators, they maintained, were often performing personal services for the laundry staff, such as making and serving them coffee, informing them of delinquent activities around the institution and so on. Secondly, these inmates were in key positions, so-called 'skilled jobs', and were paid a small wage, thus were controlled by the laundry staff. These men divided their loyalties between the laundry staff and the inmates in the institution. A common practice, for example, was for them to solicit extra services for starching and pressing creases in shirts and trousers, although this was against the rules, in return for cigarettes. They had operated a rather extensive racket successfully throughout the institution, and even some staff members were glad to receive and pay for this preferential treatment.

The men in the project contended that trying to look well in prison should not be 'illegal', but that it would help establish or maintain the inmates' self respect. They drew up a proposal to the laundry staff that the practice be made standard procedure for everyone and they volunteered to take the key jobs without pay. This would mean the end of the racket.

These solutions were, of course, too simple and were administratively disapproved. The rackets continued. The men now became suspect in the eyes of the other laundry workers, staff and inmates alike whose jobs they had threatened and whose rackets they had exposed. When the situation became known by inmates and staff on the 'yard' of the main institution, the project men were viewed with even greater suspicion. What kind of 'nuts' were they?

The men could now step up production, in quantity, but were prevented from improving quality, and often completed all the work by noon. They contended that they ought to have the additional time off, and proposed additional group meetings. Yet the laundry staff, accustomed to an inexhaustible and conforming work force, would hold the men until 3 p.m., the time for the community meeting, providing them with 'busy work' or none at all. The men, being basically restless, grew more so as idleness increased, and the conflict between work operations and the ideals of the project became more apparent.

A correctional officer in the housing unit attended a meeting one evening by the men who were most concerned about conditions in the laundry, and wrote as follows:

> B. and H. said that the laundry situation is a mess. They said that the work is not being done, there was no supervision today and when confronted with the situation, Mr. A. (the laundry Superintendent) said the best way to handle it was to send most of them to the fields to work! I believe the best way would be to send Mr. A. to the fields and let the men work it out as they have planned. Why do we, as staff, have to be so inactive about things in the laundry? Mr. A. is not going to change after 20 years. I do not believe all the fault can be blamed on the inmates.

These matters were repeatedly brought into the community meetings where the men clearly saw the discrepancies between what they were daily faced with and the philosophy being developed in the project. Their initial expectation was that the project staff, especially myself, would take some direct and forceful action to alleviate an untenable situation. The laundry staff attended the meetings less and less often as these matters came up more frequently. Some of the new men, seizing upon the conflict in the work project, aligned themselves with the delinquent activities of the inmates who were not in the project. Some collaborated, on a percentage basis, or established more exclusive, more lucrative rackets of their own. One, for example, ran a 'bakery route' around the institution, picking up cakes, burying them under fresh laundry in his cart, and delivering them to the housing units along with the laundry for a good profit. The 'older' residents in the project were torn with split-loyalties, feeling especially impotent as their attempts to change the laundry had failed, and their reporting of delinquent behaviour to the groups was ineffective. They were more upset as they saw the whole project now jeopardised. Many had considerable investment in the project themselves and had changed considerably.

The correctional officers in the housing unit, too, were beginning to respond to the laundry crisis. This seemed an area they could more rapidly identify with, and now they were beginning to see the value of the large group meetings. One wrote in the log:

> The area to really be concerned with now is the laundry. I feel we need to set up some standards for the laundry and help

the supervisors learn how to *supervise*. I do not feel we have to become authoritarian any more than we have been except in the laundry, and even there to a limited degree. I do feel that the men are capable of the work and that we should expect it of them. If necessary we should carry them awhile, but not too long unless they are not working with the problem. Then I believe a firm hand should be taken just like *dear old dad!* In the unit, I believe we can be more patient and be less restrictive in our linits and offer more of ourselves in the groups. (Opinion only.) P.S. R. felt he was both right and wrong in his action. I encouraged him to fight for what he thought right and to admit his wrongs, all in the group.

An attempt was made to improve the situation in the laundry by all the staff in the project going there and working with the men. In retrospect, this seemed to make matters worse, for now the laundry staff thought we were encroaching on their territory while we were there. The men showed us evidence of what they had tried to describe. Most of the counsellors became anxious about such a sudden shift in their roles. One said indignantly that he had not gone to college for five years to work in a laundry; he was there to wear a white shirt, not to wash one!

Meanwhile, in the housing unit, the men were relaxing their conforming behaviour. This was in keeping with the philosophy of the project as we were developing it in the community meetings. The new men especially were covering up their delinquencies less and less, and I was supporting this. The correctional officers were becoming more and more uncertain about their roles and reporting fewer and fewer violations to their superiors. Formal disciplinary charges were often being referred back to me from custodial superiors, especially from the custodial associate superintendent. I, in turn, brought them into the community meetings. The custodial staff both in the housing unit and in the main institution now believed their authority seriously in jeopardy as 'nothing happened' when they formally made a disciplinary charge; that is, no punishment followed. They thought the men in the project were receiving special immunity and believed this was not fair to the other inmates.

The weekly meeting with the officers was going well and we were finding more consistent policies for the housing unit. I was encouraging them to talk about their dilemmas. The main one seemed to centre on creating an atmosphere where there was less suppression and more expression within the limitations of the institution. We were still feeling our way as to what those limits were. How could men learn? The men we had selected for the project could obviously not learn from punishment. The dilemma of permissiveness versus punishment placed the officers in an untenable position. Some began to see the merits of what we were trying to do in the project but could not safely identify with it or support it publicly, as they had outside supervisors with differing views. As more delinquent activities were reported and no action was taken, custodial officials in the institution became more alarmed and viewed the project as a place fostering and harbouring delinquency rather than controlling and punishing it.

The officers were also becoming more open about differences among themselves. A log entry at this time states:

> It seems that our consistency as officers is falling apart now as O. seems to be fighting for something. I hope that further discussions next Thursday in our officers' meeting will help.

Officer O. replied:

> I have and will continue to 'fight for something' if I feel a strict adherence to the rules is necessary on said subject or any subject of great concern.

Another entry reveals the beginning of a cautious shift from purely custodial concerns:

> I caught G. about to leave the laundry with a sweat shirt. I gave him a chance to 'save face' and he seized the opportunity. He displayed a very good attitude.

The conflict between taking immediate action and delaying it for discussion and group resolution was highlighted in an instance when custodial officials received rumours that there were many knives and weapons hidden around the institution. A secret order was put out to the housing officers for a 'surprise' inspection to occur simultaneously in all the thirteen housing units of the prison one evening. I intercepted the order and for our unit, instead, called a meeting and read the instructions to the men. I asked that we cooperate and that they turn in any such 'weapons' to me and I would turn them over to the custodial captain. Many men had, in fact, taken table knives from the mess hall to spread peanut butter and jam on bread and biscuits, which was also against institution regulations. I suggested that they keep a couple of knives for that purpose in the desk in the office and use them when they needed them. As it turned out, our unit of less than sixty men produced more knives for the security officer (and without an inspection) than the whole institution of sixteen hundred men had found on the 'surprise' inspection.

As a result of this, the original fears of the custodial staff were confirmed. They had expected that the project would control delinquent behaviour and police the unit more than the rest. It was now clear that we would do nothing of the sort and moreover were harbouring an arsenal of weapons! We had tried to deal with the matter openly and with trust. It backfired.

From then on, the custody staff took to making frequent unannounced inspections of the men's property, usually in the evenings, late at night, or at weekends when the counsellors were not around. They watched the men's activities with greater scrutiny and peeped in the windows after dark, hoping to find them doing something wrong.

I made the following note in the staff log, summarising some of my own feelings about one week's activities:

> There are several men in the unit who are upset just now. We've been through a trying week. K. was upset on Monday, the D. incident on Wednesday, etc. Many of the men have been feeling bad this week and I don't know just why. Perhaps the more firm attitude I have taken has something to do with it. R. is depressed, H., S and S. are acting out more. C. is putting himself in jeopardy by revealing in the community meeting this afternoon that he was asked to inform on the project by the custody staff in payment for cigarettes. He said they offered him a carton. I think they suspect narcotics and homosexuality are being condoned in the unit and that we are even encouraging delinquency. Perhaps some of the men will now label him a 'snitch' and carry this out on the yard and he will be in danger. This is serious, I think, in view of his sentence for murder. He has to walk such a tight rope. Why did Lieut. G. have to pick him as an informer? He has enough on his mind as it is. B. seemed better after his family group last night. Patience, patience, patience!

An officer recorded:

> When ordered to release the men for noon chow, Lt. J.'s orders were, 'Release those bunch of snivelers!' All the housing

128

officers who were still on the conference line heard this and laughed.

The men were outraged at the constant harassment and brought their protests into the community meetings. Again, they expected me to take action. There was nothing I could do. The confrontations upset the few correctional officers in the housing unit, who were beginning cautiously to listen in and, on occasion, sit at the periphery of the group meetings. They saw themselves as vulnerable both to inmate 'attack' and open to criticism from their superiors for attending the meetings. They withdrew even more.

A series of crises brought focus to the several problems which the project was unable to handle. As all efforts to change the work situation rationally seemed thwarted, newer men organised a go slow in the laundry. They delayed so that they would not be released until 4.30 p.m. when it was mandatory for them to be in the housing unit to be counted. No one would be in the living quarters for the community meetings daily, except the staff. Only the staff appeared for the daily meetings and so the men had no chance to talk officially about their frustrations.

Also the counsellors were becoming more anxious. Their former roles as counsellors to the men individually and in small psychotherapy groups were no longer valued. In the community meetings, their continued attempts to get the men to recount and understand historical, personalised and emotional material were no longer accepted. And their clinical vocabulary, a carry-over from their former professional roles, put them at further disadvantage in attempting to communicate easily. They could not yet see meaningful roles for themselves in the community.

Relations with the main institution, both with staff and with inmates, were becoming tenuous. Inmates who were not in the project were berating those in it by continual harassment and accusations as to their 'weakness', impotency and 'sell-out' to the establishment; they were seen by other inmates as 'finks'. Staff who were not in the project were looking for things to criticise and putting pressure on the officers and the counsellors to conform with the rest of the institution. Even some administrators in the central headquarters of the Department of Corrections were beginning to become anxious as they received many distorted accounts of what was happening at Chino.

As a result of the mounting tensions the men began to break away from the project and to become involved with other inmates. We did not know enough about these things. A crucial incident involved one inmate who joined some others, not in the project, and together they stole a considerable sum from the main canteen. His participation in the burglary was not at first detected, but subsequently it came out in a community meeting. Delinquent behaviour was coming forth as desired but outside the boundaries of the project.

As if all these mounting crises were not enough, the project was besieged with visitors, from the Department of Corrections headquarters, from other prisons, and from various professionals throughout the country as well as from abroad. There were over one thousand visitors in one year alone. It was difficult enough among ourselves to live with the mounting frustrations, let alone to have them open to inspection, comment and possible misinterpretation by strangers. Some visitors were very helpful and added a great deal of support and new ideas to the undertaking. But some of the policy makers, as a result of brief visits, became concerned that the inmates had been given too much freedom and that steps needed to be taken by the staff to gain more control over them.

I maintained that the mounting crises pointed to the need for structural and administrative changes in the project in order that crises could be used as an important means for change. Yet our very existence in the prison and as a project seemed in jeopardy.

I thought the project could bear no more tension when an additional and more immediately serious situation suddenly erupted, involving us with the whole institution. But the resolution of the crisis was the beginning of our salvation, and was a clue to the strength of the project.

In a very tense meeting, a new resident was confronted with responding to homosexual advances by a negro inmate not in the project, who had recently arrived from San Quentin. Open discussion of homosexuality was rarely hinted at in the meetings—it was still within the realm of the 'inmate code of ethics'. The resident, young and attractive, was repeatedly being seen in questionable places with the man who was known to be aggressively homosexual and who had been involved in serious similar incidents at San Quentin. He had been transferred to Chino to prevent his being knifed!

The young resident originally denied the implications, which angered the group. He maintained that what he saw was friendship from the other. The group became enraged to the point of nearly kicking him out of the project. He totally resisted attempts to forewarn him.

The group's prediction suddenly came to focus when the inmate demanded the younger one now yield to him sexually. Upon his refusal, the older man enlisted the support of a large group of followers, all negro. An ultimatum was delivered to the younger man through the inmate underground at the prison to meet at a stipulated place outside the mess hall after supper, 'or else'.

When these rumours filtered out, I called our first crisis meeting. I confronted the younger man with what I had learned through official channels. To my surprise, the residents already knew the details and many that I did not. They, like the custodial force, had been tipped off by the inmate 'fink system'. They were preparing to protect the resident even though they were furious with him and were resorting to their former means of violence. Unknown to the custodial staff or to me, the men in the unit had collected an impressive arsenal of weapons, bricks, stones, pipes, boards, and so on, hidden in the housing unit, some in our office.

The chief custodial officer, I learned officially, was also amassing weapons, including tear gas, and was planning to retain an additional custodial force after normal working hours who were to stake out the area for the fight and subdue it. I was alarmed and fed this all back to the community, violating standards for prison employees. I felt that if the incident erupted it would be the end of the project.

I repeated my commitment to the restraint of violence. When asked by the men what I would do if the fight broke out, I said I would at once not only leave the project but resign from the prison service and have nothing to do with what I could not condone.

This stand, neither identifying with the establishment nor with violence, but firmly remaining with the ideals of the project and with the men who supported it, was seen ultimately by the men as strength, even if immediately unpractical.

The men, some of whom had been through similar situations which had erupted at other prisons, enlightened me about the outbreak of violence over homosexuality and racial conflicts, either one alone being the most serious cause for riots in the eyes of experienced prison officials. They briefed me and then tried to enlist me as their battle commander.

We began to discuss alternatives in order to avoid open violence. The meeting, which lasted several hours and well into the evening, eventually concentrated on evaluating the total project, looking at where we were and attempting to think together how we might change the project and put it together again.

I finally shared with the men by own mounting frustrations. I told them how I had tried to get administrative changes for the project, the work situation, the disciplinary arrangement, the housing unit, the correctional officers and so on, and had failed. I expressed my disappointment in the counsellors and their inability to change and support the project. Some, who were present, were now able openly to confront me with their frustrations and to voice their anger towards me. Staff conflicts for the first time were now brought openly into the meeting with the men. The men showed great understanding and were most helpful in trying to get the staff to work together and with them, to become colleagues in the total endeavour.

The solution to the impending crisis evolved during the meeting. We decided to call off the arms race and avoid confrontation on the 'yard' with the opposing forces of inmates and security forces. We decided to make a strategic withdrawal and everyone gave up their supper. We shared biscuits, bread and butter, peanut butter, jam and coffee, items the men had accumulated both from home and stolen from the mess hall, and continued to examine the larger issues within the security of our own 'house' and thought first how to get it in order. It was agreed that all weapons would be disposed of the next day and that the younger resident either leave the project if he wished to maintain the relationship with the other man or, if he remained, sever all ties with him. To see that he carried this out, if this was his choice, some of the older residents volunteered to go with him to see that he fulfilled his commitment. We spent the remainder of the evening planning the project —how it could be changed. There was great enthusiasm and open communication. Our task was now clearly to find a way to move the project forward.

When I was assured that everyone was in bed, that most were sleeping and that the new officer on duty was not over anxious, I went home. I had persuaded him to attend the meeting and participate with us. He was astonished, favourably, at what he had seen happen and later voluntarily became part of the new staff. I stopped by the security office to make reasonably certain that the tear gas had been put away, and relayed to the Superintendent what had taken place. I made an appointment to see him the next day to discuss the changes we wanted to propose.

THE SECOND PHASE: THE THIRD AND FOURTH YEARS

We held a series of meetings and presented plans to the administration of the institution for the changes we believed necessary in order for the project to continue to develop. We asked for separate administrative authority, separate staff, including correctional officers, a separate housing unit and new work. These requests were approved and there was a great deal of enthusiasm in everyone. I learned later that avoiding a head-on battle over the homosexual/racial incident had won the confidence of the custodial department, and they were now less worried that what the project was doing would get out of hand.

I made some unilateral decisions which I thought the community could not make at this time, to give the project some strength and establish a precedent for action.

I had known about the burglary of the institution canteen and the participation of the inmate from the project, which was still undetected. I exposed the inmate who had been involved to the custodial officials who were still investigating the crime. This was a violation of the former immunity we had given the men in the project. But it concerned a more serious form of delinquency than we had previously brought to light, and, it involved the main prison. I told the community what I had done and asked that the man involved be transferred from the unit to an isolation cell for his own protection, along with the others who had been involved, until the investigation was over. I appeared at the disciplinary committee hearing, which I usually did not do. When the inmate was found guilty, I recommended he be terminated from the project and that he be transferred along with the others to San Quentin. I fed this back to the community, saying I could not tolerate, knowingly, illegal actions outside the community, and that I had responsibilities as well as they do to the outside world, of which the prison was still a part. My actions demonstrated clearly that I was not always neutral and passive. This action seemed to strengthen the community. It made clear what could be tolerated and what could not; what was within the realm of the project and what belonged outside it; what we could have control over and what was beyond our jurisdiction.

A second unilateral action on my part inadvertently gave the community a sense of balance. Four men who had been in the project longest had recently appeared for parole consideration, and been given early release dates. From then on their behaviour changed. They became openly delinquent, and made a disruptive effect on the community, especially on the new men. They belittled the project, both within and outside it, and maintained that they had only come into it to get early paroles. They believed they had accomplished this. They flouted the efforts of the stronger men and the staff, and, we found, maintained a 'fink system' of their own in which they told tales about the staff and inmates. Repeated attempts at dealing with their destructive behaviour were to no avail. Finally I asked the parole board to have their cases reconsidered in view of what had happened. I believed these men were not ready to be released and would soon revert to delinquencies. I announced what I had done in the next community meeting; again I did not think the community was ready to take this type of action. It would have violated their prison ethics, but I hoped the community might soon be ready to move ahead with me. The four men involved, naturally became very angry with me and abusive. Most of the members of the community, although fearful of the precedent this raised, agreed with what I had done and were relieved. Almost everyone believed that I had more power than actually I had, especially in view of the recent approval of the changes in the project. The men took it for granted that the parole board would go along with the recommendations I had made.

But the parole board would not hear the cases unless I pressed formal disciplinary charges against the men, which would have to be backed by the institutional authorities. By my own recent request, I had given up this prerogative in order to allow the community more authority to deal with delinquent behaviour. I was powerless to do anything further. The men had the power of redress; my power could be checked.

I called another meeting that same evening as soon as I

had heard of the decision by the parole board. I wanted the community to hear the decision from me, and to work out the consequences with me. Where, in a usual setting, the action might have jeopardised an administrator's position, it seemed to strengthen and clarify mine. Now the limits of my power were clearer, and the community felt it was invested with greater responsibility. The meeting became a serious attempt to think through ways to help men become more involved in the project and to begin to look at what kind of means the community could establish to help men change delinquent ways.

One of these four men was arrested for armed robbery within a few weeks of his parole, a more serious offence than that which brought him to prison originally. He was reconfined at San Quentin. This incident gave the men an immediate example of the need for greater seriousness in the task confronting all of us. It seemed to underscore my belief in the project and in the men. Was it not better to remain in prison a bit longer and get things sorted out for good than to leave before the business was finished? Later in the project's history, some men even remained voluntarily in prison after the paroling authority had set their time, as they believed they were not yet ready to leave. The men were beginning to distinguish between retribution, punishment, and helping someone.

For two years the project had not 'blown up' as some thought it might. We had survived several major crises, and had learned through them. Almost all the staff was new. The men had taken considerable responsibility for their own and other men's change. We could alter the administration. And we had only two years remaining under our research grant. It seemed time to move ahead.

We needed help in rearranging the project at this juncture and again brought in consultants who were of great assistance. They helped us all think through our philosophies and fix our goals and to invent ways for carrying them out.

Maxwell Jones continued to be our primary consultant. In addition, others who were extremely helpful were LaMar Empey and Max Scott from the Provo, Utah Study (3), Albert Elias, Superintendent of the Highfields, New Jersey, Residential Group Center (2), Joy Tuxford, who had been with Maxwell Jones at Henderson Hospital, and Eric Trist, from the Tavistock Institute of Human Relations in London. Two consultants were brought in specifically to work with the residents, Betsy LaSor, a psychiatric nurse, and former social therapist at Henderson, and Leslie Navran, a psychologist from the Sepulveda Veteran's Hospital, who had pioneered a project encouraging employers to hire psychiatric patients. He had worked with the men studying methods of operation in the laundry.

The Director of Corrections, Richard A. McGee, made helpful administrative suggestions from his vast experience, as did Norman Fenton. Douglas Grant and his research staff visited the project frequently, providing professional assistance and administrative support. Many others from the Department of Corrections headquarters were most helpful.

Superintendent Oberhauser remained supportive and created a new administrative organisation which gave us greater control of the project, including the correctional officers and all activities of the men while in the project. His appointment of Robert Eklund to a new Associate Superintendent's post, and placing the project under his direction, made faster growth possible. The appointment of a new, young, understanding custodial captain, Tom Stone, who openly and enthusiastically supported the project and became keenly involved in making it work, helped me to convert those outside the project who were still sceptical. He has gone on to become the new Superintendent of the strife-ridden Soledad Prison.

The change in attitudes is reflected in an officer's comments in the staff log:

> The new captain came by the unit this afternoon to get acquainted with the project. The welcoming committee spent a lot of time with him and both seemed impressed with each other.
>
> I had a long talk with Lieut. S. and Sgt. R. in the lounge last night. We discussed the 'hassel' that exists between custody and care and treatment. Their ideas, particularly those of Lieut. S. are sound and not all against what we stand for.
>
> Sgt. H. was here for approximately 30 minutes tonight, looking for you (Briggs). He said that much could be learned here if a man applied himself. Referring mainly to the staff. We were out of clean socks and later he came by with a whole bag of them. What has happened to him?

At this time also, we chose to move to the least desirable living accommodation at the institution, and moved to an

old, delapidated Second World War army barracks, which
had long ago been condemned. It was one of seven on the
outskirts of the prison grounds, the Skid Row of the institution. Here, the men would have more freedom and the activities of the project would be less visible. The barracks was
cold and draughty, but the men could now control their own
living quarters, rearrange things for certain purposes —they
could leave their beds unmade if they chose—and we could
all learn more about their current states by seeing how they
lived when allowed to be themselves. Social and personal
behaviour could now occur more as it might outside the institution. Its effect on others could be used as important
material for confrontation, reflection and commentary.

We made a 'strategic withdrawal' from the laundry as a
work project. Changing conditions, established and maintained for over twenty years, seemed impossible in the time
we had remaining, and the conflict was more than we could
use for our purposes of changing delinquent behaviour. The
men found their own work projects after a thirty day moratorium during which they were 'unemployed'. First, they re-
landscaped the area around the barracks, and made sports
facilities, a soft-ball field, and so on, to use in the evenings
and at weekends.

The new Associate Superintendent established a screening
committee and invited any officer in the institution to apply
to work in one of the several projects. At the same time, he
invited us to sit on the committee and choose the officers we
wanted. The officers could now clearly identify with the
project and did not have to split loyalties. Most of the counsellors asked to be transferred or had taken promotions at
other prisons. The project had acquired a sufficiently unde-
sirable image among professional social workers that we had
few, and for a time, no applications for the vacancies. Lacking
professionals, we engaged instead some bright, young college
students, including the first female counsellor to be hired by
the prison. The men had a great deal to teach these new rather
naive young people, and the communication between the two
groups was honest and direct. The students constantly asked
questions which made us all think more critically about what
we were doing.

The correctional officers were appointed as 'acting counsellors'. This enabled them to remove their military-like
uniforms and gave them the freedom to experiment with

different roles. Some wore suits and ties at first, in an effort to resemble the image they had of the counsellors. Others dressed more casually.

Their experimentation, and the men's response to it, is reflected in the subsequent entries they made in the staff log:

> R. told me of some sad experiences from his youth concerning a clipping from a newspaper which he showed me. The paper said that twenty years ago a man was arrested for having his daughter beg for drinking money for him. The man was R.'s father.

> Two days ago, P. said he dreamed of me, and in the dreams I had beaten him. He said he kept saying, 'Mr. L., it's me, P., don't hit me', and I only said, 'Give him 15 more lashes!' I asked him if anything like that happened to him really and he said, 'Yes, that was the way my parents treated me.'

Many of the residents in the project formed themselves into sub-groups or committies to deal with various functions. These small groups were effective, and this in turn enabled the daily community meetings to devote themselves to the more important aspects of daily life. A 'screening committee' took on the job of selecting the new men for the project. A staff member attended and gave his opinion, revealing confidential information from the candidate's file. Final selection was still by randomisation.

A night 'fire watch' from 11 p.m. to 7 a.m. was begun by the residents for a thirty day trial, allowing all the staff to go home at night. A 'personnel committee' selected, trained and supervised watch standers. It worked well and was established permanently for the remaining time of the project.

In the previous two years, with constant custodial supervision, five residents escaped from the institution. In the last two years, with total inmate supervision, we had none although the resident screening committee was bolder than the staff had been in picking men who might run away if they became upset. The residents always knew who was thinking of running away. They worked out ways, including physical restraint if necessary, of preventing it.

The men were by now totally involved in the project. Each man could evolve a role for himself, with added responsibilities as he changed. Jobs, as they were created, were filled by the personnel committee, who set standards, established appropriate training programmes, and supported and supervised the men while they were on the job. They could and did remove men if they had reason. The work projects were conducted in small crews of six to eight men.

The residents extended the night fire watch to daytime, thus taking on total responsibility for managing the housing unit. The staff took the official counts as required by law and assisted the men when their help was requested.

Community meetings were extended to an hour and a half, where as previously they had been forty five minutes and increased from five to seven each week. We met in the mornings at 7.30 and after supper at the weekends. There was simply so much happening now that an hour a day was not long enough for the community meetings. We dispensed with reading the log and with a chairman of the meetings. They became spontaneous gatherings filled with feedback, drama, excitement, commitment and dedication. Often they opened with silence, as people were gathering their thoughts together—indeed on two occasions, no one spoke a word for the hour and a half, and I merely ended the meeting making some general comments on the meanings of silence. Most things tended to happen at the weekends as the men had more leisure time. Family visits, or lack of them, brought out feelings we needed to work on—they couldn't wait until Monday. I usually worked at weekends as I wanted to be at the evening meetings, and the other staff wanted to be with their families. We often extended the time of these meetings for two or three hours. They were more intense, personal, intimate, more detached from the normal working situation of the project. We could be more reflective and more philosophical. Often these weekend meetings were punctuated with laughter, gentle humour, and with tears—tears of loneliness, of hope, of despair.

We also learned the importance of continuity in a community; the staff were not on a rigid schedule and were familiar figures who were always around, often inconspicuous by their presence. They formed a most important continuity link, and their willingness to experiment helped greatly the whole process of changing.

A review, which now included the senior residents, was always held immediately after each meeting to discuss what had happened. We had a large blackboard and tried to reconstruct in a systematic way what we thought was going on. At the weekends we did this at the end of the group itself, and the men were keen to take part. We used a systematic means of learning about what had taken place in the meeting.

We believed this to be especially important; we had realised from visiting other projects how staff reviews of community meetings tend primarily to be dominated by the anxieties of the staff. Even skilled staff are liable to be inhibited from speaking candidly and save comments on individuals until after the formal meetings. Much of the material for learning by direct confrontation is thus lost. At Chino, having both a systematic way to explore the meetings, a visual means *vis-à-vis* the blackboard, and having residents present insured that the experience could be a learning one.

We did it like this. We noted who opened the meeting and tried to recall his exact words, as this first communication often set the tone for the meeting and was a preview of what was to follow. We made a seating chart to try to understand what significance the physical position a person took in the circle had on what he might be trying to communicate. Tony Ladiana, the correctional officer most involved in the project, and I tried always to take nearly the same positions, apart, to give it some stability, and so that we could have a relatively fixed position to see where others would assemble. I always came to the meetings a few minutes early and would not hold side conversations with anyone. I believed that a certain amount of tension was necessary for 'work' in the groups to take place. The chairs were not comfortable ones, and we did not encourage people to drink coffee during the meeting, but had coffee breaks afterwards. We did not begin until everyone was present. There was no voting, and decisions were taken by consensus. Everyone in effect had the power of veto.

The remainder of the meeting was spent in small groups.

As the project went on, crisis meetings were called more often, sometimes of everyone, sometimes of one of the small groups or committees, and sometimes for individuals who were involved in trouble. Crisis meetings often cut through barriers to communication, allowing new learning to occur or decisions to be made that otherwise could not have arisen. The men who were selected for the project were impulsive by

A THERAPEUTIC COMMUNITY

nature. What happened at 10 o'clock at night might be cold mutton by the time of the community meeting the next morning and would have lost its value for social learning. On the other hand, as men began to change, they learned patience and profited from greater reflection and understanding.

The small groups went through a series of transitions. In the early stages they were primarily psychotherapy groups. Men were assigned at random to the groups as vacancies occurred. The groups were led by the counsellors, who were trained psychiatric social workers. In the year before the project began, the counsellors had begun conducting small psychotherapy groups and were given supervision and training by an experienced senior psychiatric social worker, a clinical psychologist and a psychiatric consultant. In the first year of the project, the newly formed small groups dealt with historical material, characterised by frequent moving, emotional episodes. They were serious, close, well attended, met daily and were valued in the community. In the second year, the community became more critical of the small groups as the discrepancies between the community meetings and those of the small groups became more apparent. Men began to question the value of recounting the past, other than delinquencies. The community meetings assumed greater priority, and personal, moving material involving current feelings appeared there as well as in the small groups. In time, staff members could openly and safely talk about their own feelings in the resident groups, and there was less need to retreat to staff meetings—indeed, there were no exclusive staff meetings anymore.

Men began to become dissatisfied with their particular small groups early in the project and at times requested transfer to others. This was a frequent topic in the community meetings, recurring with regularity for a year. The staff maintained that this was material to work out in the small groups and refused to allow anyone to transfer from one group to another. At one point, we felt that perhaps we were learning nothing from this rigid approach and wondered what in fact would happen if they could transfer at will. We decided to by letting them change groups, merely asking that they discuss their discontents in their present group and get some kind of agreement from the new one. A number of shifts then occurred. The research group kept records of the transfers. After a few months, things settled down and

141

there were rarely any shifts other than a man going to visit another group for a few meetings to see how that group worked and bring back any ideas to his own. Later some residents were asked to come and serve as a 'consultant' to another group from time to time. After six months it was recorded that only two out of sixty residents had changed permanently, although many had sampled others and returned to their original one.

Then in the third year, the residents, through the welcoming committee, took more things upon themselves as they began to ask questions about various procedures. Very simply, they let new residents visit all the groups for a week or two and select the one they preferred. They seemed to have regard for the size of the groups and in time they equalled out. When a group became larger or another one was depleted, this provided important material.

With these changes, objections remained. For example, older men complained that the newer ones were bringing up things they had already resolved. Newer men complained that the older ones were not patient enough with them and prevented them from talking about things with which they were concerned.

One of the correctional officers, now an 'acting counsellor', commented in the log:

> I had a long discussion with R., H. and B. concerning maturity. They seemed to feel (H. and B.) that to continue in a program of this sort with the immature ones of lower level (who they feel are a majority just now) would hurt them or the older men since they cannot seem to communicate with them. They were speaking of all the new men who have come into the project recently.

We discussed this matter with LaMar Empey and with Max Scott, who had been using 'closed groups' in their project much as in the Highfields programme. Almost simultaneously, two of the older men presented a proposal to try a closed group for six months, which they would lead, calling themselves 'group coordinators'. The community seemed rather enthusiastic about trying the scheme and so they set up the desired conditions. They proposed that their beds be so arranged that the group, including the coordinators, could be together in one area of the housing unit. The interaction of the group could then become more intensive. They thought

A THERAPEUTIC COMMUNITY

they could get much closer to the men and be there to handle things as they arose.

They asked the psychologist, Richard Heim, one of the correctional officers, Tony Ladiana, and myself to visit the small group on separate days and then hold a training meeting with them and with the other men who were acting as 'social therapists' and developing a new role. The meeting was to be based on the observations each of us had made that day of the meeting, supplemented by the careful notes that the coordinators kept on what was happening in their project.

Each Wednesday the staff members reported to the dispatcher who was in charge of work, to be assigned to a work crew, and then to a foreman, for a job. The foreman supervised the staff member at work. Those of the staff who enjoyed the work, and new staff members seeking a role, worked everyday even when this involved working at night or over the weekend.

'This can't be true. I gotta see it for myself! The IT Supervisor with a con for his boss!' The sergeant was right, for when he passed me slowly in the patrol car, I was pushing a wheelbarrow of dirt. It was loaded extra heavily, as my foreman was angry with me just then. I had been putting pressure on him in the community meetings to make him see how, when he literally pushed people around, they were upset by it. The sergeant went on his way, amused but puzzled. But now, at the work meeting or the morning community meeting I could confront Larry with my own reaction when he had pushed me around; now, perhaps we could make a connection that had not been possible before.

We presented our television set to the main institution, as the men thought too many of the new people and some of the staff were spending too much time watching it, and missing important opportunities for being involved with one another. The research group had made a study and found that the staff were spending one fifth of their time viewing. Instead, the evenings were now spent with athletics, with committee and planning meetings, socialising and reading. The men excelled over all the institution. They began to read a lot, which formerly had been rare.

To demonstrate the increased sociability among both men and staff, the log reported at this time:

> There was a party last night in the barracks. Some nonproject men were invited and seemed welcome. It was mainly

for the new men who had just arrived and was from 6.30 to 8.30 They donated cakes, cookies and canned soft drinks. Some of the men played guitars and others performed. It seemed that 'a good time was had by all'. One of the men in the project, a new one, said it was the most fun he had had since he came to prison. Several felt it was a good healthy release of tension and a good opportunity to bring the new men into the group as friends. I was the only non-inmate present.

In order for the community to develop, further special consideration was given to the project, releasing residents from the rules and regulations of the rest of the institution, while they were in the project areas. This included the housing unit and work areas. In other places, such as the prison mess hall, they were subject to the same rules and means of discipline as everyone else. We believed that this gave them some sense of reality and offered them more choices. Within the project they were governed by the same conditions as in the outside world to which they would be returning. There was no system of reward and punishment.

In addition I made one condition. I thought some limits had to be set in order for the project to function and survive in the prison. I believed that the kind of resident we were selecting, that is, with high violence potential, aggressive and impulse-ridden, with few internal controls, needed an additional outside control. Many had histories of violence and knew no other way to resolve conflicts. While they were learning and experimenting in the project, new stresses might momentarily provoke a return to old ways involving violence. I also had strong personal convictions about restraint of violence. Therefore, in an early community meeting I said that I would not tolerate violent assault on the part of anyone in the project. This I defined simply as striking another person, staff or resident, with a weapon of any sort. This did not include fights, of which we had many. For example, I recorded:

> 7th April, 5 p.m. B. and H. apparently became involved in a skirmish this afternoon at work. The foreman brought B. around with a bloody nose and a swollen jaw. I sent him to the hospital for attention and possible X-rays. H. is very tense over his relations with his wife just now. A lot of material for his groups here.

No act of violence occurred within the project, to my knowledge, during its four years, although we did have frequent
fights. I made no threats and did not say at the time what I
would have done had violence erupted, as it nearly did once.
I simply do not know what I would have done. But with the
prospect of the incident with homosexuality, I found out.

We did have one violent act during the time we were
operating the laundry. A resident got involved in a quarrel
with another inmate who was not in the project. During the
fight he picked up a broom handle and struck the other man
severely enough for several sutures to be required. Both men
were locked up while the custodial officials investigated the
situation and a disciplinary committee meeting was held to
take action. We discussed it at length in the community
meetings several times, and held-up a final decision until we
could see more how the men coped with it. Eventually the
project men reminded me of the 'normal' conditions I had
created and suggested that the obvious thing to do was to
report the matter to the police. I consulted the local District
Attorney. He did not ask for charges to be preferred because
the man was in the project. After a series of rather dramatic
meetings, the community decided that the victim had provoked the assault and invited him to apply for admission
to the project. He was accepted. (And exception was made in
his case, admitting him to the community without randomisation, but not using his case in the research findings.)

To summarise, the first three years of the project had
demonstrated that the prison culture could be considerably
changed; the rigid code of inmate ethics could be altered, staff
and inmates could collaborate in a united effort at changing
delinquent behaviour; delinquent behaviour could, in fact,
be changed and within four to six months, the 'lowest ranking'
non-professional staff could be re-trained to become enthusiastic and highly competent. The professional counsellors were the ones who had difficulties learning new roles
within this structure. Our casualty rate for professional staff
was high. We also knew that an egalitarian-democratic structure could safely emerge and survive in an authoritarian-
militaristic traditional prison, though with great difficulty.
The project had to maintain eternal vigilance in order to
survive and continue to grow, as Eric Trist had warned us.

In the third of these years, the correctional officers had
moved into positions at first resembling those of the

counsellors.(4) The residents took on the former duties of the officers, ran their own housing unit and supervised their own work projects. They then began to take up the roles of the counsellors and the small group leaders. There was constant 'role blurring' among the staff and the residents, but in addition, there was movement of roles—role displacement—and a more fluid overall social structure. In the next year—the fourth—the officers became more involved with the administration of the project and acted as 'consultants' for the residents, who in turn were performing roles more like those of the counsellors. The officers were supportive of the men's efforts to try new things and were now able to teach them skills which they themselves had recently acquired, such as leading small groups, interviewing, intervening and using crisis situations, reviewing things they had done, and generally promoting and supporting their ideas.

In the final six months of the project, several of the residents took on these things too, they became consultants to the new inmate group coordinators. The officers moved into new areas of probing into research and evaluation, thinking, understanding, teaching, and supporting what the men were doing. All the staff spent a good deal of their time and energy keeping other staff members who were not involved in the project informed about what was going on, clearing up distortions and protecting the men and their efforts from interference. This was no small job.

I abdicated my nominal role as project administrator, and all the staff, including myself, filled it on a daily basis, were called 'administrator of the day', and were responsible for any matter that arose. Contact with families, visitors, the outside as well as internal matters were all referred to the day's administrator so that everyone on the staff shared in the administration. I did not give up my leadership role in the community meetings, however, but was considerably less active in it. I made few decisions; there was no need to make them. The community was functioning quite effectively and it was now so strong that it would not have allowed me to make unilateral decisions as previously I had done. Everyone realised that I still did have latent power, the veto kind, which could be exercised if need be. But the occasion never came.

During the third year of the project, different approaches and procedures for changing delinquent behaviour had been tried which gradually we perfected. A community with its own structure and periphery, and with clearly defined time and space dimensions had emerged. It had a housing unit which was autonomously operated by the community, and it was different in physical appearance from those in the remainder of the institution; it had changed to meet the current needs of the members.

Daily community meetings now resembled forums and kept the community members abreast of what was happening, opened up new areas for resolving social tensions and understanding, and they formed an ambiance within which the members could work.

A party of eight to ten men arriving in the project at about the same time would form a small closed living-group. This enabled its members to maintain close identification with each other. They became a primary reference group through sharing similar changes. The community was composed of three of these groups, all operating at different levels. The newest group could observe the older one and see what they might become. They didn't always like what they saw.

As time passed, an older group could see in the behaviour of the new group, how much they themselves had changed.

Others groups which assisted the community to maintain itself and grow, like the personnel committee, the selection committee, the welcoming committee, the recreation committee, the social therapists, the planning committee, and so on, gave members additional opportunities for crossing the small group boundaries, and allowed the older members direct opportunities for teaching and for increased participation. A small group could appeal to the community for assistance in matters it could not handle itself such as extreme abusiveness or the manipulation of one member. And it could share solutions which it had worked out to problems which might have significance for other groups. Likewise, the community could refer specific matters to one of the smaller groups. Fewer and fewer calls for action came up in the community meetings as the small groups were able to handle more and more matters by themselves. The community meetings became more spontaneous and were a clearing place for ideas and for working out broader philosophies. The community now had enough trust to allow autonomy to the small groups and no longer needed to know the day to day details.

The living-groups, in addition to their regular daily meetings following the large group, began 'pin point' meetings, held in the evenings. Each man was assigned a particular evening, and the evening meeting lasted as long as the group chose. It was devoted exclusively to that member. Within a week after the resident entered the project, he was expected to call a pin point meeting and review all his delinquent activities. Many of the men knew of each other or about the activities of a new member, prior to coming to prison. The encounters and details of their criminal careers, often more apparent than real, that were revealed in the pin point meetings were candid and more complete than either the officially known crime record or their clinical history. This procedure seemed to get pertinent historical material out in the open and out of the way early in a man's development. It also served diagnostic functions, for the group could see now what it had to work with. The screening committee meetings tended to avoid this material, as the groups believed that ferreting it out of a candidate would dilute the first pin point meeting. This is in contrast to professional diagnosticians who often extract and then fail to follow up important material. Screening became much more a matter of inclusion rather than exclusion as it had been earlier.

As a man became involved in changing himself, another pin point meeting was expected of him, about midway in his stay. He had to review what he thought he had accomplished and present plans for the remainder of his stay, including setting a definite date for leaving. If he changed this date, he had to call another pin point meeting and justify the change to the satisfaction of the group. Included in his plan he was required to have a realistic scheme for staying out of trouble while still in prison and afterwards. The group coordinators often taped pin point meetings, listened to them frequently, used them for training sessions, and reviewed them just prior to the subsequent pin point meetings. They would often let a man hear, in his own words, what he and the group had decided previously, and comment on what progress he had made.

We had no idealistic notions that we were curing people or changing their basic personalities, and did not value 'insight' or understanding. We had clearly established that changing delinquent behaviour had the highest priority in the community, and that was in fact the community's task. Further, it was action, rather than talk, which formed the basic criterion of whether or not someone had changed. A man would frequently be asked, 'What have you done? Name two things while in the community.' We always challenged the use of any kind of psychological terminology. The late Eric Berne spent a day with us as a consultant and made us critically aware of how inmates as well as staff quickly seize psychological concepts and use them as games, preventing real change.

There was enough information from former members who came back to visit and from the parole agents who now came around regularly and told the community about former members. We knew that significant change was in fact possible from the project. We also knew that failures were possible. One of the strongest members of the community was shot and killed in an armed bank robbery. His photograph was on the front page of the *Los Angeles Times*. He was lying on the bank of a motorway in his own blood, after a chase with the police. This situation caused a great deal of reflection, and underlined the futility of a delinquent way of life. The 'smart crooks' were obviously still outside prison and did not often get caught. We often suggested at a critical point, when a man was deciding whether to change, that an alternative was to become a more skilled criminal and to have the right connections. Change now made some sense. The culture had espoused the notion also, that part of changing oneself was to help others. In assessments, an older resident would frequently ask of another, 'What have you done to help someone change in the project since you've been here? Name one!'

In the remaining year of the project, a framework evolved in which change could take place within a shorter period of time. Here again, we enlisted the help of Maxwell Jones, LaMar Empey, Max Scott, Albert Elias and Douglas Grant. We needed a more specific framework in which to understand and conceptualise what was happening, and through which we could continue trying to evaluate alternative ways for changing delinquent behaviour within the structure of a transitional community.

CHINO

REFERENCES

1. Briggs, D. L., 'Social Psychiatry in Great Britain', *Amer. J. Nursing*, 59, February 1959.
2. Elias, A. *et al.*, *The Highfields Story.* New York, Holt, 1958.
3. Empey, L., 'The Provo Experiment in Delinquency Rehabilitation', *Proceedings of the 90th annual Congress of Corrections*, 1960.
4. Briggs, D. L., *et al.*, 'Some Observations on Staff Training and Involvement in a Social-Therapeutic Community', *Proceedings of the 93rd Congress on Corrections*, 1963. Briggs, D. L., and Dowling, J., 'The Correctional Officer as a Consultant: A Newly Emerging Role in Penology', *Amer. J. Correction*, April 1963; and Briggs, 'Convicted Felons as Social Therapists', *Correctional Psychiatry and J. Social Therapy*, Fall, 1963.

Chapter Six

FINAL PHASE

It is one of the most beautiful compensations of this
life that no man can sincerely try to help another
without helping himself.

EMERSON

WE were greatly assisted at this point by LaMar Empey and a
visit to the Provo Project in Utah, where a number of consultants were called together to take a close look at his ideas
(see ref. 3, chapter 5). Borrowing many of these we began to
formulate some basic beliefs, which could then be translated
into action. Change, we believed, could be greatly facilitated,
given certain conditions: (1) change was a group task rather
than an individual one. The small groups and their activities
became the focus of change. (2) Change must come to be related to meaningful activities in the daily lives of the men,
over which they could have a considerable amount of control.
These activities they developed in the areas of work, programme
planning, control of one another and, in fact, all areas in the
daily operation of the community. (3) Change must involve
evolutionary social roles which were constantly in flux, as both
individuals and small groups matured. We constantly questioned everything, especially when all appeared to be operating
smoothly. (4) Change should proceed somewhat rationally,
according to developmental levels or stages of social growth,
within the small groups. These levels appeared to have four
phases.

These four structural levels formed a viable social organization, enabling groups of men to change with some consis-
tency. Understanding of what point a group or an individual
had reached within this growth process enabled the staff and
the advanced residents to intervene more effectively. Intervention was primarily called for when a group or an individual
was in a transition phase, and helped them move to the next
level. Crises, confrontation, and active intervention at these
transition stages became the real work of the community.
Individuals, a small group or the total community needed

approximately thirty to sixty days to complete their tasks for each level—thus, four to eight months time was needed for the total change process to be realized. The follow-up studies later on revealed that eight months was the optimum.

The pattern which emerged was for eight to ten men to be brought into the living unit together within a week or two and to form a closed living-group. They were joined by two 'group coordinators', men who had volunteered to remain in the project longer and who had been scrutinized by the personnel committee to ensure their suitability. They presented their individualized plans to the community and these were ratified along with their conformation as coordinators. Their ratification was based on the success of the men's own change, though their original plans were not always approved. One of them usually took a more active role, the other lent support and gave criticism to the other. They often changed roles at some point in the programme. The group, including the coordinators, arranged to have their living quarters together to promote social interaction and to increase opportunities both to observe and to confront the members with the effects of their intense living together.

Originally the staff, thinking along traditional lines of psychotherapy, believed that the men who wanted to experiment with the new roles would need some distance from the men with whom they would be working. We arranged for them to have separate housing in another part of the institution, but they objected. They maintained that they would miss too much, and would not be readily available when needed. They thought they would be seen as too much like the staff.

The individuals in the small group had considerable latitude and could develop as a distinct unit. Usually they were not given a work assignment and their first task would be to find one. Sometimes they would wander about the institution. Most were cautious at first and, on seeing others working, sought to imitate them, hoping for approval. As there was no reward for their good efforts and they might even meet with disapproval, their thinly disguised conformity soon broke down and they would leave their jobs, wander around again and begin to make old delinquent associations with inmates outside the project. They might then get into minor trouble. They would frequently belittle the project. Soon they might get caught, most frequently for stealing food from the mess hall. This behaviour, readily observable by the other men, would be talked of in their small group meetings and people would begin to take notice.

Men who had been a short while in the project would often moralize and attempt to put pressure on the newer man to conform. More advanced residents made no such attempts, and the staff would reinforce their attitude.

'Hey get off his back! He just drove up. What do you expect? If he was all that perfect, he wouldn't be in prison!'

The new man, or the small group itself, would then see the unit and especially the staff and the older men as permissive, gullible, passive, naive, 'stupid', or whatever. His delinquent behaviour would continue unabated now that he thought it was sanctioned. It might even be amplified.

In addition to the diagnostic functions, at the first structural level, it was hoped that at some point the resident or the group as a whole might get into minor trouble or lose some of its rigid control. If a crises could be precipitated it would be easier to look at the futility of their previous delinquent ways. When this occurred, the staff would maintain an inactive stance, neither interceding nor taking action, but preferring to leave the structure fluid. On occasion a resident would get into relatively serious trouble outside the project, appear before a disciplinary committee and be punished. A few times, men were removed from the project by the authorities for punishment and then returned at a later date. No one interceded on their behalf. Rather we maintained that if members were upset and could not control themselves they should be encouraged to remain within the housing unit where it was safe.

This developmental level, of course, was the most important one of all, for until we could see the extent and nature of the delinquency we were working with, and the delinquent himself could experience the uselessness of his delinquency,' real change could not be expected.

As the individual began to take another look at the project and his role in it, things began to change for him, and we would realize that he was near a transitional period and perhaps ready to move on to a more advanced one. Characteristically, taking a second look, he became bewildered by the place, by the individuals in it, by the structure and the roles. He would often become angry at people, especially the men in more advanced levels, seeing them as 'finks', 'phonies', etc. Now he would not see the staff as so inane, but as having unrealistic and overwhelming expectations and power, and as very subtle and 'keen' (manipulative). The project might seem an organised plot against him. In anger, he might refer to the staff, the coordinators and the social therapists as 'God', 'J.C.', etc. Or at other extreme he might become very depressed and withdraw.

All these reactions gave indications that he was in the transitional phase and ready to move on to the next level. We became active to assist him, or the small group he was in. A more definite work assignment might be suggested for the small group, or the individual might be listened to more seriously in his proposals in the meetings. If his delinquent behaviour continued, the group would begin to ask him questions about it and to link it up with his history in the project, but not attempt to control or analyse it. The staff would frequently not shield him so much, but review what they had noticed about him in the past month or two, and begin to help him make some connections with his behaviour. (Memory, and the ability to recall events accurately on the part of any 'leader' in a project such as this, is an extremely important part of the whole process.) It plays an important part, too, in determining the size of any community or group.

Many individuals wanted to leave during this period, and some controls were needed to protect them while they were examining themselves in relation to their new surroundings. It was a terribly disruptive time for most of them, as a kind of identity crisis, long postponed, was forming. They began to question, to doubt, to become confused, to have feelings they had never experienced before, and they would often become very frightened. This was the beginning of the thawing of the 'frozen attitudes' which Fenichel believed was characteristic of those with severe character disorders. Sometimes a man might think he was losing control and that he was going mad. 'Stop messing with my melon!' he might cry out in a group meeting.

So, the first developmental level was characterised by a man finding himself in a different kind of environment and discovering that his usual ways of behaving were of no use. The second was centred on becoming more observant. Residents now began to look about more. What they saw at first as simple, was more complicated. They began to see that there were no ready-made, easy, or instant solutions to the matters which were constantly arising in the community. They became *curious* about things and about people. They began to see that there was leadership and direction, more than they had realised when they came into the project. Power and power relationships, which at first they had found confusing and frightening, were being used wisely for change. They became more confused when they began to see that power in the unit was not used to exploit people or groups, but was harnessed for the good of the community and for individuals and for long range goals rather than immediate needs.

Residents frequently became silent during this time and did a good deal of looking and thinking. They also tended to become depressed and despondent. Their former ways no longer had helped them and they knew no other ways. It was very important to allow them to become depressed and not to interfere, as many of them had not known that this emotion existed within themselves. They had been throwing it off with their aggressive activities. Thinking and feeling actually began at this level for many of them. Bruno Klopfer had just returned from Switzerland and gave us a very helpful seminar on the trends in existentialism in psychotherapy. He talked of depression and his belief that we must handle it differently. Depression must be allowed to occur, and we should assist the man to learn to recognise it and learn to live with it, instead of trying to relieve it.

Delinquent activities would generally take one or more courses during this phase. (1) They might cease entirely, either temporarily or permanently. This might occur abruptly and they might reappear later when the individual or group was under stress or when the community was in a crisis. (2) The deliquency might continue unabated much as it had existed in the first phase. (3) It might change its form, becoming group centred; for example, one man might take on a crime partner or two, or shift from stealing food to exploiting new residents. (4) It might, on occasion, go underground, and few, if any, of the community members would have any knowledge of it. This would usually occur outside the project and we might not learn of it until later when the person(s) were caught, or it might come as rumour from the custody channels or the inmate fink system. If the delinquency took the latter course, it usually caused fright over what they discovered about the unit and the power systems. They might see it as a super spy system over which they had no control—they couldn't fight it or join it successfully. The underground delinquent activity could often be seen as a man's last resort to maintaining some sort of former control and identity.

When a group had arrived at this level, a new group of men would usually arrive, which enabled it to see more clearly the movement that had been made. They could also observe the more advanced men go into action with the newer ones and now appreciate their skill or lack of it, and might want to join them. The most advanced residents became desirable examples in their eyes and they began to discuss ways they could become like them. This had occurred occasionally in the earlier years of the project, but with the closed-ended group the impact of change could be maximised and built into the system rather than leaving it to chance.

When a group or an individual reached the *third level*, there was a noticeable shift in activities. As delinquent behaviour became less of a preoccupation, the men began experimenting with new roles and with new ways of behaving. They could appreciate the complexity of human behaviour and refrain from earlier advice-giving and reprimands. Abandoning conformity and imitative behaviour, they tried out their new roles instead. An individual resident, somewhat cautiously, might venture out and make some risks, for example, by exposing newer inmates' behaviour in a meeting. He might find he could only safely do this if his own delinquent behaviour had changed. As he earned self-respect, he began to feel responsible for himself and for the newer residents. He would want to become a member of one of the committees and would make application. He could be seen as overtly anxious about his reputation where just two or three months earlier he had revelled in displaying his exploitative activities. He might decide to become a social therapist, a group co-ordinator, both positions which had high social status in the community, and would get close to one of them to learn more about how to become one. He became closer to the staff and shared things openly with them, suggesting ways to improve things. He began to share in planning and came up with new ideas which were listened to. His own delinquency was sporadic, if it existed now at all.

In this phase, we believed this man to be searching for a new role for himself, a new identity in the community; and that he was then finding ways to become proficient in it. He no longer seemed so preoccupied with getting out of prison, but began to show anxiety about going outside.

Men frequently contrasted prison life with the outside world, especially in relation to their families. Why, they wondered, were things so different at home? Many felt an increasing estrangement from their families. The Sunday night meeting following visits was often centred round the pain which resulted from trying to be candid and open with family or girl friend, only to be rebuffed. Was their present life too idealistic to be duplicated outside?

Mutual distrust began to grow also between inmates and their former delinquent friends, whom they saw as unaware and purposeless; while their friends, for their part, regarded them as weakened and 'brain-washed'. Perhaps their friends were right? They began to doubt their effectiveness as criminals. What could they become? Indeed, was there a place at all for them outside?

This was a most difficult and crucial time for many of the men, as they were neither fish nor fowl nor good red herring. Some reverted to delinquency momentarily while still experimenting with new roles. When such contradictions were exposed in the meetings, their position was devalued by the community. 'How can you offer help to someone when you're still wheelin' and dealin'?* You're a phoney!'

If the group refused to deal with the behaviour under discussion, a staff member might take a turn in the community meeting and say:

'You've been around here for nearly three months and you still haven't really changed. You *talk* a good line, but in the meetings, you are still being brought up and you are acting like a hood, like all those convicts out on the yard. When are you going to change?'

We might then review his delinquent history and ask to hear about things we had forgotten or which we did not know. We would appeal to his small group and ask if we might have a deadline for him to come up with a plan for changing. The group might suspend his status and not let him reassume his role until he had demonstrated that he really had changed and wanted to—was willing drastically to shift his priorities.

By the time the man or group had reached the *fourth level*,

* American prison expression meaning involved in delinquent enterprises, such as selling services illegally for personal gain, usually for payment in cigarettes.

they had experimented with several roles and had found one
or more in which they could be comfortable and in which they
became proficient. They were seen to have changed, and were
wanting to help others change. Committed to helping others,
delinquents became non-delinquent, they felt a strong urge to
intervene whenever they saw acts of delinquency. With rare
exceptions, each man at this stage had an official and valuable
role in the community. He was either accepted to stay longer
and become a group coordinator, which carried the most
respect in the community, or was on one or more committees, or was a work supervisor, or was carrying out some unique
and useful role which he had created. There was a closeness
and a cameraderie with the staff.

This was the usual development but of course it did not
always run smoothly or on course. In a few instances we
needed to intervene more than usual to assist a group or an
individual through the transition periods, to move on to the
next level.

On one occasion, at the end of the third year of the project,
after considerable discussion with two of the projects consultants, I took a direct, sudden action to create a crisis in the
community in order that it might re-examine its existing
position and become stronger. The community had been
struggling with one particular resident for some time who had
great difficulty moving into the final stage. He vacillated back
and forth between taking on helping roles with new residents
and maintaining his delinquent activities. His father was
socially prominent in Los Angeles and would appear at
intervals to give him large sums of money which were used to
buy favour, especially with the newer men. His small group
had held a series of crisis meetings with him, and the community seemed exhausted with him, ready to give up. Once
again his delinquencies were brought into the meeting. He
began, as usual to rationalise and explain and manipulate the
group. Someone groaned loudly, 'Oh no! Not again!'

Without explanation, I left the group, went to the telephone nearby, and within the hearing of the group asked the
control sergeant to come with another officer, remove the
man, take him to the segregation unit and hold him without
charges for an unspecified time. He was to be there for holding
until he, his small group or the community came up with an

acceptable plan to help him change. We decided to concentrate all the efforts of the community on trying to work this out. This became a moratorium where the community focused all its attention on the examination of the structure and resources available to help him to change. The situation was left fluid. This upset some of the newer residents. I was silent and, when pressed for my reasons, said, 'You know damn well why I had him transferred!' The older men were startled at first at my action, as were some of the staff. I had never before done such a thing. However they figured that there must be some method in my madness, and there was now sufficient trust in the community for them to await the outcome.

The energies of the community were devoted for the next fews days to examining the man's development, the resources we had available and the alternatives yet to be tried. The community asked to talk to him. I went to the segregation unit the next morning, prior to the meeting, and had him released into my custody. I had requested that he should not be allowed to shave, shower, or leave the holding cell, that he have no mail or outside communication. When I arrived he looked dishevelled, and alternated between being very angry and abusive with me and trying to ingratiate himself with me. He had a history of violence. I told him that the community wished to see him and we walked across the prison yard together. Taking him alone was telling him that I was not afraid of him, that I trusted him. It gave him the chance to overpower me physically or to control himself, which might be more difficult. I was the one who had had him locked up and he knew it. It also meant to him, to me, and to the community that he had changed a little and that we believed it possible for him to change more, for now he had to restrain his frustration and anger in wanting to 'clobber' me and escape, which he could easily have done. I responded to his abuse with words, and to his efforts to manipulate me with silence. It was a long five minute walk across the yard.

The community scolded him, moralised at him and tried to work with him. He turned his anger onto it, abusing it too, and scorned the plans the community had made for his release. The members, in turn, showed counter-aggression and threats. It seemed there was no solution. I escorted him back to the segregation unit with the same instructions as before. But now he aligned himself with me, and turned his anger on the community, maintaining that he was glad to be away from it, that neither the community nor his small group cared about him.

The community found itself immobilised. It cancelled all the work projects and family visits, and everyone remained in limbo for the next three days while discussions continued. The man in segregation was writing new plans daily, each of which was shared with the community and returned to him, marked simply, 'unacceptable'.

The community now set about re-evaluating the entire project, everyone's role in it, including my own, and soon came up with the idea of a stronger unit, giving the men increased responsibility. The staff now totally moved into consulting roles and together took over the remnants of my administrative role, eliminating my right to make unilateral decisions and freeing me to find a new role myself. An 'escape committee' of very select residents was formed. They released the man from the segregation unit when he agreed to a plan dealing more effectively in the future with residents who had similar difficulties.

To my astonishment, a few weeks later, when the community was facing another problem with a person whom neither the small group nor the community could help, the escape committee presented a plan to move temporarily the person to the segregation unit and calling it 'therapeutic lock-up'. They reasoned that they had seen this work effectively, not so much for the victim as for the group and the community. The community had become stagnant again and therefore could not help this new person. Everything needed to be shaken up a bit to get things going again. The committee used this tactic on four or five other occasions in the remaining year of the project, and each time it had a startling effect. Each time they discussed their expectations with the staff. I, in turn, discussed them with the Associate Superintendent and the Superintendent.

At one point, when the new Director of Corrections visited the projects, four men were in therapeutic lock-up. He interviewed them in their holding cells, and surprisingly they defended their position and maintained that they were being helped. Nonetheless when the escape committee brought them back, they were ferociously indignant.

This locking up procedure was used judiciously and was effective, but grossly misunderstood and misinterpreted, especially by people outside the project, who went back to

FINAL PHASE

their own correctional settings and used the same procedure punitively.

Unknown to everyone, a man whom the residents subsequently isolated kept a diary. As he was leaving he gave me this diary, which summarized his view of the project. He had become a social therapist and had been very effective in coping with difficult residents. He thought I might like to use this material for lectures at the university or if I ever wrote this book.

> I found myself in lock-up. Lying there night after night I found myself going back over the past few weeks, and what had been said. I tried to get these things out of my mind, but no matter what I did, I couldn't.
>
> . . . all at once life became very real and I could no longer tell myself that I was that smart person that I thought I was; but who was I? I knew I was a liar, and I knew I was not the keen person I was trying to be.
>
> Once back in the group I made up my mind to be truthful with them and with myself. I fought this very hard at first because no matter what I said it was really not heard. Not being heard made me feel bad but I kept on going because for the first time in my life I was doing something for myself that I really wanted to do.
>
> At first when the group laughed at my proposals I wanted to quit. I told myself that they would never listen to me. . . . I knew that if I gave up, who would there be to keep trying?
>
> The first time I really saw change and not just felt it, was when Al told me he didn't want to sign my proposal. I became angry and I could not say anything for a while. I cannot explain to you the feelings at him for a minute or two. I turned and walked to the next bed and asked the next person to sign. Pete also laughed at me. I was mad . . . then very proud of myself and knew at that moment I no longer had to protect even the little bit of false image I was still holding on to.

It seemed to me, moving into the final phase that the crunch came when residents moved into quasi-staff positions. The staff with formal training had trouble both in learning how to use their expertise and how to be helpful.

161

In the approach developed in this project where emphasis was on creating a structure in which individuals could shape social roles, tolerate role conflicts, analyse role performances and both perfect and change role expectations, knowledge of dynamic forces in individuals behaviour could be a hinderance as well as an advantage. In the seminars for the correctional officers, when residents were included, and in the educational courses for the more advanced ones, we were constantly impressed at how quickly so-called non-professionals could grasp sophisticated concepts, translate them into action, observe interactions and then return to the seminar with examples for further discussion. They could, more easily than the professionals, keep out technical jargon and explanations, and they were not under the same pressure to talk. They were keen on and highly adept at putting concepts into action and testing them for effect. Unlike the professionals they could happily abandon an ineffective course, and try something new.

Doug Grant, Chief of the Research Division of the Department of Corrections, his wife Joan, in paroles research, and I, convinced of the merits of the self-help and non-professional approach and trying to move with the times—the exciting movements launched nationally by the late John F. Kennedy in the peace corps, the poverty programme and other self-help approaches for disadvantaged people—decided to move outside the limits of the prison.

Under a federal grant we undertook the New Careers Development Project.[1, 2, 3, 4,] Eighteen prisoners, selected from the therapeutic community projects in operation at the various prisons, were moved to the California Medical Facility at Vacaville, equivalent to Grendon Underwood, for a four months intensive development programme. They were trained to become non-professionals and we hoped to find them jobs in the helping professions—social work, youth work, community development, education and especially in corrections. When the first graduates were ready for employment, we found most of these agencies were loath to have them—they were too threatening. Ironically, the employers in the correctional field were the most resistant.

And so we re-grouped our resources and decided on a long range approach to assist the agencies to expand their horizons and examine themselves critically.[5] Instead of developing non-professional aides, we created a series of 'Change and Development Teams' each composed of two inmates, a university graduate student and one of us as a professional consultant. These teams could then offer an agency a new service and not immediately threaten its established structure or way of operation.[6, 7, 17]

Incidently, Larry Dye, the lad who over-filled my wheelbarrow and pushed me around while acting as my work supervisor, volunteered for the new project. Thus, five years later, Doug Grant reported:

> By age twenty-two, Larry Dye had been confined with a Los Angeles Forestry Camp, The California Youth Authority,* and the California Department of Corrections. His highest academic achievement was a high school equivalency which he obtained while with the Youth Authority. At twenty-seven Larry is a doctoral candidate and on the staff of the Department of Education in the University of Massachusetts. He has served as a researcher with the Joint Commission on Correctional Manpower and Training and on the staff of the Office of Youth Affairs for the Department of Health, Education and Welfare. This is one, but not necessarily the most outstanding, example of new careers being pursued by fourteen of the eighteen Department of Corrections confinees who took part in a National Institute of Mental Health sponsored program to develop offenders as social change agents. Only one of the eighteen is reconfined.[8]

The current prison crisis facing both the United Kingdom and the United States is attributed to overcrowded conditions, lack of trained staff and of enough funds to handle properly those who offend. If this crisis forced us into taking revolutionary and truly imaginative leaps in the training and employment of delinquents and those seemingly destined to become delinquent in new careers such as has been described elsewhere [1, 2, 3, 4, 10, 12, 18] the crisis could rapidly be reduced in intensity. For example, they might work with children in schools as assistant teachers,[11] as play and youth leaders especially on adventure playgrounds and in youth clubs; in communities as 'trouble shooters' and 'linkers' with the poor; and in control and prevention of crime and delinquency as

* Equivalent to Borstal.

police assistants and probation officer assistants. They work splendidly with other disadvantaged people—the mentally retarded, the mentally ill, the physically disabled, the immigrants, and the elderly.[13] One of the most exciting areas of all would be working in what are now probation and aftercare hostels, making these transitional places where troubled people of all sorts might stay temporarily to learn about their social behaviour through interaction with others rather than merely being housed and contained.

The Urban Programme of 1968 in the United Kingdom makes all these alternatives possible and the British Government has subsequently made generous finance available to local authorities. In the field of Mental Health the Secretary for the Social Services has announced the Government's plans to close the large institutions for confining disturbed people within the next fifteen years. The problem will be met by the establishment of a variety of small, local units, designed to meet different needs. With the new Criminal Justice Bill, the opportunity likewise exists for putting an end to imprisonment as we now know it. The implications are staggering for Borstals and prisons in the next decade, yet at the same time we make elaborate and costly plans to continue building new prisons in the old tradition. Imaginative alternatives to confinement ought to be a challenge to everyone engaged in the helping professions, particularly the courts, and to all those who care about offenders. But the moments of time in which we can still choose which course to follow are rapidly ticking away.

Appendix to Chapter Six

RESEARCH AND EVALUATION

RESEARCH DESIGN

The research staff in central headquarters chose the method of random assignment to an experimental and to a control group, to test the effectiveness of the programme. From a pool of eligibles, the individual inmates were selected by a table of random numbers; two-thirds of the men were placed in the project, the remaining one-third received regular institutional programming in the prison.

TABLE 1

Flow Chart: Selection Procedures

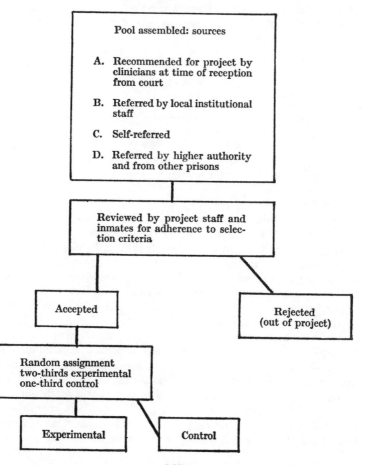

Randomisation: Comparability of Groups

A 'risk score' or base expectancy, (B.E.) developed by Leslie Wilkins, formerly of the Home Office, based on certain items from the case history, was calculated at the time of entrance to prison for all the men who were selected and placed into the pool of eligibles.[15] The mean B.E. scores of any two sub-groups of the total sample could be compared to see if the potential for favourable parole performance was equivalent. If the randomisation was successful, then there should be no significant differences between the base expectancy distributions of any two groups to be compared. A lack of significant differences confirmed that similar 'risk levels' were represented in all of the basic sub-groups compared in this study. Thus, there was no selection bias operating to enhance parole performance for any one of the groups involved in the comparison (see Ref. 14).

TABLE 2

Mean B.E. Comparisons

Scores

Experimental Group	Control Group	
49·0	50·1	(Difference not significant)

Selection

All the candidates were volunteers. In phase one, they were selected by staff who saw them individually in an interview, after having screened their histories for eligibility. In phase two, they were selected by a group of residents, chosen by the personnel committee, and usually one staff member. They were interviewed now in a group situation, which became an additional selection factor, namely, to see how the candidates could handle personal matters in a group and with fellow inmates.

Adult felons, recently remanded to the Department of Corrections to serve a minimum of one year in prison, were considered favourable for selection if they were under twenty five years of age, had at some time had a close relationship with some adult such as parents or substitutes, a marital or common-law relationship, some ability to relate to peers, such as crime partners, and rated at the higher levels of four or five on the Interpersonal Maturity (I level) scale of Grant. Briefly, this meant that in an interview they showed some evidence of internalised conflicts, anxiety, a discomfort with their current status, some motivation to change, and ability to differentiate social roles and to recognise responsibility for their own behaviour, sufficient ego strength, some flexibility and overall, some capacity to change.

Candidates were seen as questionable if over thirty years of age, had a record of prolonged institutionalisation from early childhood through adolescence, a record of long-term satisfactory military adjustment (two thirds of the sample had had some military service), long history of varied offences rather than related ones, and a record of either absolute conformity or many rule infractions in prior juvenile confinement.

Adult felons were considered ineligible for the programme if they tested below the eighth grade (age 14) had an intelligence test rating of below low average, were ever diagnosed as psychotic, had been treated with electro-convulsive or insulin coma, or were obviously isolates. In addition, certain men were not eligible such as the non-English speaking, those with a natural life sentence, a person given exceptional publicity or notoriety, and those with long-standing addiction to drugs or alcoholism.

If recommended, candidates were placed in a pool of eligibles and their names were drawn at random as vacancies occurred in the programme (see Table 1). In the first phase, a constant total population was maintained and the men were taken into the project on a weekly basis. In the last year, they were admitted into the programme in groups of eight to ten men at one time. All those who were not selected automatically became the controls. Men who were not initially chosen, of course, could not be reconsidered, and once terminated from the programme a resident could not be readmitted.

There was continual pressure from various officials to relax the selection procedures and to take men who fell far outside the criteria. Earlier pilot projects with this method convinced us of the soundness of the criteria we had established. When older, less overtly aggressive men were taken in, more like those described in the next chapters by Turner, they not only had great difficulties, but for some, their delinquencies took on a new course. They now became upset, often escaped and committed more aggressive offences. We eventually designed a new approach for them. But for this programme we clearly wanted men whom we could place under a great deal of pressure at the times we felt they might be susceptible to change. And we had the means to cope with their disturbances.

CHINO

Criteria of Success

Favourable performance on parole was defined as either having no arrests, being arrested and released, having no outstanding felony warrant, being assigned to a short-term narcotic treatment unit, and having a misdemeanor-type conviction resulting in fine, misdemeanor, probation or jail sentence under ninety days.

Unfavourable parole conduct was defined as an individual absconding with an outstanding felony warrant, death while committing a felony, awaiting trial or sentence for felony at end of follow-up period, a felony-type conviction resulting in a suspended prison sentence, a felony probation, a jail sentence of ninety days or longer, being returned to prison to finish term or being returned to prison with a new conmitment.

RESULTS OF ONE YEAR FOLLOW-UP STUDY

Seventy-five per cent of the men in the four year study and their controls had been on parole for one year or longer when the evaluation was undertaken.* The differences between parole performance of those treated and the control group were statistically significant in favour of those who were in the treatment programme.

TABLE 3

One Year Parole Outcome (Total Four Year Programme)
(75% sampling)

	Mean B.E.	Favourable Outcome
Experimental Group	48·5	79%
Control Group	49·4	71%
	(Difference not significant)	($\chi^2 = 4·66$. $p < 0·025$: one-tail)

* A two year parole performance study for this project is being undertaken. A 43% sampling, representing all those available on parole for two years at the time of the one-year study, yielded slight but not statistically significant differences in favour of the men treated. It should be kept in mind, however, that it was the performance of the men who were in the second phase of the study which accounted for the magnitude of the differences and most of the men in this phase had not yet been out of prison for two years when the current study was undertaken (see Table 3).

APPENDIX: RESEARCH AND EVALUATION

The median period of treatment was eight months. Those who remained in the programme over eight months did no better than those who remained in it for eight months or less.

TABLE 4

Time in Treatment and Parole Performance

Time	Mean B.E.	Favourable Outcome
Eight months or less	49·2	79%
Nine months or more	48·0	79%

The parole performance of the men who had participated in phase one of the programme was compared with those who had participated in phase two. Here, rather striking differences emerged. The differences between the performance of the men who participated in phase one with their controls was slightly higher for those in the programme, but was not statistically significant. But the differences for those who participated in the second two years with their controls was statistically significant, high enough

TABLE 5

One Year Parole Outcome (Phase I vs Phase II)

	Favourable Outcome	χ^2	p. (one-tail)
Phase I (First Two Years)			
Experimental Group	74%	2·15	0·1 (N.S.)
Control Group	69%		
Phase II (Second Two Years)			
Experimental Group	84%	3·29	0·025
Control Group	76%		

TABLE 6

Difference in Outcome between Phase I and II

	Favourable Outcome	χ^2	p. (two-tail)
Experimental Groups			
Phase I	74%	4·84	0·05
Phase II	84%		
Control Groups			
Phase I	69%		
Phase II	76%	0·16	N.S.

to account for the magnitude of the differences when the two phases were combined and compared with all controls. When those who participated in the programme for the first two years were compared with those who participated in the second two years, the differences were also statistically significant in favour of those who were in the second phase. These results, while awaiting the two year follow-up study, are powerful indications of the strength in the self-help aspects of this approach.[16]

REFERENCES

1. Grant, J. D. 'The Offender as a Correctional Manpower Resource', in Reissman, F., and Popper H. I. (eds.) *Up From Poverty*. New York, Harper and Row, 1968.

2. Grant, J. D., and Grant, J. 'Contagion as a Principle in Behavior Change', in Rickard, H. (ed.) *Unique Programs in Behavior Readjustment*. New York, Pergamon, 1970.

3. Hodgkin, N. 'New Careers for Ex-Convicts', *London Times*, January 8, 1971.

4. Hodgkin, N. 'The New Careers Project at Vacaville', *The Howard J. of Penology* (in press).

5. Grant, J. D. 'The Use of Correctional Institutions as Self-Study Communities in Social Research', *Br. J. Delinquency* 7, 301–8 (1957).

6. Grant, J. D., and Grant, J. 'Client Participation and Community Change'; in Adelson, D., and Kalis, B. L. (eds.) *Community Psychology Perspectives in Mental Health*. Scranton, Pa., Chandler, 1970.

7. Grant, J. 'The Industry of Discovery: New Roles for the Non-professional', in Pearl, A., and Riessman, F. *New Careers for the Poor*. New York, Free Press, 1965.

8. Grant, J. D. 'Delinquency Prevention Through Participation in Social Change: New Careers in the Administration of Justice', paper presented at Juvenile Delinquency Task Force, California Council on Criminal Justice, 1970.

9. Hutchins, R. M., 'Are We Educating our Children for the Wrong Future?' *Sat. Rev. of Lit.*, September 11, 1965.

10. U.S. Joint Commission on Correctional Manpower and Training, *Offenders as a Correctional Manpower Resource*. Washington, U.S. Government Printing Office, 1968.

11. Jackson, K., and Briggs, D. L. 'New Careers for Delinquents in Education: An Alternative to Confinement', *Amer. J. Correction*, May–June 1966.

12. Empey, L. T. *Alternatives to Incarceration*. Office of Juvenile Delinquency and Youth Development. Washington, U.S. Government Printing Office, 1967.

13. Rutgers University (New Jersey) *Innovative Programs for the Treatment of Juvenile Offenders—Alternatives to Confinement.* (Department of Social Welfare, 1970.)

14. For details of the one year parole follow-up study, see Robison, J., and Kevorkian, M. *Intensive Treatment Program, Phase II, Parole Outcome Interim Report.* Sacramento, California Department of Corrections, 1966. For a description of the project and two others, together with a seventy-six item bibliography of published papers and unpublished documents on the projects, see Fromm, F. *The Intensive Treatment Program, Phase II: A Condensation of Working Papers.* Berkeley, University of California, School of Criminology, 1966.

15. Meuller, P. C., and Gottfredson, D. 'A Shorthand Formula for Base Expectancies', Sacramento, California Department of Corrections research report number 5, 1962.

16. For practical applications of the method begun in this project applied to prisons generally, and to begin new programmes, see Fenton, N., *et al.*, *The Correctional Community: An Introduction and Guide*, Cambridge U., 1967.

17. Jones, M., Briggs, D. L., and Tuxford, J. 'What has Penology to Offer Psychiatry?' *Br. J. Delinquency*, January 1964.

18. Empey, L., and Lubeck, S. G. *The Silverlake Experiment: Testing Delinquency Theory and Community Intervention.* Chicago, Aldine, 1970.

19. See for example, the brilliant studies of Basil Bernstein of London on the relation between social class and linguistic development, and the further studies of Robert Hess in the U.S. with urban, negro, pre-school children. Bernstein, B., 'Social Class and Linguistic Development: A Theory of Social Learning', in Halsey, A. H. *et al.* (eds.) *Economy, Education and Society.* New York, Free Press, 1961. Bernstein, B. 'Elaborated and Restricted Codes: Their Social Origins and Some Consequences', in Smith, A. G. (ed.) *Communication and Culture.* New York, Holt, 1966. Hess, R. D. 'Educability and Rehabilitation: The Future of the Welfare Class', *J. Marriage and Family* 24, 1964. Hess, R. D. 'Maternal Attitudes Toward the School and the Role of the Pupil: Some Social Class Comparisons', in Passow, A. H. (ed.) *Developing Programs for the Educationally Disadvantaged*, New York, Columbia University (Teachers College) 1968.

PART III

NORMAN HOUSE
By

MERFYN TURNER

Chapter Seven

THE NEED FOR A HOSTEL COMMUNITY

THE twenty prisoners who stood in a line were about to be discharged. They showed no sign of joy or of excitement, but stood staring stupidly about them. The Governor went up to them, and after congratulating them kindly upon regaining their freedom, added, 'Now that you are going to have your liberty, I hope I shall not see you again. Seek the Kingdom of God and his righteousness, and, depend upon it, you will prosper.'

So Mayhew[1] describes the discharging procedures of 1860, and they were not greatly changed eighty years later when I first had contact with them. The prison Governors of that time did not pronounce benedictions or congratulate prisoners on their release, but merely barked, 'Don't come back again!' and after-care continued to be largely a matter of chance or divine intervention.*

THE DEVELOPMENT OF AFTER-CARE

Parliament had recognised as far back as 1792 that prisoners needed help to return to their parish, and later Parliament conceded that 'deserving prisoners' should be given food and clothing, tools for work, and some measure of financial help, but the State was reluctant to become directly involved in helping prisoners on discharge. It did accept responsibility for prisoners serving sentences of penal servitude—a numerically insignificant proportion of the total of the prison population—but even that responsibility did not entail material and financial help until 1910 when the Central Association for the Aid of Discharged Convicts was created. The main burden of after-care during the second half of the

* I received this treatment when I left prison after serving a brief sentence as a Conscientious Objector together with the admonition—'And don't let me see you here again'.

Eighteen months later I returned to prison as an Official Prison Visitor to be shaken warmly by the hand by the Governor and thanked for all the good work that he felt I was about to do. Needless to say it was the self-same Governor who failed to recognise his old client!

nineteenth century and the first half of the twentieth century fell on the Discharged Prisoners' Aid Societies who had little understanding of the needs of the prisoner and only inadequate resources to meet such needs.

At the end of the Second World War, when even the prisons were caught up in the wave of reform that swept the country, the whole system of after-care was subjected to criticism. Emphasis was now laid on professionalism in social work, and anything voluntary was suspect and regarded as amateurish and second-best, the workers were untrained and unqualified, and their role obsolete. Following the recommendations of the Maxwell Committee which had been set up to advise the Government in matters of prison after-care, the Discharged Prisoners' Aid Societies were themselves discharged from the prison scene and told to work in the virgin field outside prison. Gradually trained workers were brought into the prisons to replace the agents of the Aid Societies and to apply the new casework techniques which were more in keeping with contemporary thought and pratice in the field of professional social work. It needed but one step to complete the development and that step was taken in the Criminal Justice Act of 1967 when the after-care of all offenders was made the statutory responsibility of the Probation Service. What happened to the prisoners on discharge was no longer to be a matter of divine intervention or of chance, or of mere aid on discharge; it would be the result henceforth of sound collaboration between the Probation Officer within the prison and his colleague who worked in the community outside. The service may not have operated so far as smoothly and as effectively as was expected, but no critic would deny the progress that has been made in the last ten years.

When I became a prison visitor at the end of the Second World War the concept of the 'aid' on discharge was by no means dead. On two afternoons a week I sat on the discharging panel of the Prisoners' Aid Society and helped to dispense 'aid' to men who, for the greater part, were destitute and homeless.

> 'Well, Mr. Smith, ' the Chairman would say, 'you are going out in three weeks. You've no place to go to, no money, nor a job. It doesn't look so good does it?'
> 'No Sir.'
> 'That's the reward of crime isn't it?'

THE NEED

'Yes Sir.'
'Well there isn't very much we can do. We'll give you a letter of introduction to the Labour Exchange. They'll give you a B.1 form to take to the Assistance Board. We'll give you a little money to help you on your way. But you'll have to stop at a lodging-house, won't you?'
'I'm not stopping at no lodging-house. I want a room on my own.'
'Beggars can't be choosers, Mr. Smith. You've only got a penny in your property and you won't get a room for a penny, will you? Our advice to you is—*stay in a hostel*—then when you've saved a pound or two you can move into a private room.'

The prisoner may have been inclined to prolong the discussion but the Chairman would have other ideas, for on average the time we could allocate to each prisoner was less than four minutes.

Of the men who appeared before the Discharging Committee four in every ten were homeless and rootless. They spent their lives between prisons, common lodging-houses and the open road—but not, it seemed, at a reception centre which they said was for those who had reached the end of that road and —'Thank God I haven't come down to that yet'.* This was the picture they painted for me when I talked to prisoners in the privacy of their own cells. However much they might want to break with tradition—and many claimed they wanted to do so—they had no prospect of succeeding because they never got the help that they needed to set themselves on their feet. 'A couple of bob and a ticket to the Sally Ann gets you nowhere unless it's back to these places. If you could find me a room and get me a job as well—I promise you—you will never see me in these places again.'

THE COMMON LODGING-HOUSE

When the Chairman of the Discharging Committee said to the homeless prisoner 'You'll have to go to a hostel, won't you?' I had a very poor idea of what constituted a hostel. I knew that in London there were large lodging-houses and hostels accommodating between 100 and 900 men—and one hostel

* Mayhew[1] writing in 1862 on Holloway Prison describes a comparable scene: 'He (the Governor) advised him to go to the union. The prisoner replied, "he would rather stay out at night than go to the union".'

for both men and women—which were run by religious societies who claimed an interest in the redemption of their lodgers, or by private individuals, companies, and trusts who claimed to do no more than provide cheap lodging for those who could afford no better. These lodging-houses, hostels and working men's homes were located in depressed, deprived neighbourhoods, but it was probably also true to say that it was the location of the hostels that brought into the neighbourhood this type of client and thus created the need in the locality.

What sent me to live at a large common lodging-house in East London was the need to discover for myself the influence a hostel could have on a homeless isolated prisoner who wanted to break away from the tradition of hostel, prison and crime. The Victorian argument was that the professional vagrant could no more change his ways than could the leopard his spots, for vagrancy, it was argued, 'had become an institution which supported able-bodied men and women in a state of idleness, thieves of every sort, deserters from the Army, bad characters, run-away apprentices, prostitutes, vagabonds of the lowest class who worked in gangs, and many wretched beings who could not take any effective step to change their position. Outcasts from society by their crimes, or their vices, unpleasant ways or unbearable temper.'[2]

It seemed reasonable to me to assume that if the contemporary lodging-house scene was a similar haven for London's social deviants then the optimism of the Discharging Committee of the prison when they referred homeless prisoners to the hostels could not be justified. The truth was that neither hostels nor prisons were really concerned about deviancy. The religious organisations might talk about making the crooked straight, but they would have been totally demoralised if they had recognised the immensity if not the impossibility of the task which they set themselves. Clearly the lodging-houses were places of shelter and protection for those who were homeless for a variety of reasons. They could not make the crooked straight but they helped to make the handicap bearable.

I did not need to stay at my common lodging-house for three months to realise how unsuited it was to cope with the problems of homeless discharged prisoners. I had calculated that the latter accounted for 40% and possibly more of the total population of the recidivist prison to which I was attached as a visitor, and it seemed to me that such men accounted for perhaps a half of the lodging-house population. It seemed fair also to assume that for the greater part they were one and the same people. On my first morning at the lodging-house I was accosted at the canteen by a lodger who was a complete stranger to me.

'I've seen you before', he said, 'I know I have.' He pondered for some time, and then his face lit up. 'I've got it,' he said, 'I know where I've seen you—in *the nick.*'

Other discharged prisoners similarly identified themselves from time to time, and particularly if they were short of money.

Stuart Whiteley, in a study of the mental health of homeless men in London[3] which was written sometime after my sojourn in the common lodging-house, identified and described the inadequate homeless men who use London's lodging-houses and Reception Centre. If he had also been examining the inadequate recidivists in a London prison his findings would not be greatly different, for they are very much the same people whether they are in prison, in a mental hospital, in the lodging-house or the Reception Centre, or on the open road.

When my stay at the common lodging-house[4] convinced me that hostels and Reception Centres had no solution to offer for the problems of the homeless prisoner, I returned to the prison to seek the answer.

The homeless men I talked to in their cells saw their problems largely in terms of lodgings, money and work. They rarely confessed a need for people. 'If I had my own room to come back to at night and a radio, I would be satisfied. I have never been one for going out. I like to keep myself to myself, and when I do feel like a bit of company, I can always go out for a pint, can't I?'

An exaggerated concern with the problems of lodgings, and work, and money, could well be expected in men who had spent so much of their lives in institutions of one type or another and which had provided them with food, shelter, and weekly issues of pocket money. When they were discharged from the Services or from prison they would look for work which offered shelter as well as money. In particular they regarded hotel work as the best hope of survival for them, for their histories showed that they could not withstand the loneliness of bedsitting rooms, nor the anonymity of the common lodging-houses.

PRISON TYPES

During my first years as a prison visitor and as a member of the Aid Society's Discharging Committee I kept my own records because I had no official access to prison and welfare records. As a member of the Committee I would see approximately 1,500 prisoners in the course of a year who represented a fair cross-section of the prison population. Most of them, of course, I saw only once when they appeared before the Discharging Committee. As a prison visitor I would see in addition some 50 prisoners who were selected for me, most of whom would be classified as *passive inadequates*, and who never questioned or protested but accepted submissively whatever was prescribed for them.

> 'I'll do this twelve years: it won't kill me', I would be told.
> 'But you are going to appeal surely?', I would say.
> 'Me appeal? I've never appealed against anything yet, and I am not going to change now.'

For my own convenience I divided the men I saw during the course of a year into three groups.

1. *The Aggressive Recidivist*

I recognised the *aggressive recidivist* who sought nobody's help and would not have accepted help even if he realised that he needed it. He had roots outside the prison. He had family and friends and criminal relatives by inter-marriage. He belonged in his community, and he followed a pattern of life which that community created for him. Crime was usually a strand in that pattern. If he liked you, he offered you hospitality. He would also accept yours. But it was implicit in the relationship that just as he did not attempt to change you, so you made no effort to change him.

Sid was just such an aggressive personality who had spent the greater part of his 35 years in penal institutions. He had been taken into care when he was a child and had escaped from children's homes and Approved Schools and returned home to his family. He had been to Borstal and he had absconded. He was conscripted into the Army, and he deserted. He was sent to prison, and he fought it as he fought everything that others prescribed for him. He was a thorough-going extrovert who challenged his environment, and was happiest when he was fighting it. The real people in his life were his family and his criminal friends. He belonged to them and they made no attempt to change him. 'We never want to change straight people. And we don't expect them to change us.'

Officially he was classified as *a prisoner who needed to be watched*. He accepted his imprisonment as a penalty for his failure, but he had no intention of conforming to prison rules and regulations. He broke them whenever it suited him, and if he was caught he accepted his punishment without complaint.

Over the months I developed a good relationship with Sid. This aggressive type of psychopath is always more stimulating company than the passive, inadequate psychopath. But I knew that the friendship that grew between Sid and myself would not be allowed to influence his way of life when he returned home to his own people and his own environment. This unwavering loyalty to a way of life was typical of the other aggressive recidivists I met in prison. It was their main driving force but it was also what made a return to prison inevitable, for it greatly simplified the work of the police who kept good account of the *'villains'* who lived on their *'manor'*.

By my rough calculations this type of aggressive psycho- path accounted for one-third of the prison's true population. That is to say they amounted to two-hundred and fifty men who constituted a serious penal and social problem.

2. *The Disturbed Group*

In my second group I placed prisoners who were so *mentally disturbed* that it was clear to me even as a layman that prison would do nothing to alter their behaviour. Some of them had received psychiatric treatment at one time or another but others appeared to have escaped such notice. They would leave prison to assault children yet again, to burn down empty buildings or smash the glass of telephone kiosks. They would always accept the offer of a place to go to on release for it was something that they had been waiting for over many years. It would be a turning-point. But when they were released from prison and joined the new group, they failed to withstand the different social pressures, or resist the urgent demands of their own damaged personalities. Sooner or later they would be back in prison, bewildered by their failure, and once again anxious about the next release to freedom.

In this group there were men like *Stan* who often conducted conversations with me as he faced his cell wall. He was in prison for demolishing a night watchman's cabin because the watchman had refused to let him sleep there. He would have demolished the night watchman, too, if he could have caught him. There was also *Alfred* who was showing advanced signs of senility although he was not yet 60. He lived in a state of pathological anxiety which his fellow-prisoners recognised and used for their own amusement. There was *Lawrence*, a West Indian immigrant, whose only conversation was 'I am coming out tonight Jack!', and *Lou* who had cut off his right thumb because it offended against him, and *John* who had slept next to God in the Reception Centre, and seen Lord Nelson driving a 'bus'.

Stuart Whiteley describes similar personalities in his study[3] and concludes: 'This group of eccentrics is made up of a mixture of schizophrenic and organic defect states, bizarre and unstable personalities who have been down and out for some time. It is probably increasing age and the consequent increasing difficulties in adaptation which drives them into the Reception Centre.'

They would leave prison as lonely, isolated and unfitted for life in society as they were the day they were removed from it. The present offered no respite for them whilst the future offered more prison committals, lodging-house sojourns, the railway stations, and the open road, until ultimately, as Whiteley states the ageing process would produce its solution. When that occurred society was required to supply only the bare necessities of food, and shelter, to sustain lives that had lost all meaning.

3. *The Passive Inadequate Group*

It was my third group of *passively inadequate* prisoners that offered the greatest hope. They were not homogeneous although their histories showed some striking similarities. Some were rejected at birth, and others very soon afterwards, and would have been handed over to the care of Local Authorities or charitable institutions. Those who had been brought up at home only exceptionally knew the affection of both parents. Some had run away from their unhappiness whilst others remained in the family home to invite parental punishment for their difficult and unruly behaviour. Ultimately they would have been sent away to Approved Schools and later had called in at Borstal on their path to prison. In

THE NEED

many instances the period they may have spent in the Armed Forces had been the most successful part of their lives. It was undistinguished, but it had given them the security they needed within a framework that was approved by society. Prison may have given them the same security, but it gave social disapproval also. Although their crimes were only rarely serious ones—an expression of their incompetence and inability to survive in society on society's terms more than a desire to pursue a criminal career—the Court punished them for their failure to survive with increasing terms of imprisonment which ultimately ended in *Preventive Detention* and which the criminal fraternity regarded as the end of the road.

Prison offered them nevertheless a breathing space and a respite from the strains and stresses of life outside. During their imprisonment they recovered their limited stamina and convinced themselves that there would be no next time, although this was more an expression of hope than a confession of confidence. When they were finally back in prison they still claimed some measure of success—'I was three months out this time—it was only two months last time.'

Walter was forty-five. He had served one sentence of *Preventive Detention*, and he was now serving three months for shoplifting. When he appeared before the Discharging Committee he was guarded and suspicious. When the Chairman asked him what plans he had made for his future, Walter was unprepared for the question. 'Prisoners can't make plans,' he said, 'that is why we come to you people.' Such remarks were unlikely to impress the Committee members who always looked for some evidence of willingness on the prisoner's part to assist his own cause.

> 'How do you expect us to help you if you're not prepared to help yourself?', the Chairman asked him, looking at the Committee members for approval.
> 'I'll go thieving', said Walter, 'that's what I'll do, go thieving. I won't ask you people for anything.'

He got up from his chair in high temper and signified that so far as he was concerned the interview had ended.

I saw Walter in the cell later that evening. He was quiet and respectful now. He had not intended to say what he did in front of the Committee, he said, but the truth was that he was desperate about his future. He had been in prison six times, and each time he came out the Welfare put him in a doss-house. 'I'm telling you, Mister, you don't stand a chance in them places. You got men there who are real villains, and you've got men like me who aren't villains at all really, but we have a lot of form behind us.* You've got "con" men there, and ponces, and foreigners: the place is crawling with them, Mister. It makes me sick. A man can't get a fair chance in his own country any more.'

Walter had no contact with his family. He had never married, and was not interested in marriage. 'But don't get me wrong, I'm not one of *them*—you known what I mean.' The best time in his life, he said, was when he was in the Forces. He had been in North Africa and he had spent a year in Italy, although most of it, from what I could gather, had been spent in detention. 'This isn't living any more—going to work with foreigners all around you, coming away with £12 clear, paying for your bed in a kip house, and spending what's left on beer. That's not life, not for me it isn't. You may think I am a bit of a moaner but I'm not you know. The only reason I get like this is because I get browned off. Everything seems so useless. I see other blokes—Greeks and Cypriots and what have you— I see them doing well—it makes me mad. So I go out and get drunk and then I find myself in these places.'

What Walter and all the other inadequate offenders were saying both when they appeared before the Discharging Committee and when I spoke to them in their cells was that they did not want to spend any more time in captivity, but that without help they could not keep out of trouble. What they understood as help—clothes and money and a place to live—was in reality only the trimmings. They needed a framework which would support them as a family supports its children. In particular they needed such when their stamina was waning, and the shine of freedom had worn off, when working for a living had lost its thrill, and life was proving to be dull, dreary and purposeless, and quite unlike what they unrealistically pictured for themselves when they were inside.

It seemed to me that what the passive inadequate offender needed was the protection and support of a substitute family which would direct his coming and his going, praise him for his success, and admonish him for his failures. It would notice his existence, listen to his tales of woe, laugh at his jokes, and

* In *London Labour and the London Poor* (1848), Mayhew describes the lodgers of more than 100 years previously in almost identical terms!

respect his points of view. He could grow in such a climate whilst previously his experiences of life had diminished him. Childhood institutions, prisons and lodging-houses with people numbered in hundreds, were unlikely to foster growth in the inadequate personality. They emphasised his handicap, and aggravated his state of dependence. A small group instead of a large one, a house instead of an institution, and people who cared instead of officials in authority, might provide an answer to the problems of these homeless inadequate offenders. These were assumptions that could be easily tested, I felt, if money could be made available to finance an experimental project.

The beginnings of norman house

It was the financial support of the London Parochial Charities that translated this thinking into a practical attempt to provide the inadequate offender with a substitute home and family, and in 1954 *Norman House* was born—the first of the half-way houses.

The scheme envisaged a group of a dozen or so people living together in a family setting with a warden in charge, and one, or perhaps two, 'non-offender' residents following their own occupations by day and contributing to the life and well-being of the house by their mere presence rather than by the performance of any specific duties. A warden would be expected to possess insight into the problems of individual offenders and some skills in helping to resolve them. But it was important also that he would see the individual offender in a group setting, It was one thing to come to know a man when he was in the loneliness of his cell, but quite another to see him when he was responding and reacting to the pressures and influences of a dozen others who had once been solitary individuals like himself.

It was considered important for the warden to select his residents whilst they were still in prison, partly so that a sound relationship might be developed between himself and the offender before the latter went to live at Norman House, and partly because it aimed to ensure that only those offenders were selected who, it was thought, could most profitably benefit from the help that the House was designed to give. Although Norman House was later to be criticised for its selectivity the selection of residents has remained one of the cardinal principles.

NORMAN HOUSE

The House, which was located in a good residential neighbourhood in North London but close to the sources of work and recreation, had accommodation for 14 people. Fifteen years later this was increased to 20 by the acquisition of a basement flat. It was decided that rooms should not be partitioned but be shared by the men, as bedrooms and not used as an escape from human contact, which is what prison cell had afforded. The *life* of the House would be on the ground floor—in the kitchen, and the dining room and in the lounge. At the front of the house there was a garden and at the back a large lawn and a derelict greenhouse which was soon to be replaced by a workshop. So it was neither a hostel nor an institution, but a large suburban house indistinguishable from its neighbours in the quiet backwater, of a private park.

It was to be expected that Norman House would attract attention for there was very little in the early 1950s, either by way of treatment in prison or care outside it, that could excite anybody's interest in penal matters. The deliberate policy of bringing offenders to live together under the same roof—and not first offenders at that—invited criticism, for it ran contrary to the doctrine of separation which had been preached so successfully in the 19th Century, and perpetuated in the 20th Century without question. What was exciting, however, was that an approach that had been recognised and applied by progressive workers in the field of child care and development was now to be applied to adult offenders. The implication was that although chronological age placed these offenders in the late twenties, thirties, and even forties their emotional development fitted them more readily into the world of maladjusted children. Pioneers like Homer Lane[5] and A. S. Neill[6] had demonstrated the correcting and healing potential to be found in communities of children and adolescents allowed to develop their own resources, and what Norman House was about to do was to apply some of those lessons to the field of adult offenders.[7]

REFERENCES

1. Mayhew and Binney (1862). *The Criminal Prisons of London.* Frank Cass, 1968.

2. Ribton–Turner. *Vagrants and Vagrancy.* Chapman & Hall.

3. Whiteley, J. S. 'The Mental Health of Homeless Men in London' (1956). Unpublished work.

4. Turner, M. *Forgotten Men, a Study of a London Common Lodging-House*. National Council of Social Service.

5. Wills, W. David. *Homer Lane. A Biography.* Allen & Unwin, 1964.

6. Neill, A. S. *Summerhill: A Radical Approach to Education.* Victor Gollancz, 1962.

7. Turner, M. *Safe Lodging: the road to Norman House.* Hutchinson.

Chapter Eight

EXPERIENCES IN THE HOSTEL
COMMUNITY

NORMAN HOUSE set out to work with the *individual* offender.
The aim was therapeutic, and the setting was that of community, but neither in its origins nor in its development was
it a *therapeutic community* as the term is commonly understood.
It was paternalistic. The rules, such as they were, were
imposed on the residents, and the community had no authority over their selection, nor over their departure. On the other
hand the organisation of life within the community was
simple, and the degree of participation was high. There was
fair equality between residents and staff in that the same
conditions applied to both. Neither staff member nor resident
occupied a single room.* In fact the assistant warden generally
shared a room with the most disturbed or difficult resident.
Household duties were shared and nobody used keys. Neither
staff nor residents were permitted to bring alcoholic drinks
into the house. Courtesy to visitors was demanded whether
they were friends of staff or friends of residents. In the
earliest stages nobody occupied a permanent place at the
table and residents and staff took it in turn to sit at the head,
which carried authority and responsibility for callers and
visitors.

As time passed, however, this arrangement declined into
disuse because residents were identifying more with the staff
than with each other. This was partly an expression of their
dependence and partly the result of their institutional experience which, for many, was considerable. It was a continual need to prove himself that most notably revealed the
offender's dependence on other people. Throughout his
institutional life, from children's homes to prison, he had
been urged on to good behaviour, to prove to others that he

* There were occasions when a resident was temporarily placed on
his own because of sickness or behaviour difficulties.

188

could attain the ends that they set for him. Conformity with the regime earned him the approval of the matron, housemaster, officer, and occasionally the Prison Governor. He lived by the consent of these authority figures, and never in his own right. When he was offered a place at Norman House he accepted the rules that shaped the framework within which he would live so that once again he could prove to someone who cared that he could reach the set target. He would find a job, he said, and keep it for a whole year—'to prove'. He would save a weekly sum of money to buy a tailor-made suit, again—'to prove'. He would dig the garden and mow the lawn when the spring came—and again he would 'prove'. But the stamina he had seemed to recover in prison was rarely equal to the task when it became fact.

It was customary also for the isolated offender to equate terms like 'going straight' and 'good citizenship' with the life his captors lived. It was the way of life of the judges who sentenced him, the lawyers who prosecuted or defended him, and all those who supported his imprisonment. They were to blame for his recurring failure—the people who wouldn't give him the chance to prove that he too could be a success. By relating 'going straight' with the way of life of those who apprehended, judged, punished and rejected him, he was making his own failure less painful.

When he was in prison the offender had stated what he thought he required on his release and in turn he had reacted to the chance of participating in the Norman House experiment with enthusiasm. But frequently it was necessary to create in him a more sober appreciation of the situation in which he would find himself. 'The house isn't an easy place to live in.' I would warn him: 'there will be a dozen men there, you know, and they've all been in trouble.' 'That won't bother me. I'm sharing a cell now with two Paddies, and believe me, if I can put up with them I can put up with anybody.' I would try again. 'There's a lot of control at this house. There's discipline there you know.' 'I've been under discipline most of my life—Approved School, Borstal, the Army, and now here. I'm used to discipline. That's what I want, somebody to tell me what to do, where I go wrong, and things like that.' 'All the men at the house go to work. . . .' 'Suits me fine. I'm a good worker. Ask my landing officer: he'll tell you.' 'If you spend all your wages on drink. . . .' 'I never touch it.' 'All right: if you spend all your money at the dogs. . .' 'I never gamble.' In the end one could be excused for wondering why such virtuous citizens should ever have come to prison!*

Despite the unrealities of their assertions it was probably true to say that prospective residents accepted the rules of the house put to them because it was these rules that would help to create the conditions that they called 'a chance'—to find work, and earn money and buy clothes, and to go straight. However, going straight did not mean just a mechanical adherence to a non-delinquent way of life. It developed more as a consequence of attachment to people. The new resident fresh from prison, intoxicated with the joy of his new-found freedom, might not at that moment see the need for anybody's support. He knew what he had to do. He had to sign at the Labour Exchange, collect his grant from the Social Security Office, and, if there was still time, find himself a job. So far he had no reason to recall his condition of social isolation. But once the shine of freedom had worn off and working for a living had become unexciting, he would be faced with his loneliness again and the bleakness that the future offered him. Working at an honest job for fifteen pounds a week to pay for lodgings, food, and new clothes that nobody notices, is pointless unless it is related to people who matter. Thieving produces quicker results.

It is likely that the rules of the house would have been more stringent if they had been formulated by the residents. Unlike the *aggressive recidivist* who fights his environment, the *inadequate recidivist* has been conditioned by experience to accept it. But contrary to expectation, perhaps, his tolerance of nonconformist behaviour in others is low, and his treatment of it is generally severe. Few residents at Norman House would have been given a second chance if the authority had not rested with the staff. What was important was not where authority rested but how it was used. It had to be seen to be fair, and in that sense it had something of the quality of the authority that is vested in the true therapeutic community. It meant close involvement by the staff in the life of the community. That is why, perhaps, some of the staff as well as some of the residents failed to last the course.

The selection of staff and the selection of residents were the

* One aspect of imprisonment is the respite it gives the prisoner from the pressures that may have overwhelmed him outside prison. Prison, therefore, restores his stamina for all that awaits him on release, but it does not infuse reality into his state of preparation.

cornerstones on which the house rested, and experience has not diminished their importance.

THE SELECTION OF RESIDENTS

We recognised at the outset that not all homeless offenders would want to come to the house. Some were unsuited for it. Men who were addicted—to drugs, or alcohol for example —needed more specialised help than the house could give, as did offenders who specialised in false pretences, and frauds. What the house was looking for was men who said they wanted to finish with crime and prison, but who, because they were homeless and friendless, stood little or no chance of changing the pattern of their behaviour.

As a prison visitor the information I received covered only the prisoner's name, the location of his cell, and the date of his release. The argument ran that as prison visitors only talked with the prisoner they did not need to know anything about him. Prisoners are people with problems which they are more or less helpless to resolve, and the coming of a stranger into the cell does not suggest aimless conversation to the prisoner, but a possible source of support in the battle with his wife's family, his employer, or the Inland Revenue. In other words, however zealously the official policy of non-involvement has been preached by the Prison Visitors' Association, the real value of the prison visitor as often as not lies in the opportunity he gives for the development of a relationship that will affect the prisoner's living when he has been released. Reliable information about the prisoner is a valuable ingredient in the development of this relationship.

It was in my capacity as a prison visitor that I made almost all the selections for Norman House in the first year. The Discharging Committee was enthusiastic about the new project and referred men to my notice. The Chaplain was a supporter also and he arranged that only homeless, inadequate prisoners were placed on my list of prisoners to be visited. Other visitors as they came to learn about the existence of the house interceded on behalf of their own prisoners, and occasionally, even in the first year, a prisoner either communicated directly his own need or that of a fellow prisoner.

There was, therefore, no shortage of candidates for the dozen places that the house provided. The problem was to select from among the many the few who could profit most from the service that the house offered.

In a recidivist prison where the experience of prison may be in excess of four sentences per man, it is as likely as not that the prisoner is as familiar with interviews as he is with the more commonplace aspects of crime and prison life. When I talked to people in their cells, therefore, having explained my connection with 'a house in Highbury' as the reason for my visit, they would provide answers to the questions I asked which they felt would best commend them in my eyes. 'Of course' they preferred *a house* to a large hostel. Large lodging-houses, they said, were breeding-grounds of crime. People didn't live in big crowds, did they? They lived in *families*. They had never had a family, they said, not a real family anyway. They were brought up by step-fathers, or step-mothers, and with children who weren't their real brothers and sisters. They had truanted from school, and wandered away from home until they were '*put away*' because of it. And, they said, somehow or other they had been put away ever since. They had never had probation, the Magistrate *always sent them down*. Some people did far worse things—murder for example—and got off much better in court. All the same *all they wanted was a break* to prove what they could do. The house I had mentioned was the break they had been waiting for.

I had no means of checking what the prisoner said or of discovering the omissions which could be more important than what was disclosed. But I learnt to interpret what the prisoner was saying. For example, whenever he said he had lived at Sutton it was safe to assume a connection with the Henderson Hospital or Belmont as it was known in the early days of the house. Men who claimed to be farm workers, or to have worked on farms, were disclosing their Borstal history as the older men who had been in 'the Boys' Army' were almost certainly declaring their orphanage upbringing. Whether they communicated by euphemism, omission, or simple confession, what they were saying, it seemed to me, was that they had failed in freedom because they lacked support, and supervision, and a strong, positive leadership.

The prisoner may have believed implicitly what he said about himself in the insulated unreality of his cell. But I had no means of determining how he would respond to living at the house. 'I'm a good worker; ask anybody who knows me,' might or might not be true. But there rarely was anyone within reach who could corroborate or contradict what he said. 'I don't like hanging around. I like to be told what to do and left alone to get on with it. If I came to your house,'—it was always *my* house—'you wouldn't get any trouble with me so long as you told me what to do.' If prison records had been available it is likely that they could have denied the claims the prisoner was making for himself. It was hardly surprising, therefore, that during the first months I made errors of selection because I had allowed myself to be persuaded by the prisoner's confession of his need. Experience taught me to be more discriminating.

Another selection difficulty was that inside the prison I was talking to individuals who spent at least eighteen hours of every week-day in their cell, and twenty-one hours on Sundays. The older recidivists had been doing this for many years until their ability to socialize had been seriously damaged if not totally destroyed, and although they quickly maintained that if they were offered the one thing they had always lacked—a home and the atmosphere of family—they would know how to use their chance, it was doubtful in fact whether they were any longer capable of relating to anything except the four walls of their prison cell.

It went without saying that a certain degree of mental and physical fitness was looked for in the men who were accepted as residents. On the face of it they had some ability to do the things they said while they were in prison, that they wanted to do when they were outside but the strongest men rarely turned out to be the best workers and it was those with the keenest minds who most quickly seemed to work towards their own destruction.

Selection was crude, unscientific, and highly subjective, but in those early days there was probably no other method that would have proved more satisfactory. One of the advantages of the selection method was that it was possible to establish a relationship with almost every resident while he was still a prisoner. In later years when the demand for a place at the house came from courts and prisons in widely separated parts of the country it was not possible to see the prisoner more than once, collaboration from other social workers, and a willingness to make available information about the offender, was compensation for the loss of opportunity of forming these pre-release relationships.

During the first year thirty-one men lived at the house for periods ranging from five days to five months, and averaging overall six weeks. Five offenders proved unsuitable. That is, they were incapable of making the degree of adjustment to the life of the house that would make them acceptable to the group. Two of the unsuitable residents were psychotic, and had been accepted so that proper provision elsewhere could be made for them. The group showed slightly more tolerance towards them than it did to the other three, two of whom were alcoholics, and the third a wayfarer of long experience.

The remaining twenty-six were considered suitable. On the face of things they were the inadequate, passive recidivist offenders for whom the house was designed. By inadequates we meant persons who were not mentally or morally ill but were adrift in society, and, having difficulty in establishing lasting and satisfactory relationships, expressed themselves through drunkenness, vagrancy, crime and personal eccentricities.

Over the next four years there was no great change in the number of men selected annually or in the proportion of unsuitable choices. Of two hundred men who lived at the house in its first five years approximately one quarter failed to fit into the group. This proportion has remained fairly constant. But in the last eighteen months when exceptional attention has been given to selection for long rather than short-term residence, the proportion of unsuitable residents has dropped dramatically as it could be expected to do when the element of risk, inherent in the work of selection for the house, has been reduced to a minimum.

THE SELECTION OF STAFF

If the selection of residents was one of the corner-stones on which the work of the house rested, the selection of staff was the other. It had been assumed in the planning stages that the role of the staff would be decisive, for the basic reasoning was that inadequate men failed in part because they desperately needed leadership. Experience of the first year indicated the validity of our assumptions. If the men at the house were deprived of leadership they languished in the evenings, at the weekends, and on Public holidays. Like young children they made unrelenting demands on the staff. If they had no real problems to discuss they would invent them, and when invention was exhausted they clung as children cling when they are jealous of the attention the parents are giving to an activity that excludes them. The staff soon learnt that the pursuit of private activities when the residents were home from work was interpreted by the residents as an act of rejection.

The experience of the second year confirmed what the first year had indicated particularly in the sphere of personal relationships. Dependence on the staff continued to be great. Diary entries of the period make interesting comments and observations. There was *John A.* who found great difficulty in relating to staff or residents. An entry in the diary reads: '*February 2.* John eats little at supper and rushes out. Talk it over with him later. Confesses he is frightened of people. Trembles visibly when I speak to him, or, he says, the boss at work, or the police. I suggest he sits by me at mealtimes. John accepts, saying this will help.' A year later John was participating fully in the life of the house.

Another entry, referring to *Bill* who had moved to lodgings nearby, read: 'February 8. Bill calls twice bringing presents for S. (my wife) and me on both occasions. Follows me into the garden, then the workshop, where he sits quietly and contentedly while I get on with a table.'

During the first five years there was no change of warden, and only a few changes of assistant wardens. Such a relatively sustained continuity contributed greatly to the security that communicated itself to the residents. It fostered in them a sense of belonging to *something* or *somebody* which was the starting point of the therapeutic community. Residents could be themselves as children are themselves in their own family. They could discharge aggression that had previously been dammed up under the threat of punishment. They could behave like children and expect, with the expectation of children, to be noticed.

They could exhibit switches of mood. They could be cheerful at tea and sulk after it. They could pour out their troubles and fears and not be diminished by it. They accepted criticism and correction because they knew that the underlying relationship was one of affection and respect. This after all was the way families developed and prospered. Occasionally a resident was unbelievably offensive to me—but never so offensive to my wife or to my assistant. I was, after all, the father of the family who had acquired other people's grown-up children. Under the stress of frustration they were telling me how much they hated not only myself but their real parents also. It needed only a new situation —a visit from the Police for example who might be enquiring about an ex-resident—to change the mood and erase the memory. There were no hard feelings on the resident's side and he assumed there would be none on my side either. I remember a particularly offensive attack by a resident who was about to leave. Four weeks later he was writing to me from prison asking me to go to see him, and to take some tobacco also 'to show there's no hard feelings'. It could be said, of course, that the man was more interested in his supply of tobacco than in resurrecting our relationship but I incline to the latter view.

In the second five years there were two changes of warden, but after the first decade the picture changed seriously and the sense of continuity virtually disappeared. Suitable staff seemed almost impossible to find and there is no doubt that the unregulated development of other small hostels and half-way houses about the country contributed to the change, for there were now too many houses seeking too few suitable staff. There are implications in residential work that are mandatory for those who undertake it, but under the pressure of shortage of workers there is a temptation to compromise. The results are almost always likely to be disastrous. In its second decade Norman House was to learn the bitter lesson that, in the sphere of its work, at least, half a loaf is no substitute for no bread at all. Expediency debases the service and the community at the house becomes a collection of residents. The experience may help the staff but it injures the residents for certain.

The period of staff unsettlement was not entirely negative however. Crises in staff relationships and the catastrophic events that sometimes overwhelmed them inevitably involved the residents just as parental disharmony involves the children.

In some situations the residents collectively became protective to a staff member, as, for example, when one warden's wife left with one of the residents who was playing the part of the shining knight, rather than the less romantic role of the wife snatcher. This warden was not particularly popular with the residents but nevertheless they forgot their dislike of him in a wave of sympathy, and they assumed control of the house when he neglected his responsibilities and drank himself into an alcoholic stupor. In the short-term these crises caused by staff irregularities had a cohesive effect on the community but in the long-term they became forces of disintegration, reinforcing for me the belief that a community of offenders could only be as therapeutically effective as the staff were skilled to support and foster it. Without the unifying influences of the staff the community languished and collapsed.

EXPERIENCES

Ideally the house should be in the care of a married warden supported by an assistant warden who may well be someone in training for the social services. The warden and his wife are able to play the part of parents to the offender residents and thus create the sense of family that the unmarried warden finds it difficult to achieve. The warden's wife may or may not be employed as the official housekeeper but her presence in the house makes its own impact. It is possible for the work of the house to flourish under an indifferent warden if his wife is exceptionally attuned to the community around her. But it would need an exceptional warden indeed to promote growth in the community if his wife were antagonistic or indifferent to the idea. It is when both husband and wife are in harmony with the work that the house fully prospers.

There must be in the staff an intuitive feeling for people which then communicates itself simply and honestly. The best workers come with an aptitude for the work and an awareness of its demands and dangers, and they will recognise their own limitations and work within them. Training and experience will deepen their understanding, and to some degree, perhaps, modify those attitudes that require correction. But without a willing and realistic acceptance of the fundamental implications of residential work training will avail them nothing, and experience will have no value.

It is important also that the staff are shock-proof against both the actions of community and the attitudes its members reveal towards judges and lawyers, the police and all those others who uphold law and order. Offenders who have, as they see it, suffered throughout their lives at the hands of those who constitute a society which they resent and sometimes despise, can be expected to proclaim their hostility towards its representatives with a vehemence which betrays the guilt and shame they feel for their own failure as citizens more than for their acts as criminals. Authoritarian staff nurtured in the Victorian concept of discipline may see in such uninhibited and unchecked condemnation of society allowed to go unchecked a condonation by the other staff of the criminal and anti-social behaviour of the offender. If this were so the house would cease to operate therapeutically for the offenders who come to it expect to find in the staff total incorruptibility, although they may be cynical of their ability to achieve it. They may well hold a poor opinion of police, politicians, priests, and public servants in general. But wardens are a different matter. It could make life easier for the offender if the image were not so, but it would mean disillusionment also. However seriously or persistently the offender may have failed as a citizen, he has his own ideas of what constitutes happiness and good citizenship, and when he comes to Norman House he identifies those ideas with the staff. If they were to fail, the offender's own failure would seem less important.

It goes without saying that the senior staff of Norman House should be well-balanced, mature, and integrated people who have insight into their own needs and motivations as well as into the needs of the residents. It is imperative that they have friends and interests outside the house, and that they can withstand the pressures which life at the house puts upon them to abandon such personal pursuits, for to do so would make them inward-looking members of an inward-looking community, and cause them to lose sight of that ultimate goal which lies outside the protective framework of the house. Staff who do become enslaved by the community soon become devoid of new ideas and leave to take up what they see as more exciting work in some other field. They have failed to comprehend both their own needs and the needs of their family of offenders.

As the regime at Norman House is authoritarian it is important that staff who are appointed know how to exercise authority, for the wrong use of authority spells disaster for the offender. It re-emphasises the paramount importance of maturity. Time and again staff reach a critical point of anxiety because they feel their authority threatened by the refusal of an individual resident or by the group as a whole to conform to their own wishes. Considerable personal maturity is required to cope with such a situation, and in the most permissive communities as in authoritarian groups much depends on the quality of the leadership. Recognising that indifferent staff are not equal to the demands which this type of work makes and that the availability of suitable staff diminishes as more and similar after-care houses open, Norman House has established its own staff training scheme, and so far this policy is succeeding in its primary aims.

THE DEVELOPMENT OF A COMMUNITY

There was little evidence during the early stages of the development of the house of a feeling of *community* amongst the residents. The relationships that developed between individual residents were superficial. Sometimes plans would be made for a common enterprise such as a visit to a cinema, or a football match, but usually on the initiative of the staff. Those who responded would be those who had a particular friend among the other residents but also those who related to nobody except to the staff. When the time came for the group to set out on the expedition, one member would be missing, another would be in bed, and a third would be sulking on the sitting room settee. A weekend camping expedition which got off to a shaky start ended on a highly successful note, partly because the period was short and the weather was favourable, but largely because the lead was taken by two members who were not typical of the types at the house, for they were both men of good intelligence and attainment and infinitely more socially adequate than most of the men who came to the house. Both had been patients in mental hospitals where group therapy was practised. They were active participants in, and leaders of, the life of the house and by our standards they were quite exceptional.

All the same as time passed there were unmistakable signs that the group at the house was acquiring something of the character of a therapeutic community. New residents who had nothing to support them except the stamina which they had rebuilt during their period of imprisonment were helped by the attitude and example of residents of longer duration. The newcomer fresh from prison knew what he had said he wanted to achieve—even though in some instances this was no more than the intention of keeping out of prison. At the house he found himself living with men who were already *doing* what he had promised himself; they were getting up in the morning and going to work; they were collecting wages at the end of the week and paying for their board and lodging; they were watching the television at night, playing billiards, talking with the warden's wife and trying out their hand in the workshop. In its own ways this kind of behaviour was contagious, just as less constructive behaviour was contagious also. The staff supported the newcomer but it was the support of his peers that gave him the greater reassurance.

The contagiousness of constructive and destructive behaviour was similar to that often seen in maladjusted children who are housed together in the same school, or home, or hospital. One abscondence may be the prelude to a series, and one act of vandalism may be the beginning of a spate of destructive acts. The inadequate offender is influenced similarly by the behaviour of those who form his community. It needed only one man at the house to change his job for others to follow his example. If one resident took to his bed with a common cold, others followed with influenza. If one said he was saving money to buy a suit others would immediately declare their intention of saving for overcoats, despite the fact that for these men who had lived so much of their lives on pocket money handed out regularly by institutions saving money was an achievement in itself and almost outside the bounds of reality.

The sense of isolation and individuality was slow to disperse however. When a new resident arrived at the house he encountered some hostility but little else, and it was often the fringe member of the community who then took the newcomer under his wing to initiate him into the ways of the house. Again when residents left little interest would be shown in their departure, although this could be expected in men who had only the experience of artificially formed communities, in prison, or in hospital. As patients in hospitals are concerned only with problems of health as it applies to them, so the prisoner recognises freedom only as it applies to himself. If he is made happier by the release of a fellow prisoner it is because he interprets this as a step nearer to his own freedom, for while he is deprived he cannot be happy for others. It was an exception within our community for any concern to be shown about the fortunes of a departed resident.

There was one occasion in the first year, however, when such concern was expressed to a high degree. One of the younger residents, whose moods swung from high elation, when he was the life and soul of the house, to a depth of depression that cast a darkness over all, left for work in the morning and telephoned later in the day to announce that he was leaving. That evening the conversation over the meal centred on the absent member. Somebody suggested the likelihood of suicide, by drugs or by more dramatic means. Others said he would return to crime and that would mean more prison. It was this spectre of prison rather than of death that finally stimulated concern. Two search parties were spontaneously organised to comb the known haunts of the missing resident. Both parties searched without success and they gave up at midnight, returning home in a spirit of some accord. The expedition may not have produced the missing resident (he produced himself two days later). But it served to bind the men more closely together, while the emergency lasted at least.

Any challenge from outside the house produced a similar show of unity, most noticeably when the challenge came from the police. Occasionally a resident was asked to visit the local police station, for instance about a routine matter relating to some incident that had occurred before he came to the house. But sometimes a more serious matter. The sexual offenders were particularly vulnerable, for the police kept a list of known sexual offenders and they checked their movements whenever serious sexual offences had been committed not only locally but in any part of the country. The interrogation of one of the residents invariably provoked strong reaction from the residents against the police which temporarily overcame their own condemnation of sexual offenders.

Outward expressions of solidarity would be short-lived, however, for by breakfast-time the following morning the group would once more be a collection of individuals dependent on the staff for enough stimulus to make the prospect of work bearable. They left for work as anxious children leave for school. They were leaving their security behind them. They returned in the evening cheerful, or chastened, or charged with aggression, but secretly happy to be back where they felt they belonged.

The sense of community developed slowly as a pattern of life emerged. Whenever the house was challenged by developments ouside, the residents adopted protective roles. Group solidarity increased also when a resident announced the loss of money. When that happened the self-righteousness of the innocent exceeded even the virtues of the saints. It only needed *John D.* to lose six shillings for *Alf* to report the loss of eight shillings and a shirt, and for *Mick* to recall that he was ten shillings short one morning although at the time he had given it no more thought. But *now it all seemed very clear*. He knew who had taken it. He wouldn't name him. But if he should catch the culprit at it he would deal with him in his own way — and there would be no psychology about his technique. Such declarations won general approval from the residents. They improved the individual's image of himself for although he may have stolen from strangers, he declared he never stole from friends. Similarly residents maintained that they would never commit offences whilst they were living at the house: 'I would never give the house a bad name,' they frequently said. It was perhaps the spreadover of residents from the first year into the next that gave some momentum to the development of a community, for it created a nucleus around which other residents gathered and encouraged the development of a group ethos.

THE RESIDENTS AND THEIR NEEDS

An analysis of the men who lived at the house during the first five years places them for convenience into three categories.

1. In *the first group* there were *those who needed permanent support*. They were unemployable except in sheltered occupations and without support they begged, or stole, or stayed pathologically apathetic. Placed in a hostel or a Local Authority home they drifted away, wandering by day and sleeping out at night. It could be argued that they should never have been accepted at the house in the first place because their need was for permanent support whilst the house offered support only for a short period. In some instances the extent of their dependence was only revealed during their stay at the house, but even when it was known beforehand it was fair to say that they lived more happily and less inadequately whilst they were at the house than they had done elsewhere for a great many years. That at least was preferable to the aftercare arrangements that merely deposited them in a common lodging-house.

Ernie and *Stan* were characteristic of the men in this category. Both were in their mid-fifties but were prematurely old, and both had been married and lost their wives, their children and their homes. They had reacted passively to the loss, Ernie making no attempt to maintain himself so that ultimately he was committed to prison for debt, and Stan becoming vagrant. When they were in prison they were both apathetic, expressing no interest in their situation nor concern for what might follow it. They accepted what they were given and made no requests, wrote no letters, and sought no interview with the staff or with the welfare officer whose compassionate plea it was that brought them both to the house.

It was clear from the outset that Stan was unemployable by virtue of subnormality of intellect. A pathological apathy enveloped him in a cloud of hopelessness and communicated depression to the others in the house. Ernie appeared to have been fitter mentally and physically up to the breakdown of his marriage which had lasted twenty years, during which time he had an impressive work record. Work was therefore found for him, and for three weeks he was supported in it. But even if his employer had been a charitable agent it is unlikely that he could have continued Ernie's employment, for the latter's speech, comprehension, and movements were slow. He was not living in a world of fantasy even, but in a vacuum which suggested not so much protection from further pain but indifference to it. Within the house the two men sat and ate and sat again, never initiating conversation nor participating in a discussion which others had started. It was possible to interest Stan in the workshop, although that was at a childish level, but Ernie was frozen. It was the sadness of his countenance that pleaded for further kindness. Neither Ernie nor Stan was really accepted into the community of the house, for it was wrongly argued by the group that they contributed nothing to it and therefore could expect nothing in return. They stayed because the staff protected them, for otherwise the residents would have helped them quickly back on to the road of vagrancy and destitution.

The residents rejected them chiefly because they lowered their own status and threatened their image of themselves. 'This is becoming a doss house' or 'We have become a home for nutters', were comments made at the time. They were unhelpful comments but they provided interesting insights into the resident's attitude to the community. They were as jealous of its standards as are the most reactionary members of the exclusive St. James' clubs.

Ernie eventually departed for lodgings and soon collapsed. Stan was placed in the care of the Local Authority but three times he returned to the house for an overnight stay before he himself finally gave up the struggle and disappeared.

2. *The second group* compromised *those residents who were too psychologically disturbed for the house to do more than exert a temporary control over their disturbed behaviour.* Some were recognisable in the prison setting, but others revealed the extent of their problems only when under the pressure of close community living. In this group were the wayfarers who showed signs of mental illness, alcoholics, sexual offenders and those with a history of fraud or false pretences. Their underlying emotionally disturbed condition demanded greater specialist attention than the house was able to give.

Offenders with a history of false pretences made a marked

initial impact on the community and were quickly accepted into it. They impressed with their claims to affluence and association with persons of good standing. They borrowed money from their room mates and the other residents to tide them over until their allowance or dividends came, or loans which they claimed they had made to friends in need were repaid. They claimed contacts with yachts and girl friends, and they promised lively weekends for those of the residents who could enjoy them. They usually disappeared from the scene when their creditors could no longer be stalled or their phantasies continue to remain unexposed. It was a source of mystery to me nevertheless how offenders who claimed with pride such a high degree of wisdom in the field of crime and the quick recognition of those who commit crimes should so easily and unfailingly fall prey to the fabrications of the false pretender, unless it was that it pleased them also to accept the phantasy lives of their more imaginative fellows.

Homosexual offenders who belonged to the group presented difficulties by their tendency to involve the whole group in their ambivalent relationships. They formed a group within a group which was rigidly exclusive and caused tension and ill-feeling. This imposed a strain on staff and residents, for the egocentric urgency of the homosexual's problems took him outside the controls created by his group or by individual residents or staff. When a relationship changed and the excitement waned the homosexual would be consumed by his own feelings of guilt. If he was religious it was then that he sought refuge in his religion. For him the answer lay not in his relationship with man, but with God. It was a defence that effectively protected him from the need to make an honest appraisal of his problem.

3. It was the men in *the third group the inadequate, passive, repeating offenders who benefitted most from living at the houses.* This was our anticipation when we established the house. Always labelled 'below average'—intellectually, educationally and socially—they revealed a common history of broken homes, a material as well as emotional deprivation. They had arrived in their position of social isolation as a result of repeated failure, particularly in the field of personal relationships. They had failed at school, at work, and in some instances in the Services also. Mostly they were unmarried and without friends to support them. They drifted into crime but always protested that this was the last time. Yet they were

EXPERIENCES

ill-equipped to achieve a permanent change in their pattern of life. More imprisonment was not so much punishment for them but depressing evidence of yet more failure in life. Approximately 60% of the men who lived at the house fitted into this category. They demonstrated that they could succeed within the limits set by their own handicap but they relied heavily on the guidance and direction of the staff coupled with the support of their own peer group. It was when they were deprived of both staff direction and peer group support that they faltered and many failed.

The causes of failure were manifold, but two were pre-eminent. On the one hand there was the long-standing difficulty of the residents in developing satisfactory relationships with others. And on the other hand there was the real difficulty of finding a community outside the house which would accept them, and into which they could happily fit. Even if the men had been more adequate in social interchanges it is doubtful whether they would have suitable ground in which to grow roots. Three former residents who had stayed in lodgings for a year and a half and were well-liked by their landladies preferred to keep themselves to themselves, as they put it. 'I stay in every night except weekends,' they would say. 'I have my tea when I get back from work. Then I have a wash and a shave, and I have a read. Then it's time for bed.' It seemed that rather more than a half of the residents who lived satisfactorily at Norman House were unable to cope later with a sudden transition into the cold reality of the outside world. This reflected in part the lack of suitable lodgings for this type of isolated personality, and of sympathetic landladies who could take a friendly interest in their tenants. Even if such lodgings with their motherly landladies existed it was still very doubtful whether they had sufficient resources to meet the needs of these residents.

What was needed now was an intermediate stage between Norman House and the normal world—a 'second house' which was less protective than Norman House, and more closely resembled the community in which the ex-prisoner must ultimately live, yet at the same time was not as cold or as indifferent as the outside world. Such a house need not be run by a trained social worker, we felt. A landlady or landlord of the right kind was wanted rather than a surrogate 'head of the family', and the house should also include a fair proportion of residents who were *not* ex-prisoners, but who were generally

205

typical of those members of the normal community who lived customarily in lodging-houses and private bed-sitters. By introducing these non-offender residents into a 'second house' the hope was that they would develop relationships with Norman House residents and encourage the latter to adopt and share interest and follow the recreations that were normal and popular in the society outside the house.

THE SECOND HOUSE

This was our next intent but it took three years to find a suitable house, and another year to make it ready for occupation. In the meantime ex-Norman House residents who were surviving unhappily and uncertainly in lodgings heard about the new house and asked to become residents even before it opened.

It was difficult to refuse these requests even though the house was not ready for occupation. Over the first few months of 1962 an interesting situation developed. A group of ex-Norman House residents who had been tottering uncertainly in their lodgings were allowed to move in. They lived in spartan conditions which they would not have tolerated in any common lodging-house or private lodgings. They also lent a hand with the work of adapting the house to its new function. Gradually the house attained its full readiness for occupation and we looked around for staff. The first two appointments of a landlady were brief and unsatisfactory but a third proved to be the success we had hoped for and during her three years of occupation the Second House was able to establish itself on a firm and secure foundation.

THE PLACE OF THE NON-OFFENDER IN THE SECOND HOUSE SCHEME

It has already been stated that the intention at the Second House was to have a balance of ex-Norman House (offenders) residents and 'ordinary lodgers' (non-offenders) recruited in the usual way from newspaper adverts and the cards in shop-windows. These of course made no mention of the population at the house for we wished to create a very 'ordinary' atmosphere different from the specialised care at Norman House.

We still rather simply believed that there was a place for our residents somewhere in normal society and that these 'ordinary' representatives of society would somehow influence our residents into making the transition.

It transpired, however, that our first unknown lodgers were no more interested in fraternising with our ex-Norman House residents than were our men interested in associating with the strangers. The unknown newcomers remained individuals who merely used the house for shelter and their impact on the Norman House residents was to force them closer together and so shape them into a new type of community.

It was a misjudgment on our part that we could believe that there really were well-balanced young, active and sociable citizens living in lodging-houses and private bed-sitters and working on building sites, who yet had the personality and resources to exert a healthy influence on our own residents. In their turn the 'ordinary lodgers' numbered psychotics, 'drunks', 'layabouts'—and ex-prisoners

With the recognition of the dismal failure of this experiment we turned our attention to the recruitment of mature students attending training courses at the local Polytechnic, school-teachers, and an occasional prison assistant governor to produce the stabilising influence we were seeking. It was unquestionably their intervention that finally prospered the development of a healthy and stable community, and at any time there would probably be just over a third of the population of the house made up from these sources in the early days.

There was one more fundamental misjudgement on our part in that we had hoped that the house would be a half-way stage between Norman House and the outside world. This hope turned out to be illusory at least in the short-term. The men who came from Norman House did not move on but instead showed every inclination of making the house their long-term home. No decision was made in the early months on the question of length of stay but ultimately it was decided that it should be indefinite, even though such a term might include permanence. For once at least in a lifetime of movement decided upon by others, the resident would be able to decide for himself the time of his next departure. The average length of residence so far has worked out at three years, and what the men have demonstrated is the simple truth that if left to themselves they move away from the house when they feel competent and adequate to survive outside it and only then.

One of the interesting differences between Norman House and the Second House is that it was part of our deliberate policy to create a community at Norman House, whilst it was never part of our policy to create a community at Second House. It is interesting to note that the community that eventually developed at Second House was infinitely stronger than that which existed at any time at Norman House. One of the influences in the development of the community at Second House was the failure of the experiment with the 'ordinary' (non-offender) lodgers, which had the effect of bringing the ex-Norman House residents more closely together, for this was the time when they began to talk of 'our house' in a way in which they had never associated themselves with Norman House. The Management Committee had not foreseen the creation of a strong community at Second House. Their intention was to provide lodgings which gave considerably greater freedom to the individual resident than he received at Norman House— for example by giving the residents keys to their rooms and to the front door—so that they were encouraged to take the final step into unsupported lodgings in the neighbourhood. The Second House residents were told also before they moved in that they would be required to live in the house on the housekeeper's terms, in much the same way as they would be told by any landlady what she required of her lodgers. Whereas landladies in general looked on their activities as commercial ventures and may only have been exceptionally interested in performing a job of social support, the housekeeper of Second House was selected not merely because of her ability to manage a house but also for her capacity to see the lodgers as people who needed warmth and affection. Even so on the face of things it was an ordinary boarding-house in which the residents went to work, paid their rent, and fraternised together or kept their own company. Whereas at Norman House they were encouraged and even directed into a new job if they lost their old one, at Second House there was no official intervention. As in any lodging-house, they were told, 'You must pay your rent or go'. In the early days it was almost always the unsatisfactory non-offender residents who left. As they were replaced by the mature men of our own choosing the unsettling movement in and out of the house ceased, thus giving the residents who remained a breathing space to consolidate their position in 'their' house.

It would be wrong to pretend that Second House survived its troubles and crises without some degree of the specialised social work help that the offender residents received at

Norman House. It was my responsibility to provide that help because there already existed a personal relationship between myself and every ex-Norman House resident, and I made it my duty from the beginning to spend part of almost every day at the house, and my presence at any time excited no particular comment for I was looked on almost as part of the furniture.

Sometimes it was an individual who needed help, in which case it became very much a private transaction between him and me. But there were occasions when the troubles affected the whole community and it was necessary to sit around a table together to seek the solutions. Countless hours were spent also in communal discussions of problems that sometimes did not merit such formality, but they played their part in the shaping of the community, and in producing its leaders. During the first five years eighteen Norman House men lived at Second House, and at the end of five years eight were still there, including two who had come to the house when it first opened. Of the ten who had left seven had continued free of trouble. These included three who had married, one who had returned to his home, one who became reconciled with his wife, and one who had set up a stable home with a woman to whom he was not married. Of the remaining three, one was dead, one was in prison, and one was in a mental hospital.* Thus at the end of five years fifteen out of eighteen ex-offenders who had come to Second House were surviving out of prison. The past histories of most of our residents would have suggested that without the house they had a very poor chance of remaining free for any length of time, and it can reasonably be claimed that the house was primarily responsible for keeping most of the residents from returning to prison and enabling them to live useful and increasingly self-directing lives in the outside world.

One consequence of the state of relatively permanent residence at Second House was that the house was not able to help Norman House in the way which had originally been intended. So far as Norman House was concerned, therefore, it looked as if the answer was in the establishment of a *third house* which would continue the task which the Second House had begun. As the community of Second House settled, however, it was possible with continuous steps to reduce the number of the non-offender residents at the house which at the beginning accounted for half of the total, until at the end

* Since released and resident again at Norman House.

of the fifth year there were only two non-offender lodgers in residence, and thus more places could be given to ex-Norman House residents.

There were some occasions too when we were deprived of the services of a housekeeper, and whilst the house was able to organise its life by its own efforts it is dangerous to over-emphasise the contribution that the inadequate offender is able to make to the running of such an enterprise. Our experience is that however far he seems to develop a com-munity spirit his own underlying condition changes but slowly and he is therefore liable under pressure to suffer some degree of relapse. It should always be borne in mind that however industriously, and patiently, and with support and guidance, the residents of Second House have developed their own com-munity, their continued stay at the house is also an indication of their continuing need for support. If it were not so they would all have left to create homes of their own. The pattern of living that developed both at Norman House and at Second House in these first five years was more or less repeated in succeeding years. Norman House has continued to be paternal-istic. Second House has continued to prosper on shared responsibility. At Norman House the support given both to individuals and to the group has been considerable whilst at Second House the support has remained a minimal, but never-theless vital factor for the existence of the community.

In the last four years we have opened yet another house—the *Third House* which it is intended to operate more in the Second House pattern than as a Norman House. It made an enthusiastic start which almost led to total disaster. It recovered, faltered, and recovered again. It is now set on an even course. But it is too soon to draw conclusions.

REFERENCES

Turner, M. *Norman House, the first Five years;* The annual Reports of Norman House; The Second House, first and second Reports, are available in reference libraries or at Norman House.

Chapter Nine

THE IMPACT OF NORMAN HOUSE

WHEN Norman House was started in 1954 its concern was to give the homeless inadequate offender the chance that he said he wanted, to settle to a useful happy and crime free life. We maintained that any man leaving prison with the intention of 'going straight' had a right to conditions that constituted a 'chance'. Whether he succeeded or failed was a separate matter.

Later we recognised that Norman House did not constitute a chance for all homeless offenders, but only for some. Homeless prisoners accounted for almost half of the recidivist proportion of the prison population, and we considered it essential that we should select from amongst them those whom we felt could put the chance to good purpose. Our early experience then revealed the depressing truth that it was not enough to provide a man with a chance to settle, but that he had also to be helped to use that chance.

During the first year our records consisted almost entirely of information volunteered by the prisoner in his cell, and hurriedly recorded after the interview. Later, when we were more adequately staffed, and more time was available for recording information, the official information that we might be given about a prisoner was still scanty and unreliable. It offered no basis for an objective and systematic recording system. The introduction of the Home Office grant scheme and the involvement of the Probation Service in after-care helped greatly to standardise the information that was required about the offenders. But a system of recording of information is only as good as the staff who operate it, and the methodical keeping of records is not Norman House's most shining achievment.

It could be argued that Norman House was never intended as a research organisation. We were concerned in a practical way with the problems of inadequacy. We recorded information not because we thought it could have significance in the penal and criminological field generally, but because it helped us to improve our selection, and subsequently our understanding—and therefore our treatment—of the offenders who came to us.

In the sixteen years of its life rather more than 500 offenders have lived at Norman House. For the greater part they were regarded as filling the criteria for selection—that is, they were inadequate homeless offenders who wanted to stay out of prison, and who seemed to possess a relative ability to do so if they were given their 'chance', and for the greater part, at least while they lived at the house, they succeeded in these aims. They did not commit crime, they maintained themselves in work, paid their taxes, and contributed to the life that the house collectively created for them. It was fair to assume that they would have been back in prison if they had not been at the house. Thus the taxpayer was being saved an expenditure of some eight pounds a week per man which was the cost of keeping a man in prison in the early 'sixties. The cost of maintaining a man at the house exceeded our charge to him for room and board by slightly more than two pounds a week, but as this subsidy came from Charitable sources the taxpayer could not be unhappy about it. For the taxpayer, therefore, the work of the house was a success.

If it was the aim of Norman House to help to keep its residents out of prison it succeeded beyond question *whilst the offenders were members of the community of the house*. For example, in the first five years only one resident returned to prison whilst he was living at the house. When residents left, however, rather more than one half declined again into criminal behaviour, and only one-third could be said to have continued successfully beyond the probability of a relapse.

The subsidy towards the cost of living at the house was deliberately incurred. In the early years of Norman House, prison food was of poor quality, and there was too little of it, the prisoner's cell was invisibly and erratically heated and the help he could expect on release was minimal. When he came to Norman House, therefore, we provided more food than he could eat, coal fires that he could see burning, and the opportunity to save so that he could buy for himself the many essential articles that he lacked on his discharge from prison. We believed that such luxuries were a vital element in the overall treatment that the House offered its residents.*

* The Second House also maintained a high degree of comfort and provided meals of good quality but without involving the house in a subsidy. This was possible because the Second House did not employ—

THE IMPACT

The records that Norman House has kept over the 16 years do not allow us to draw reliable conclusions about the influence of the house on the residents but merely permit us to make observations. We may know that 100 recidivist offenders who had had indifferent school and work records, averaged between them four-and-a-half convictions per man, were aged between 28 and 45, and for the most part had no family or friends outside the house, have since adjusted to life outside prison, but what we do not know is the part that Norman House played in their resettlement. Our belief is that it was a vital contribution but we have no means of measuring the extent of it.

There are on the other hand Norman House residents who have maintained contact with the house although it has been punctuated by terms of imprisonment. It could be said that such contact helps the maturation process and is therefore a factor in their continuing development which may ultimately lead them into a satisfactory adjustment to a life in which prison no longer plays its part—which is what we believe.

Reconviction of itself tells us very little. Some men left Norman House because they could not withstand the pressures of the community at the house. They knew—as we knew—that they could not survive outside the house, but they sought a respite in prison and, having found it, immediately looked with eagerness to their return to the house. For some residents committing an offence when they had moved into lodgings which we had found for them was a desperate expression of their feeling of abandonment and rejection. Other offenders committed offences after leaving the house for a variety of reasons which had little or nothing to do with dependence, and in their cases the house had merely suspended their criminality for a brief period.

What matters most for the public, of course, is the knowledge that offenders who come to Norman House from prison or the courts are unlikely to commit offences whilst they live at the house, but for those of us who are involved in the work, although the committing of a further crime affects us, what matters most is what may be happening to the individual offender whilst he is with us, and after he leaves us. He may well commit further offences; that is not in itself regarded as

---

and therefore finance—a social worker, but received social work support and help from Norman House for no charge to itself.

failure and we may accept him for a second and, indeed, a third stay so long as we believe he is continuing to grow towards a time ultimately when he will be able to stand on his own two feet. We are clear in our own minds that our function is to give the individual offender an experience of personal and community living which will help him eventually to settle independently in the wider community outside the house. It is this experience itself that makes criminal behaviour super-fluous for almost all the offenders whilst it lasts, and for approximately one-half thereafter.

RESIDENTS AND THEIR RESPONSES

1. An analysis of our records indicates very clearly that in general *the house is not able to help the aggressive psychopath*, although it may not automatically reject him. Experience of recidivist offenders in prison long before Norman House was started had indicated the difficulties of helping the aggressive psychopath in any setting and by any sort of regime. For such a venture to be successful demands a high degree of knowledge and skill on the part of the staff that should not be required of hostel workers. It calls too for some self-awareness on the part of the offender—of his defects and his needs—sufficient to motivate him to join a small community whose very living together limits his area of personal freedom and is painful in the process. If he did show the insight that is necessary to bring him into such a community of handicapped men it was unlikely that he could withstand the stress and strain of involvement in the community, or that the passive inadequate members of the community could withstand the threat that *he* posed for *them*. Unless there was some degree of physical restriction on his liberty, he would leave, usually on impulse, and he would be unlikely to return.

Pat was intelligent, omniscient, and supremely egocentric. His defence in the face of criticism from the staff or from fellow-residents was simply—'I am a psychopath. I can't help it, can I?' This suggested not so much a personal belief as the repetition of many pronouncements made by the social workers who had worked on him in the past. His resources of destructive and disintegrative ability were greatly disproportionate to his physical size, which was unusually small. He made a seemingly unprovoked physical assault on a particularly docile resident one evening and when called to account for his behaviour before a meeting of residents and staff, he made fierce verbal attacks on those who contributed to the discussion. He disclaimed all responsibility for the assault on the resident who, he said, having provoked the incident, had clearly only received what he richly deserved. 'I know I am on trial,' he said, 'but you can't kick me out for what I did.' When asked for assurance that there would be no further such assaults, he characteristically turned to his favourite defence, 'I'm a psychopath. I can't change.'

What Pat was in fact claiming was a special dispensation from the conditions that governed the community of the house and gave it some cohesion. He would get up in the morning when it suited him and would go to work only if it pleased him to do so. He would eat or not eat according to his whim. If he had money he spent it and when he was without he expected to borrow. If debts became inconvenient they could be cancelled (by him) and he would start again with a clean sheet. When it was clear to him that he could expect no further tolerance he disappeared to the Continent, leaving his meagre store of belongings behind as some visible sign of his intention to return. Within a fortnight at most he would be standing on the doorstep, chastened and contrite, and professing the strongest determination to succeed now where previously he had failed.

It was only exceptionally that the aggressive psychopathic offender succeeded in conforming to the requirements of the group at the house. The inadequate offender is supported by the example that the group sets but the aggressive psychopath rebels against it. Collective example helps the inadequate offender to be like the others but it aggravates the attitude of the aggressive psychopath. A degree of mutual trust is implicit in the successful ordering of a community of inadequates, and the inclusion of an aggressive psychopath exposes that element of trust to a strain it is unlikely to survive, and the whole group suffers. Whatever facilities are available for aggressive psychopaths in therapeutic communities they are clearly not to be found in the sphere of Norman House as it is at present constituted.

2. Our experience at Norman House indicates also that there are homeless *inadequate offenders who are too intellectually subnormal, damaged or disturbed in personality to profit from living at the house.* The tolerance of the group of inadequates is low. The interplay of the group is threatened as much by the inability of these subjects to adapt to the life of the group as

it is by the more positive and disruptive impact of the aggressive psychopath. Whereas the latter generally leaves the group fairly soon, the subnormal of grossly damaged personality leans heavily and gratefully upon the others. He cannot contribute to the solidarity of the group but remains a liability that threatens and angers the group whose immaturity and insecurity is in some ways its most distinguishing characteristic.

In fairness to the low-grade psychopath who may come to Norman House, it should be borne in mind that he has probably defeated the efforts of socially and medically trained workers over a long period of time and accustomed himself to repeated rejection. Children's officers may have described him as 'A lovable child who needs great affection', and housemasters as 'A likeable lad who needs firm handling and constant supervision'. But by the time he reaches prison he is 'a problem case'.

Tommy came to Norman House with the blessing of his Children's Officer to whom he faithfully returned from all his wanderings. She had been kind and affectionate to him when he was first taken into care of the Local Authority, and in Tommy's mind, at least, she had substituted for the mother who had rejected him. Tommy was twenty-two when he came to the house. He was almost illiterate, 'read' children's comics and played Cowboys and Indians either alone or with neighbouring children, and his proudest boast was that he was the fastest gun amongst them.

He could, perhaps, have been contained within the rural community where he had his roots but he could not hope to survive in the town. He was employable only in sheltered conditions and under close supervision. A member of staff at Norman House once entrusted him with the work of minor repairs to a set of dining-room chairs, and within an hour Tommy had converted them into stools—at which point he proceeded to paint them pink. When he was set to work in the front garden he whistled after the girls and engaged the elderly in unending conversations which unfailingly caused him to wander away in the direction in which they were heading. He would return, usually before nightfall, with flowers which kind people, he said, had given him, but which one suspected he had himself picked uninvited from their gardens. Sometimes he stayed away overnight having been admitted into hospital with suspected appendicitis. On two occasions his stay in hospital was longer, but his discharge was brought about less by his physical fitness than by the need to save the ward from total disruption. One one occasion he was transferred for observation to the psychiatric annexe of a London teaching hospital, but he escaped at bed-time by wearing his clothes underneath his pyjamas which he then discarded in a lavatory before walking out through the main entrance. He shot himself in a busy street and was rushed to hospital by ambulance only to be discharged into police custody for committing a nuisance: he had used a blank cartridge which merely singed the jacket he was wearing.

When he was in physical residence at Norman House he hoarded other people's property and intercepted the mail, and he remained supremely innocent when his fellow-residents questioned him about the disappearance. Money vanished also. But perhaps the greatest worry of all was the moral danger to which he exposed himself when he wandered away from the house into cafes reputed to be the centres of homosexual activity, and where he was easy prey to men older and more worldly-wise than himself. Norman House could not give him the degree of supervision that he required for his protection, nor did the community at the house have the degree of tolerance that was needed for his development to proceed. It was inevitable, therefore, that he should move into a hospital community that could give him the protection he needed although, sadly, it also deprived him of his liberty.

There was also *Harry* who had been declared unemployable by a City Corporation Cleansing Department, and that in itself must be almost a declaration of subnormality. He had also been deemed a total economic liability by private employers and industrial retraining units. He was illiterate, and though he was still young—that is, in his early thirties—he had a history of vagrancy covering a period of nine years. He had lived at home with his subnormal parents until they had refused to continue to maintain him, and then had moved into a lodging-house and tried his hand at working for his living. His employers dismissed him, Harry claimed, before he was given time to prove himself. His longest period of employment had been five days and his shortest twenty minutes.

Harry then turned his hand to crime. He was convicted of stealing bread rolls and a bottle of milk and was fined ten shillings, and given time to pay. He left his home-town and took to the road. But it was winter and the weather beat him. He was convicted of begging and sent to prison for seven days, and on his release he returned to begging and a second conviction, followed by fourteen days in prison. He then abandoned professional begging in preference for State aid. But when he abstracted from the Assistance Board more money than one man was permitted to receive, he was apprehended and sent to prison for three months for what the Magistrate described as a clumsy fraud.

Harry was a failure as a worker, a thief, a beggar and a fraud. For him, as with others like him, there remained only vagrancy and the open road. He travelled south, sleeping at Reception Centres where they existed and in barns and outhouses where no other shelter was available. He reached the northern outskirts of London when it was late and night was closing in. He sought shelter in a disused building only to be arrested for being on enclosed premises 'with intent'. His only intent was to secure for himself a place to sleep. But even if Harry had been adequate enough to speak on his own behalf he would not have been understood in Court, for a raw Northern accent coupled with a cleft palate rendered his speech almost unintelligible. It was far easier for the court to find him guilty than it was to decide how to deal with him. Harry was remanded in custody whilst the Magistrates sought a solution. Eventually they felt they had found it at Norman House.

Harry accepted his disposal without protest. It is probable that he had never protested in his life but had accepted quietly whatever had come his way. His chances of survival in any organised community were small. His behaviour was primitive. But unlike that of the aggressive psychopath it was not intended to be disruptive. In the early days Harry intrigued his fellow-residents. With good humour they attacked his appearance. They required him to wash himself, change his clothing, and comb his hair. But Harry never seemed to learn, and the group's good-humoured patience faltered under the strain of repetition. Hostility took its place. Harry childishly exposed himself through the lavatory window, and offended them. He sat on the lavatory seat without first closing the lavatory door, and such behaviour outraged them. But their reactions left Harry unperturbed. He remained cheerful, primitive, and cunning, and for a time it seemed that he might settle after all.

In reality that was asking the impossible. One morning, three weeks from the day of his coming, he announced his departure. He was returning to the road and the endless journey that has no purpose or destination. But it came closest to meeting Harry's needs. It made almost no demands upon him, subjected him to no authority, imposed no limitations on his whims and impulses, and gave him the company of others who, like himself, were finding their escape on the open road.

Over a period of fifteen years 34% of the residents proved themselves to be similarly unsuitable in the sense that the house could only help them superficially. They needed long-term or even permanent support as in the case of subnormal men like Tommy, more specialised treatment, as in the case of men addicted to alcohol, or sheltered employment as part of a sheltered life as in the case of those offenders who became prematurely senile and apathetic about life in general when they could still have been expected to retain some years of active and useful living.

3. On the other hand rather more than 60% of the men selected over the fifteen year period proved to be *men suitable for this approach*. They were the homeless recidivists whom we designated as inadequates, the men who were always labelled 'below average', and who semed to have arrived at their position in life as a result of repeated failure, at school, at work, and in some instances in the Services. For the most part they were unmarried, without friends except the superficial contacts they made in lodging-houses, and the offices of the Ministry of Labour and the Assistance Board. They drifted into crime, and in prison they said there would never be a next time, but they were not competent to prevent the cycle continuing.

They did not fight their environment as the aggressive psychopath fought it. They tried to survive on society's terms, and sooner rather than later they failed in the attempt.

We have already stated that our conception of success was less concerned with reconviction than it was with the growth of the resident, for experience suggested that our inadequate offender was more likely to grow out of crime than he was to abandon it for fear of punishment or other reason. Working at a job that suited him encouraged his growth, as did interaction within a community of men with whom he recognised a kinship. It could be claimed that his growth was vitally affected by the *length of residence* at the house, for inadequate offenders who were isolated and homeless were unlikely to respond deeply to a short stay. The residents who stayed longest at the house were those who settled most successfully after leaving it, and not all by any means had the advantage of a further long stay at the Second House. Over a period of fifteen years the average length of stay at Norman House has not exceeded six months but in the last eighteen months it has risen, by design, to eleven months. At Second House, over a period of nine years, the average length of stay is three years.

THE VITAL ROLE OF THE STAFF

We have never doubted that the role of the staff is central to the work of Norman House. Norman Houses are the wardens and their wives, and their assistants, who run them. Old residents never return, from success or failure, to see 'the House': they come to see the staff who cared for them. Our early thinking, which was based on some knowledge and experience of inadequate offenders, suggested a family approach similar in its essentials to the work that was being done in homes for maladjusted and deprived children. Although I was unmarried during the first year of Norman House I had to play the part of both father and mother to the group. I was the father when authority was called for—to see that the men went to work and generally did what they had said in prison they had wanted to do—and I was the mother when I cooked breakfast and dinner, and provided medicines for minor ailments. I did not create these roles for myself but they evolved naturally as an answer to the needs of the inadequate men. Later, when I married, my wife took over the mother role in the house, although for some of the group who were her contemporaries in age her position was not so clear-cut.

During the first five years of the life of Norman House the place of the warden and his wife as the father and the mother became firmly established. During the following five years there were two changes of warden, but the house had acquired a certain stability that enabled it to function satisfactorily nevertheless. It communicated an atmosphere of friendliness and belonging which reflected the high qualities of both the senior staff and their assistants. There were strains and tensions, quarrels, disagreements, and untimely departures. But they were part and parcel of the experience of family life.

The role of the assistant warden was very much that of the oldest son in any family. He was heir to the father's authority and during the first ten years the house was served by a number of exceptional assistant wardens who worked effectively with the Warden to produce a team of workers who knew what they were doing and were happy to do it together. In the following six years, however, the staff picture changed. Married wardens became hard to find and assistant wardens suffered because they relied in varying degrees on the Warden for leadership and encouragement.

The Second House was spared the problem of finding wardens and assistants, for it functioned solely with a housekeeper, but when the first successful housekeeper left* after working at the house for three years the Management Committee experienced great difficulty in replacing her. It was the virtual self-appointment of a grand old Irish lady that saved the day and guaranteed the house another period of productive stability. She left after two and a half years to return to Ireland, and her job is still vacant. The house has continued to flourish nevertheless, for now all the residents are directly involved in the management of their affairs. Leaders emerge and work to create a strong community feeling. Younger residents are critical of them but the leaders are not aggressive psychopaths and they do not fight, but take offence and withdraw from the scene. Dissension grows until it threatens the total breakdown of the community. In the absence of the old guard the aspiring leaders falter. A deputation of older residents† asks the former leaders to return to active service. The house, they say, cannot run without them and the old leaders gladly take over again. It is the intervention for which they have been anxiously waiting and the community flourishes once more.

In these cycles of changes there has always been an element of outside support both for the individuals and the community, for without this support from the Management Committee it is probable that the community would have destroyed itself.

THE FURTHER DEVELOPMENT OF THE NORMAN HOUSE IDEA

Paradoxically it was the development of the Norman House idea that was chiefly responsible for the later staff shortage. For example, in 1954, only one warden was needed because Norman House was the only centre then in existence, but ten years later the scope of hostel care was wide and varied enough

* She married a resident.
† Younger and older in terms of residence at the house. The average age is 38 to 40, and the average length of stay remains at three years.

for the Government to have introduced a scheme of financial help for the support of hostels.

One important stage in the development of the Norman House idea was the setting-up of the Margery Fry Memorial Fund to commemorate the life and work of Margery Fry by the establishment of more Norman Houses. The first house opened under the Margery Fry Fund umbrella was Newell House in Birmingham in 1961. Leicester followed in 1962 and Sheffield and Hull in the following year. William House in Manchester, also opened in 1963 and although it was not officially another Norman House its ideology was essentially the same.

Not all the after-care houses that were opened closely followed the pattern set by Norman House. Organisations like the Langley House Trust welcomed the basic idea but adopted it to suit their own purpose, which had a strong religious motivation. The first of the Langley Houses opened in Hampshire in 1959. Bradford, Reading and Cheltenham followed in the next four years.

Christian influences inspired the Anglican St. George's House in Wolverhampton and Faith Lodge in Leeds, as well as the Goldborne Centre in London which was the outcome of the individualism of Dr. Peake, a Free Church minister at Notting Hill. The Society of St. Vincent de Paul opened houses in Liverpool and London. The Society of St. Dismas opened Dismas House in Southampton. The first Warden, Anton Wallich-Clifford later established the Simon Community which differed from most other organisations in offering long-term and even permanent residence to those who seemed to need it.

A group of prisoners at Wandsworth Prison formed themselves into an organisation they called Recidivists Anonymous, and ultimately established their own house in London. The Griffins, which was the voluntary body that succeeded the Discharged Prisoners' Aid Society at Holloway Prison for Women, opened a house for discharged women prisoners, and the Borstal After-Care Association made similar provision for selected homeless Borstal 'boys' who were planning to come, or return to, London on their release.

Local Prisoners' Aid Societies became sponsors or supporters of houses in different parts of the country, and the National Association for Prisoners' Aid Societies established a Housing Trust.

THE IMPACT

These were only some of the developments that followed the lead given by Norman House* but they tended to concentrate on the provision of services for offenders and failed in the earliest stages to give sufficient thought to the quality of the service that was being offered. This was corrected to some degree when special provision was designed, for instance for homeless offenders who were addicted to alcohol. The lead in that direction was given by Rathcoole House whose first warden, Timothy Cook, had once worked at Norman House. St. Luke's in Kennington which had worked with alcoholics for many years was also influenced by the new wave of activity So too was the Helping Hand Organisation and the Social Service Unit of St. Martin-in-the-Fields.

By 1970 there existed a network of services in the country that was created specifically for homeless offenders. Opening houses had become very much a fashion but the problem of staffing them was altogether a different proposition.

In the years between 1966 and 1970 Norman House experienced nine changes of staff, and the house lost all feeling of continuity. Wardens, deputy wardens and assistant wardens came with great expectations but left dispirited, or dismayed, or resentful of the demands the community made upon them.

What was happening to Norman House was also threatening the work of other houses in different parts of the country. A myth was built around the work that it was too demanding, hours of work were too long, or the time off was too short, pay was too small, and the service lacked status and offered no prospects for the future.

There was truth in some of these complaints but they could not of themselves explain the failure to recruit suitable staff. Norman House experimented with a wide range of conditions of employment and pay without at any time successfully resolving the problem.

The Management Committee therefore, decided to find *potentially* suitable workers and train them for work at Norman House and similar houses. Already some progress had been made when NACRO (National Association for the Care and Resettlement of Offenders) which had succeeded the National Association of Discharged Prisoners' Aid Societies, instituted training courses and seminars for workers and potential

* For an exhaustive list see the NACRO Handbook, available from the Director, NACRO, 125 Kennington Park Road, London, S.E.11.

workers in the field. It was a commendable first-aid effort which could help houses to continue operating until the time that the Government instituted a comprehensive system of its own. The Norman House training scheme was much less ambitious but it aimed both to find staff and attract attention to the problem. In its first year it succeeded in some measure in both of its aims, whilst it also extended placement facilities to students of probation and Child Care.

The staffing problems of Norman Houses and similar centres are not yet solved and whilst they persist they debase the service until it may become only a matter of providing food and shelter.

In its earliest years Norman House had concentrated on the homeless men who were already in prison. Gradually, however, the courts asked for its assistance as an alternative to imprisonment and with the introduction of the Parole System, and the increased use of home leave facilities for prisoners, the demands made on the house on behalf of offenders who either had not been sentenced or had not completed their sentences clearly indicated a preventive service that houses like Norman House were qualified to give. It is in this field in particular that the wider implications of Norman House will lie for the future.

Conclusion

MATCHING THE DEMANDS

In the preceeding chapters we have described three experiences of 'dealing with deviants', and in this final chapter we present a *summary* and an *analysis* of the projects.

The projects, whatever their differences of technique, share a basic *ideology*, and the implications of this for the understanding and treatment of social deviance are discussed. A scheme for the *management of delinquents* broadly based on the three projects is then put forward.

Summary

The Henderson Hospital

The medical preoccupation with deviance is long standing. Whilst at times doctors have sought, in a rather omniscient way, to explain aberrations of social behaviour in terms of 'illness', equally some sections of society have tended to thrust those who did not conform upon the doctors for explanations of their behaviour and for a remedy.

The *Henderson Hospital* is a unit where a treatment programme for social deviants has evolved. The Henderson was one of the pioneer centres for the development of Therapeutic Community techniques in psychiatry in the post war years. Never a follower of strictly group-analytic practice, the Henderson from the outset learned to take cognisance of sociological theory and method. Although Therapeutic Communities originally developed as part of the wider range of psychotherapeutic treatments, the Henderson came to modify its own Therapeutic Community methods further in order to meet the needs of a growing influx of people with more of a social than a medical disability—although in medical terminology they were loosely defined as psychopaths. It remains nevertheless a hospital with all that such implies. It is administered by the Department of Health and staffed by psychiatrists, psychiatric nurses and the allied professions, apart from a small staff group who have no such medical background but are usually young students during or about

225

to embark upon a career in sociology, psychology, social work and so on. These non-professionals are still therefore somewhat representative of the 'healing' professions in interest if not in age and experience.

The Henderson utilises a twenty-four hour, very intensive and residential 'living and learning' situation around a structure of skilled group psychotherapy. Whilst all residents take a full part in the running of the community, there is a definite staff–resident differential which is acknowledged but is utilised in terms of psychotherapeutic transference interpretations. There are many for whom this respite in a protective environment can be of value. A certain tolerance of misbehaviour exists in hospital and regression is allowed. There is an aura of support and encouragement which promotes rehabilitatory efforts, and trained psychotherapists have much to offer the well motivated individual. The hospital setting, however, inevitably creates its own limitations and pitfalls.

There is a tendency for the staff to feel that they are primarily engaged in making people 'better', and for failed residents to plead non-responsibility for their actions. Parents and outside agencies expect the doctors and staff to provide a 'cure' for the 'patient'. Dirt, untidiness, overt sexual activity and alterations in or interference with the hospital's services, such as the feeding arrangements, the furnishing or fittings, can become foci of tension between the residents and the staff. In their turn the staff must answer to distant and often little comprehending Committees of Management, higher up the administrative chain of command. These areas of potential crisis naturally became exploited in the acting out of conflict situations between staff and residents.

The Prison At Chino

At the other end of the spectrum social deviance is regarded by some not as 'illness' but as 'badness', requiring punishment and control of the deviant individual in prison.

The idea of a prison as a rehabilitatory institution has nevertheless had a long history, and one reformative project after another has been introduced into the basic situation of imprisonment, but with only limited success. Prison imposes a restriction on the liberty of the individual and some control over his activities. Life is reduced to its raw essentials, and the individual is somewhat isolated from reality, but at least attention can be focussed without interference upon some of these basic issues. At Chino the California prison service made an attempt to carry over some of the ideology of the Therapeutic Community from the psychiatric hospital to the prison setting. Under a non-medical administration and staffed by non-psychiatric personnel (apart from the academic psychological training of the adminstrator) there could be a distinct move away from any concept of 'illness'.

But the prison setting had its own deleterious associations and handicaps too. The prisoner and the prison officer were representatives of different factions of society with different attitudes to crime and punishment. Some re-training of the prison officers in sociological observation and group dynamics was therefore necessary before any shift in their traditional attitudes to social deviance could occur. Furthermore the participants were compulsorily detained and they were all of the same sex. Certain limits on behaviour had to be set. There was an overall control from the authorities, and many areas of responsibility were just not open to the residents. The project therefore concentrated more upon the resolution of its 'here and now' problems than on any longer term psychotherapeutic exploration, but the lack of emphasis on the latter meant that more use of the residents themselves in the rehabilitatory programme became possible than was usual in the hospital setting, with its professional and non-professional participants.

The Norman House Hostel

The third approach to social deviants is that of the residential hostel. The traditional aim of hostel care has been to subsidise the lives of the lodgers, to make up for their social and material deficiencies in order that they can be maintained in the community as less of a liability. Without such material assistance many people would undoubtedly remain in a handicapped position, for their deficiencies are more than they can compensate for unaided.

At Norman House a small, more personalised hostel for men leaving prison was set up which was intended to provide not only the material things that were lacking but also the physical and emotional environment in which the individual could find the resources within himself to grow out of these long standing deficiencies. There was a deliberate effort to constitute a type of family atmosphere with the warden,

CONCLUSION

supported by his wife, directing and guiding and setting an example in a strong but benignly paternalistic way.

No treatment programme as such was envisaged but the opportunity for talking over the problems of the day with other members of the 'family' and particularly with the 'parents' was provided. The staff who come into this type of voluntary welfare work, however, are largely untrained and have difficulty in maintaining a professional objectivity. The residents can remain in some degree of ambivalent dependency which there is little prospect of working through, for the organisation is not equipped for that type of work. A hostel, registered as a Charity, financed by voluntary contributions and clearly subsidising the welfare and comforts of the lodgers, even though the residents are working and paying a rent, also has its unfortunate associations and limitations.

ANALYSIS

Psychiatric hospitals, prisons and hostels with their varied resources all have something to offer towards the management of deviance, but at the same time the very nature of the institution can limit or even be a handicap to the task in hand.

However, the psychiatric hospital, the prison and the hostel described in this volume are not typical of the majority of such institutions and have come a long way towards a better understanding of the deviant and his real needs, and have greatly modified the traditional approach. There is an overlap in their spheres of interest and activity. They have less allegiance to the original disciplines. They become more representative of an entirely different model of a rehabilitatory system, but with modifications to suit their own particular situation.

(a) All three share a certain *basic ideology* in that they regard deviance in social behaviour partly as the outcome of personality maldevelopment and partly as a result of the individual concerned seeing a situation from another point of view. Simply to suppress the deviant and his behaviour could be to fail to learn something from his way of looking at things. It therefore becomes more reasonable to search for ways of resolving the conflict situation between the deviant and society. The repetitive deviant act is itself seen as an expression of the conflict, and a commentary upon the divergent views which needs to be understood.

In the three projects described the conflict is allowed

expression and the differing views are accepted. More than this, a situation is set up which is optimal for the resolution of the conflict situation and which will demand moves from both sides, in contrast with the idea that established society should impose its will upon the deviant individual in order to make him conform.

If this procedure is primarily one of self-discovery for the deviant individual, it is also a process of re-discovery for an all too often complacent society.

(b) One point can certainly be made about the three different settings described, and this is that at different stages in the life of a deviant, particularly of a delinquent, the pressure and power groups in society allow or direct the adoption of different attitudes towards him.

The disturbed family life, the parental splits or childhood rejection, the restless search for identity, and the social isolation and inadequacies are common features in the long histories of the people described in all of the three sections. The three projects are in fact dealing with one and *the same individual* and merely focussing upon different levels in personality development.

In other words, early in the career of a young delinquent society's demand is for a cure, hence the hospital referral and psychiatric interest. At a later stage when crimes may have been repeated, or if the crime was regarded at the outset as of a more seriously disturbing nature, the demand will be for punishment and containment in prison. Still later, if the deviance persists, a seemingly more charitable attitude is adopted in that neither cure nor retribution is demanded, although the individual is written off as a liability that has to be borne and the After-Care Hostel is provided.

The Henderson thus finds itself dealing with the young delinquent or even pre-delinquent in late adolescence. The Chino experiment dealt with young adult men already committed to prison for quite severe offences, whilst the chronic and middle-aged recidivist makes up the bulk of the Norman House clientele.

We know that men who turn up in later life at Norman House have often been in Henderson. A follow-up of Henderson cases has shown us regrettably that some who fail to achieve stability at Henderson may go on to commit crimes of a more serious and violent nature as described in the histories of the men in Chino.

(c) Each project has its *limitations*, however, and it is equally clear that for some individuals no conflict resolution or personality growth occurs in the particular setting described. At best the man is only temporarily contained, accepted and to some extent controlled by the project.

Those who remain out of trouble only so long as they remain in Norman House have been alluded to, and it is clear from both the Henderson and California experiences that for some the constant questioning and counter-questioning, the manipulation of the rules and the playing of the treatment game became a way of life in itself, and that relapse into deviance soon occurred when that person left the unit and had to contend with the different and real world outside.

(d) Not only may someone be no more than contained, he may be further damaged by exposure to stresses which he cannot stand, or he may be damaging to others—which further emphasises the need for *correct selection*.

The Norman House system was unable to cope with the type of con-man who would find at Henderson fellows well able to challenge his fanciful stories and indeed proffer him interpretations of his need to live out his fantasies. At Norman House he materially damaged others by the frauds and deceits he practised, and emotionally further belittled and hurt those with whom he came into brief contact before usually taking his own departure, having in no way benefitted from the experience.

Both Henderson and Norman House find the aggressive type of psychopath, with his quick resort to actual violence when confronted or put under stress, almost too much to deal with. He brings discussion and examination to a cursory level at Henderson. No one dares venture too far, and whatever progress that person may make is limited whilst others may choose to opt out of the situation altogether rather than risk being damaged in a fight.

(e) The *available resources* differ from project to project, however, and make it possible to cope with different problems by different methods. In the California project the physical controls and limits of the prison, the particular methodology and staff functions, were clear and observable. Simple, clear-cut authority to deal head-on with potential violence made it possible not only to cope with it, but to encourage 'acting out' (i.e. as delinquency) within the limits of the project. There were the necessary controls to handle violent behaviour should it erupt. It is significant that in the study reported, negligible violence occurred amongst a group of young men who had records of causing considerable destruction.

To take another example, if the inadequate psychopath coming into Henderson is able to persist in his former pattern of behaviour, then his treatment fails, He will try to set up the accustomed patterns of behaviour whereby he is the unfortunate delinquent and 'society' alternately punishes or supports him, but always from some authoritarian position over him.

The Therapeutic Community group will challenge this behaviour when they recognise it and he must then make the choice of a change of role or of opting out of treatment. If he were to succeed in changing the system so that it did emulate the response of the outside society and in its turn punish or support him whilst he remained in a subjective role, then he would make no progress towards personality growth. The very inadequate personality finds it difficult to respond to the Henderson approach and often leaves or remains unchanged until he is finally discharged.

At another level of interaction, however—in Norman House, for instance, with its rather benign but directive paternalistic approach—he may be less forced into a defensive persistence with his own inadequate role and find that he is able to shift his perspectives and behaviour more easily.

(f) Whilst we recognise the defects of such 'labelling' and exclusion from one project or the other as offering the wrong type of treatment, what we contend is that for each individual there is a *level of interaction in which he will feel sufficiently secure* and competent to be able to put aside his accustomed defensive ploys and be able to work towards further maturity. Recognition of his needs in this respect is of paramount importance.

(g) The resolution of the social conflict situation does not, however, depend entirely on changes in attitudes on the deviant side. The communities described are introspective and self-examining and in constant flux as their own attitudes are amended. Through the experiences of those who work in them or visit them, they become *workshops for the promotion of social change*. An understanding of the problems and how they have arisen brings about changes in the attitudes of the staff involved in the treatment interchanges.

CONCLUSION

Society, with its generally conformist attitudes, its tendency to keep things under control, to suppress and to inhibit exploration of feelings and experimentation with interactive processes, succeeds only in stereotyping the deviant as one or another type of drop-out, and he then becomes as trapped in his behavioural role as are those members of society who can see him only in this particular light. When the formalised and customary attitudes of the hospital, prison or hostel to the deviant are abandoned, the stereotyped and repetitive responses of the latter are in their turn left behind.

In a *situation of interaction* the prospect becomes alive and more dynamic and eventually more hopeful. The delinquent who is formally interviewed in his cell by the psychiatrist or probation officer functions very differently when he is seen in an argument with his peers over an immediate matter that concerns him.

The interactive projects described in this book offer a respite from the established social controls, with the object that the individual should *be*, should exist in freedom and find out again what is required of him in, and what it is possible for him to gain through, inter-personal encounters with his fellows. They are living situations where real responsibility can be given, where situations arise in which he and his colleagues work out a solution themselves, and where for the moment the set behavioural patterns of society are put aside. Thus an individual is free to experiment with different ways of acting and to arrive at last at a free choice of future behaviour, knowing the options that are open to him.

In our three projects we have encountered the same individual but, seeing him at different levels or in different modes of inter-action, we have found one approach appropriate to one level, and individuals at another level more responsive to a different approach.

It is difficult to be concise or definitive about the behaviour patterns or levels of personality development that we may recognise without leaning excessively on psychological or sociological theory. However, we must make some attempt to clarify the various levels about which we are writing if they are to be of practical value.

Although in all three projects we have used descriptive

terms such as aggressive, demanding, inadequate, immature, and so on, in effect we have been observing a cluster of behavioural attributes around the central theme of *the individual's interaction with his fellows*.

A pattern of *egocentric* behaviour occurs early in the course of personality development and can be identified in the descriptions of some of the deviants encountered in all three projects. The individual is concerned primarily with himself, his own needs and feelings, and the needs and feelings of others become secondary or hardly recognised.

Along with this egocentricity goes an immediacy, an urgency, a simplicity which sees action and reaction in cut and dried terms. The conflict is around his very existence as an independent being and with problems unresolved at this early level his behaviour in adult life is seen by others as impulsive and without forethought. It can be exaggerated and uninhibited so that intense feelings are expressed in violent and aggressive actions. Action rather than thought predominates.

Later in the process of personality maturation and socialisation the individual takes more cognisance of those around him. The infant separates from the breast, the child goes to school. Whatever terms one wishes to use, the individual in our society has to become aware of the needs of others and to make compromise reactions so that each can live in harmony and equality alongside his fellow. *Dependency* needs are preeminent at this stage and are shed with difficulty. Overdependence on the stronger figure, whether parent or one of the many parent substitutes our society offers, may manifest itself by a passive helplessness or a provocative demand for continued attention. On the one hand the adult with problems persisting in this area wants more and more help and support but on the other hand he resents his subordinate situation and rages against those on whom he is dependent.

Later still in the progress towards personality maturity and independence these early exaggerated needs and later dependency problems may seem to be successfully overcome, but the individual whose social learning has been defective may then be caught up in a late adolescent type of rebellion which persists and remains unresolved leaving him out of harmony in his interactions with society. Whilst he has reached a certain independence and maturity of personality it is in relative isolation so far as inter-relationships with others are concerned. There seems to be no acceptance of him by others nor does he accept the values and standards of the rest. He is a misfit in society and is forced to function below his real potential, for he has no acceptable outlet for his energies and talents however creative they may be. Although he seems to have dropped out of society or turned his back upon his fellows in anger he is uncomfortably aware of his inability to fit in or to gain acceptance from others. It is a position of spurious or *pseudo-independence* for his very deviance is bringing him into constant contact with society as long as his conflict remains unresolved.

For the reasons why personality growth may have become fixated or deviant at these or intermediate levels we have to look at the many situations and factors which could have impinged on the developing awareness of social conduct and resulted in a misunderstanding or mislearning of interpersonal behaviour which has then become perpetuated. This is largely the province of academic sociologists and psychologists, but at best their findings can be of value in preventive work.

With treatment in mind it is necessary to *re-create the social learning atmosphere appropriate to the particular level of personality development.* Dependency needs tend to be worked out in 'family' situations, egocentric demands in a more basic expeditious and simplified setting with less competition or stress from sibling rivals and more directive control. The divergent attitudes of the more sophisticated and less markedly immature social deviant can be explored and worked out through the free and uninhibited exchange of opinions in a democratic and egalitarian community.

The projects described have all centred on one or other of these *levels of interaction* because the resources available evolved with particular pertinence for one or other group. Chino was a controlled situation, more immediate, directive and straightforward. Norman House set out to provide a good supportive family, and the Henderson offers the opportunity for problem solving on a truly democratic level but with considerable responsibility for the self put upon each individual.

In all the projects there is a process of self-discovery through role playing and testing out the latent potential of the individual, but the resources available facilitate various stages of the growth process.

What is important for those concerned in dealing with deviants is to be able to recognise the particular needs of the individual and make possible his entry into the appropriate treatment area.

A misplacement only serves to reinforce the conflict, whereas with an appropriate start some movement up the scale becomes possible as difficulties are overcome.

For instance, a young man with a long history of foster-care and residence in juvenile penal institutions suffered from psychosomatic ailments and a dependence upon hospitals and doctors. He found himself quite inadequate for the intellectual give and take of Henderson, and his asthma increased to a state in which he was almost permanently lobsted-hued through using his adrenaline inhaler, whilst in group encounters he was mute (breathless) and bewildered.

Finally discharged as being 'untreatable' (by methods used at Henderson) he was found a place in a hostel for recidivist ex-prisoners run paternalistically by a priest and from which he could go out to work. There was some semblance of sharing and solving the problems of living in the regular evening discussion groups, and at this slower and less demanding pace he found that much of what he had watched and heard at Henderson took on meaning. He was able to participate here with his peers, particularly so with his 'pre-training' at Henderson, and seen some months later he was articulate, alert and self-questioning, and making some progress towards further responsibility for himself.

TOWARDS A UNIFIED SYSTEM FOR DELINQUENCY MANAGEMENT.

In the history of attitudes to social deviance the pendulum has swung between the two poles of thought that the deviant is just 'bad' and needs punishment or that he is in some way 'ill' and requires medical treatment.

One way or the other the attitude and hence the management approach has tended to be holistic. At the present day, on the one hand we are facing an outcry for the stricter punishment of criminals, and on the other hand the penal institution for women in Holloway is being rebuilt on the same site but now with a psychiatric hospital orientation.

This is a confused state of affairs, for the majority of offenders fit neither into the extreme of pure criminality nor into that of mental illness. Whilst it is not disputed that both prisons and psychiatric hospitals are necessary parts of the developing management spectrum for the deviant, there are many possible intermediate but linking steps along the way.

A system based on a more sociodynamic attitude towards

CONCLUSION

deviance could offer opportunities for conflict resolution at many different levels. The possibility of linking these then arises, with transference up or down through the various levels. A unified system with resources integrated and geared to meet the demands of the deviant could simplify the management of delinquents overall.

Rather than the offender being referred to a certain type of prison and its attendant regime, for a fixed length of time on the basis of the category of his offence, or conversely being referred for a particular type of medical treatment, e.g. alcohol or drug withdrawal on the basis of the particular association of alcohol or drugs with his offence, it would be possible to consider the treatment of the offender in terms of his conflict with society. Selection to the appropriate regime would be determined more by recognition of his needs than solely in response to the dictates of society.

A group with a diagnostic mix of 'illnesses' and 'offences' would result but, as we have seen, that is already what happens in an established unit such as at Henderson. Thus within a supervised hostel for the more inadequate and dependent type of deviant could be both young and older men, those who shelter behind alcohol or behind drugs, some with trivial offences of an irritating nature and others who have provoked society less repetitively but with more lasting effect by committing a more serious offence. The focus would not be upon the deviance that the group had in common but rather upon aspects which were open to a constructive approach.

The common problems of social isolation, inability to exist without dependent links, and the need for strong parent models with whom to identify would be shared, and the conjoint group effort directed towards a goal of fuller personal independence.

Similarly the selection for an open or a closed Therapeutic Community of the types already described would be dependent upon the level of personality and emotional maturity in terms of the individual's ability to fit into and utilise such a process and his needs for more or for less external control, for freedom to experiment or the need to be supported and guided.

That such a plan for an approach to deviance, orientated more towards the deviant and his demands, is feasible is supported by the work of the established but often small and isolated ventures into penal reform such as the prison type of Therapeutic Community at the Van der Hoeven Clinic in Holland and at Grendon Underwood in England.

The California experience, however, shows that within a prison setting the degree of an inmate's participation in the determination of his own future course can profitably go much further even than in the examples given above. Similarly in the field of juvenile delinquency the 'permissive' living and learning type of community has always aroused much interest and some acceptance from the days of Homer Lane onwards as far as juveniles were concerned. The Henderson, however, has been able to extend into the treatment of young adults and in a unit of both sexes many of the principles of those juvenile social learning situations.

Finally, whilst hostel care of some sort for the socially inadequate has long been an accepted fact, the widening and deepening experience of Norman House has shown how much more of a rehabilitatory process can be injected into hostel care. Even in its own enlightened approach a further calculated decrease in the authoritarian and restrictive control over the residents as shown in the Second and Third Houses has allowed for increasing powers of self-help and self-responsibility to emerge.

The practicality of such an overall plan will doubtless be challenged on the grounds of numbers alone, but at the present time we have a unique opportunity in England to take a bold step forward in the reorganisation of the facilities for female offenders, for example.

With approximately 1,000 women in prisons an initial division into three geographical areas would reduce the number to be dealt with in any one complex to around 350, with the advantage of treating the offender near to her home, family, after-care and future work prospects. Allowing for 50 to be in need of strict security in the orthodox type of prison, because we know of no other way of dealing with them, the remaining 300 could be dispersed as follows. Two closed therapeutic community units of the California type operating at slightly different levels according to the actual needs, and one more open Henderson type of therapeutic community each could function at a level of 50 inmates. This would leave a further 150 women to be dealt with in varying kinds of hostel accommodation. Some of these would be hostels with more control and direction, and possibly incorporating an industrial section on the premises, whilst others would be

CONCLUSION

more open and the residents engaged in outside employment. Certainly some dispersal of the units in the outside community would be advantageous, rather than concentration within a central institution which inevitably leads to a stereotyping of behaviour on both the staff and the resident sides.

In Conclusion

An aspect of deviance that has been referred to several times in this book is the need of the deviant to establish an identity as somebody who is acknowledged by society as an integral part of society.

'Even to be a drop-out, I mean', said one Henderson resident, 'it's better than nothing'.

In persisting largely with the traditional and profession orientated approaches to deviance, whether they be medical, penal or social work programmes, perhaps we meet the demands of the deviant too readily and paradoxically confirm him in his deviant role.

Put in an over simplified way, does the presence of an active drug addiction centre, for instance, give some youth who is lacking identity a reason for existence—as a junkie—in which role he at least belongs to something? (A similar argument could be levelled at the staff who see their function only in terms of a narrow professional skill and need to have clients with whom to interact in a formalised way.)

The aim of a rehabilitatory programme should be to facilitate the re-entry of the deviant individual into society by a recognition and reinforcement of his more positive qualities rather than exclusion from society by concentration solely upon the negative aspects. As well as lessening the ties to one or other of the professional codes and involving the deviants themselves in the reformative process, the gap between society and the deviant would be further narrowed if the general public could be more involved in the day to day dealing with deviants and educated to an understanding of the meaning of deviance. In the last resort violence and social disorder erupts in the urban streets. In Holland, for instance, the Probation Service selects for a particular client an ordinary citizen of similar social, religious and employment background and suggests he works with the offender, in the belief that this man is more likely to make the contact that is necessary for the emergence of these more positive qualities.

If, as suggested in this final chapter, we can establish

238

suitable and more appropriate meeting points between the deviant and society where the conflict between the two can be worked out, the rising tide of delinquency may be checked if not reversed. We have to comprehend what the deviance means before it can be resolved.

Obviously not all delinquents can be managed by the methods outlined here. There are those who present too severe a threat for conflict resolution to be attempted with our present resources or where our knowledge of how they could be approached remains inadequate. More time and more attention could be directed toward these people, however, if more effective measures were applied to the large group of deviants who are inappropriately treated in existing circumstances and who only serve to impede the system as a whole.

Those who as professional workers in the field come into contact with deviants should take the lead in trying out new methods of working within the resources available to them and in refusing to persist with methods which clearly do not work.

Finally the policy makers must be influenced to discard methods which are unprofitable in the treatment of social deviance and to provide other facilities. Now is the time to adopt new methods. The past decade has seen a move away from the drive for Penal Reforms alone, for instance to an extending search for alternatives to penal treatment culminating in some of the proposals of the Criminal Justice Bill.

Whilst on the one hand the Bill re-affirms the needs of society for control over deviance by the increased powers and restrictions implied, on the other hand the way is thrown open for an approach to deviance which offers opportunities in which social conflict situations can be examined, understood and resolved.

Such proposals as Deferment of Sentencing, Day Attendance Centres, and Community Service for example provide the framework for a more flexible approach to the treatment of deviants. What we put into that framework depends upon all of us and this is an opportunity which society cannot afford to miss.

INDEX · NAMES

(r = reference cited)

INDEX

INDEX · SUBJECTS

INDEX

INDEX

project liaison officer (PLO) in work (Henderson) 74

Provo project (see Lamar Empey)

psycho-analytic theory 21

psychopathic disorder
brain damage 22
environmental factors 21
genetic factors 22
institutionalisation 22
Mental Health Act 22
natural history 69
paternal influence 22
results in treatment 58, 69, 70
sociological thought 73
vagrancy 59

psychopathic states (Henderson's classification)
predominantly aggressive 24–5, 71–2
predominantly inadequate 24–25, 72
predominantly creative 25–6, 71

psychotherapy vs. rehabilitation (Rapoport) 38

Quakers (U.S.) and early use of confinement 95

Rathcoole House 223

reactive fear 73–92

Reception-Guidance Centres in Prison (California) 98, 106, 112

Recidivists Anonymous (RA) 222

restrictive solutions 73–92

risk prediction devices (see B. E.; Wilkins)

ritual in community meetings 41

role-playing 40, 50–1

role displacement 146

roles of staff by patients/residents 50

St. Dismas Society 6

St. George's House 222

St. Luke's 223

St. Martin-in-the-Fields 223

San Quentin Prison (California) 96, 100

screening committee (see also selection) 148

segregation, therapeutic use of 158–61

selection of residents/patients 54, 71, 72, 106–7, 166–7, 190–4
(staff of, see also staff selection) 211, 219, 230, 236

sex offenders and offences 201
(see also homosexuality)

Simon Community 222

size of communities 107, 110, 117–119

small groups 45–6, 53, 122, 140–1, 147, 152

social activities 143

social change 151, 231

social conflict theory 9–11

social conflict resolutions 231

social learning situations 234

Social Rehabilitation Unit, Belmont Hospital (Jones) 36

social therapists 143, 147, 226

Society of St. Vincent de Paul 222

sociopath (Partridge) 26–7

Special Intensive Parole Unit (SIPU) (California) 102, 116

staff
meetings 122, 127, 139–41
roles 126, 137, 145
by patients/residents 123
of administrator (Chino) 132–134, 146, 210
medical director (Henderson) 47–8
warden (Norman House) 185–6, 195–8
selection 194, 220–1
strain, demands, problems 58, 194–5
training 105–6
uniforms 47, 99, 137–8

INDEX